Discover what peop

Pure Gold is a lifeline for toda
the virtues that sustain joy, te. ⸻ ⸻ ⸻ ⸻ ⸻ in our marriages. It
provides valuable tools of understanding, reflection, and action, leading
each couple to their own path of lasting transformation.
~ Linda Kavelin Popov, author of *The Family Virtues Guide* and
   A Pace of Grace; married 23 years to Dan Popov, Ph.D.

ක්‍යෑ

Intimacy, love, and partnership in marriage develop when spouses
commit themselves to one another and develop the ethical strength
to abide such commitments, even though they may call for significant
sacrifices and compromises. With a refreshing openness to the
common insights of both faith and science, *Pure Gold* lays out some
simple steps couples can take to form and maintain this type of mature
marriage.
~ Jason S. Carroll, Ph.D., coauthor of *Premarital Predictors of Marital
   Quality or Breakup*; School of Family Life, Brigham Young University

ක්‍යෑ

I have been happily married to my wife Jody for 23 years, a marriage
therapist for twenty years, and the author of several books on marriage
and family life. Yet I was learning new things as I devoured the pages
of Susanne and Craig's latest book. *Pure Gold* is a pure gift—engaging,
wise, and chock full of ideas that can be immediately put into action
and make your marriage a pure joy.
~ Paul Coleman, Psy.D., author of *How to Say It for Couples:
   Communicating with Tenderness, Openness, and Honesty*

ක්‍යෑ

Pure Gold is a solid formula for those who are willing to work on their
marriage relationship and personal growth. God bless you both for
your obviously demanding labor of love for Love.
~ Greg and Ann Miller, Executive Directors of Open Door Family
   Ministry; married 23 years

ක්‍යෑ

The authors work like detectives in discovering the solid evidence that supports the reasons why good marriages last—by putting together the essential clues of the healthy relationship puzzle. We see *Pure Gold* as a useful and positive tool for the earnest couple to discover the spiritual gold in their own marital treasure-trove. A job well-done!

~ Michelle Thelen-Steere, M.A. in Clinical Counseling and Certified Hypnotherapist with Native Intelligence, Consultative Educators (cross cultural specialty) and John Thelen-Steere, M.A., Environmental Planner; married for 14 years

80CR

Pure Gold is an absolute Must-Read for any couple planning to get married in the future. It's not enough to plan just for the wedding, but to plan for a future as husband and wife. This book is a tremendous and inspiring resource, providing thoughtful conversation topics, deep questions to answer, actions to take, and a priceless collection of insights into the top virtues and qualities each strong marriage partner should not only possess, but practice.

~ Sharon Naylor, author of 25 wedding books, including Y*our Special Wedding Vows*

80CR

One of the most important ingredients for any marriage is the commitment by both parties to growth. This book enables couples to explore the true meaning of growth based on the development of character qualities and virtues. It is set out in a very clear and readable way with the addition of exercises to practice the relevant skills.

~ Fiona McDonald, Marriage Educator, Manager of Education Services and Professional Development for Relationships Australia

Intended Audience

Pure Gold will be useful for the following:

♥ *Married Couples* to nurture and solidify your relationship

♥ *Dating/Courting/Engaged Couples* to assist you with understanding one another's character and determining if you have the qualities to sustain a marriage

♥ *Religious Leaders/Clergy* to use in pre-marital and marital counseling and in nurturing marriages in your congregations and communities

♥ *Workshop/Study Session Leaders* to use with individuals and couples interested in exploring marriage in group settings

♥ *Relationship Professionals* such as mentor-couples, marriage counselors, relationship coaches, social workers, and others to use as a tool for supporting couples to move in positive directions in their relationships

♥ *Parents* to assist you with supporting the relationships of your children and with understanding the characters of potential new family members

To All Readers

We welcome your feedback for future editions. Please feel free to email us at staff@marriagetransformation.com with "Pure Gold Feedback" in the subject line. Learn more about us on our website at www.marriagetransformation.com.

Handwritten inscription:

July 30, 2005
To John, In appreciation of your masterful teaching and enlightenment about the true spiritual path of love,
Ruth Twaddell

PURE GOLD

ENCOURAGING CHARACTER QUALITIES IN MARRIAGE

Susanne M. Alexander

with Craig A. Farnsworth and John S. Miller

A MARRIAGE TRANSFORMATION™ BOOK

Pure Gold
Published by Marriage Transformation LLC
P.O. Box 23085, Cleveland, OH 44123
www.marriagetransformation.com; 216-383-9943

International Standard Book Number/ISBN: 0-9726893-5-4
Library of Congress Control Number: 2005923130

See page 271 for extension of copyright notices and permissions.

This book is designed to provide helpful educational information about marriage and relationships. It is sold with the understanding that the publisher and the authors are not engaged in rendering legal or clinical advice. No information, advice, or suggestions are intended to take the place of a therapist or licensed professional. If expert assistance is required, the services of a competent licensed professional should be sought. The authors and publisher shall have neither liability nor responsibility to any person or entity with respect to any loss or damage caused, or alleged to be caused, directly or indirectly by the information contained in this book.

The examples and stories in *Pure Gold* are fictional. The authors created the stories from their own knowledge, observation, and experience to illustrate key concepts. Any similarities to situations or people, living or dead, are coincidental.

Cover and Layout Design: Joyce Ashman
Cartoons: Catherine F. Hosack (www.catherinesart.netfirms.com), Brenda Brown (www.webtoon.com), and Randy Glasbergen (www.glasbergen.com); licensed for use; copyrights held by artists
Back Cover Author Photo: Steve Petti, new image media, www.newimagemedia.com, 216-514-1835

Acknowledgements

The process of creating a book requires the dedicated, unified effort of many people. We are grateful to the following:

Linda Kavelin Popov, co-founder of The Virtues Project™, and her husband, **Dan Popov, Ph.D.** with Wellspring International Foundation, researched the scriptures of the world's religions and found that they all focus on qualities of character (virtues). The Virtues Project shares the language and tools of the virtues with others, and Linda Kavelin Popov generously allowed us to build on their foundation. We have drawn on Linda's expertise and appreciate her body of materials, including *The Family Virtues Guide, The Virtues Project Educator's Guide*, and *A Pace of Grace*. (www.virtuesproject.com; www.paceofgrace.net)

John S. Miller, Character Coach, B.S. Psychology, is very passionate about character. As the author of the Solving Conflicts™ character education system, John's focus is on identifying personal character strengths as the basis for reducing personal and interpersonal conflicts (www.solvingconflicts.com). His perspectives present you with new ways to look at your character, manage your choices, and strengthen your relationships. We honor John for his dedication and excellent work, as well as his willingness to participate in expanding this edition. We also give special thanks to John's wife, Cindy, for her loving support and inspiration throughout the process of incorporating the principles of their Solving Conflicts system into this second edition.

John Gottman, Ph.D., emeritus professor of psychology at the University of Washington and executive director of the Relationship Research Institute in Seattle, Washington, determined through studying couples that one of the most destructive interactions they can have is to attack or criticize the character of one another (*The Seven Principles for Making Marriage Work,* pp. 27-29, coauthored with Nan Silver). His finding led us to look at how we can assist couples to encourage one another's character development instead of engaging in criticism. We believe this positive and nurturing practice is vital in building strong and lasting marriages.

Honoring the Team

We are honored and thankful for the friendship, support, and service of a great team of people, who generously provided insights, advice, edits, technical support, graphics, financial backing, and testimonials to the two editions of *Pure Gold*. Our deep appreciation to all of you:

Anita Armstrong, Viki Ashchi, Joyce Ashman, Bruce Barick, Cindy Bender-Clarke, Brenda Brown, Don Brown, Jason S. Carroll, Hillary Chapman, Jennifer Coates, Paul Coleman, John Covey, Jim Dalenburg, Krsnanandini Devi Dasi, Richard Eastburn, Deborah Evans, Leah Farnsworth, Lu Farnsworth, Tamaura Foley, Ron Frazer, Randy Glasbergen, John Grinder, Allison Grover, JoAnn Harris, Mike Hillis, Kimberly Hopwood, Catherine Hosack, Katrina Jarman, Daniela Kantorova, Linda Kavelin Popov, Khalil Khavari, Kim Klein, Landmark Education, Sue Martin, Fiona McDonald, Johanna Merritt Wu, Charlie Michaels, Ann Miller, Greg Miller, John Miller, Louise Mosher, Ed Muttart, Kay Muttart, Sharon Naylor, Jan Perry, Steve Petti, John "Yakov" Phillips, Dan Popov, Tariq Saleem Ziyad, Cheryll Shuette, Melanie Smith, John Thelen-Steere, Michelle Thelen-Steere, Jean Taber, Michelle Tashakor, Sharon Toerek, Ruth Twaddell, Erik Unterschuetz, Hank Wich, Barbara Whitbeck, Jack Wolf, Lynne Yancy, and the many attendees of our workshops.

Table of Contents

PART 1 ~ ALL ABOUT CHARACTER

Introduction ~ Creating New Hope for Marriage　　　　3

1 ~ The Gold Mine: Transforming Your Marriage　　　　5
What is Transformation? • Stages of Development • Dealing with Reality

2 ~ 24 Karat Gold Nuggets: Digging Deep into Character　　　　11
Developing Character • Many Character Qualities • Assessing Your Characters • Handling What You Find • Vital Qualities in Marriage

3 ~ The Gold Standard: Affirming Your Friendship　　　　23
Friendship in Your Marriage • Qualities of Friendship • Character Friendship

4 ~ Golden Treasure: Taking Time to Talk　　　　27
Describing Consultation • Supporting Effectiveness • Consultation Topics • Supportive Structures and Practices • Communication Skills in Consulting • When Agreement is Difficult • Ongoing Development

5 ~ A Gold Key: Learning by Listening　　　　46
How to Listen • Conscious Listening • Listening Challenges

6 ~ Refined Gold: Influencing and Supporting One Another　　　　58
The Value of Influence • Refining Character • The Influencing Process • Maintaining Harmony

7 ~ The Golden Rule: Sharing the Positive　　　　68
Character Quality Language • Appreciation, Affirmation, and Encouragement • Five Love Languages • Balancing Toward the Positive

8 ~ A Gold Star: Giving and Responding to Feedback　　　　79
Complaints and Criticisms • Ensure a Positive Outcome • When You Trigger Emotions • Ways to Influence • Making Requests • Stopping Character Attacks • Motives

9 ~ Gold Rings: Interacting Qualities　　　　95
Misusing Character Qualities • Balancing or Moderating Qualities • Misusing Dominant Qualities • Misusing Creative Imagination • The Missing Quality • Decisions Follow Events • Responding to Misuses

10 ~ Solid Gold: Building Intimacy　　　　108
Vulnerability • Intimacy Through Communication • Physical Closeness • Shared Experiences

11 ~ A Golden Gift: Uncovering Sexual Oneness　　　　115
Character Qualities and Sex • Care in Touching • Having Children • Discerning Standards

12 ~ The Gold Medal: Creating a Lasting Union　　　　122
Staying in Action • A Spiritual Connection

Table of Contents

PART 2 ~ ENCOURAGING CHARACTER QUALITIES

Introduction and Instructions   129

Acceptance	132	Idealism	188
Assertiveness	134	Integrity	190
Beauty	136	Joyfulness	192
Caring	138	Justice	194
Chastity	140	Kindness	196
Commitment	142	Love	198
Compassion	144	Loyalty	200
Confidence	146	Mercy	202
Contentment	148	Moderation	204
Cooperation	150	Patience	206
Courage	152	Peacefulness	208
Courtesy	154	Perseverance	210
Creativity	156	Purity	212
Detachment	158	Purposefulness	214
Discernment	160	Respect	216
Encouragement	162	Responsibility	218
Enthusiasm	164	Self-Discipline	220
Equality	166	Service	222
Excellence	168	Sincerity	224
Faithfulness	170	Spirituality	226
Flexibility	172	Strength	228
Forgiveness	174	Tactfulness	230
Friendliness	176	Thankfulness	232
Generosity	178	Thoughtfulness	234
Gentleness	180	Trustworthiness	236
Helpfulness	182	Truthfulness	238
Honesty	184	Unity	240
Humility	186	Wisdom	242

Table of Contents

APPENDICES

A ~ Communication Skill: Consultation in Marriage — 247

B ~ Communication Skill: Agreed Consultation Practices — 250

C ~ Consultation Practice: Service and Time Commitments — 251

D ~ Consultation Practice: Your History With Money — 254

E ~ Communication Skill: Tone of Voice — 256

F ~ Communication Skill: Making Requests — 257

G ~ Communication Skill: Stop Misusing Creative Imagination — 259

H ~ Communication Skills: Humor and Fun — 262

I ~ What's Character Got To Do With It? Enhancing Sexual Intimacy in Your Marriage — 263

J ~ Permissions and Copyright Notices — 271

K ~ About the Authors — 274

Part 1

All About Character

The Structure of Pure Gold

Pure Gold is set up in three parts:

Part 1 ~ All About Character

12 Chapters about Character and Communication

Part 2 ~ Encouraging Character Qualities

56 Character Qualities for you to discuss

Appendices ~ Activities and worksheets for building your skills

Note: Throughout the book, the Character Qualities that are covered in depth in Part 2 are *italicized*. This will draw your attention to using them, as well as let you know that there is more information available. There are exceptions in some instances for either readability or because the qualities are in a quotation from other sources.

LIBRARY HELP DESK

"Marriage and relationships?....That's under the Arts and Sciences."

Creating New Hope for Marriage
An Introduction by Susanne M. Alexander and Craig A. Farnsworth

Over the last few years, our family and friends have grieved over short marriages, struggled through painful separations, chosen cohabitation instead of marriage, and experienced difficult divorces. We started asking "Why?" and "What could have made a difference?"

Pure Gold: Encouraging Character Qualities in Marriage is part of our response. It developed out of our personal experiment with what would keep our marriage, the second for both of us, *strong* and lasting. Our experience has been very positive with practicing powerful and sustaining character qualities, such as *truthfulness*, *faithfulness*, and *love*. We are *confident* this practice will be a gift to your marriage as well.

Often, marriages flounder simply because the couple does not have the knowledge and skills to make it work. For this reason, *Pure Gold* is set up to *help* you understand character and practice character qualities effectively. It also includes the opportunity to learn and practice vital communication skills to *strengthen* and enrich your relationship.

When researching character, we came to realize that most people learn about it from the world's religious scriptures. The books of these religions—Bahá'í Faith, Buddhism, Christianity, Hinduism, Judaism, and Islam—consistently mention such character qualities as *kindness*, *courage*, and *compassion*. These qualities are often referred to as "virtues," and some of the quotations throughout *Pure Gold* draw from these sources. We *encourage* you as a couple to turn to God, or whatever *spiritual* source is in your lives, for assistance in practicing these qualities—it is often not easy! [**Note:** At times in this book, we refer to "God" or "the Creator." If these terms do not match your beliefs, please substitute with what works for you.]

Pure Gold also includes quotations from philosophers, marriage researchers, relationship experts, and character experts to provide a well-rounded perspective on this topic. Two of our key resource people were Linda Kavelin Popov and Dr. Dan Popov, co-founders of The Virtues Project (www.virtuesproject.com). It is a global initiative that inspires the practice of virtues in everyday life by providing programs and materials that *help* people to awaken and cultivate these timeless qualities of spirit and character. The United Nations secretariat honored the Project as a "model global program for all cultures."

It is our conviction that positive and *cooperative spiritual* actions can draw married couples more intimately together. For us, this means most days we pray together, read a *spiritual* quotation, and read a few sentences from *Pure Gold* about one of the qualities. We then take that quality and focus on it for the day. When we have more time, we go through an in-depth discussion of how we are incorporating one of the qualities into our married life together. We *encourage* you to develop such practices in your marriage.

Marriage is an adventure, and it takes conscious choices and abiding *commitment* to maintain and enrich it. We urge you to use *Pure Gold* as an investment in this vital endeavor and create a happy and lasting marriage.

Fundamentals of a Strong Marriage

(Copyright 2005 Marriage Transformation LLC)

1 ~ The Gold Mine: Transforming Your Marriage

This book is about the adventure of transforming your marriage into pure gold. Challenging? Of course. Worthwhile? Absolutely! And definitely possible. When you find gold in a mine, it needs processing and polishing to transform it into *beautiful* objects. Similarly, caterpillars go through a complex and miraculous process to transform into colorful butterflies, but they achieve this successfully. With focus and effort, you can take your marriage through a transformation process so it achieves its highest potential.

As an individual, you are already engaged in the vital and life-long personal transformation process of developing your character. Some faiths describe this process as developing the ability to reflect the qualities of God, such as *patience, justice,* and *wisdom.* When you effectively practice character qualities in your marriage, you contribute to transforming one another and your relationship in the best possible way.

Whether you are aware of it or not, your marriage is transforming. Life itself has a way of changing each of you. If you are not mindful, it can change you into something you do not want to be. In turn, this will negatively affect your marriage. Yet, if you are deliberate and mindful, you can *purposefully* work together to transform your marriage into the very best it can be.

WHAT IS TRANSFORMATION?

Transformation is a deep and vital shift in something or someone, a change from one state to another. Sometimes transformation happens rapidly and unexpectedly. Either of you might have an experience or significant realization that causes a breakthrough in using a character quality effectively, and you might never be the same again. Other times, transformation happens over a long period and requires *commitment* and *perseverance*. The process is often so slow-moving, that it is difficult at any particular time to see the progress that is taking place.

Transformation is a fascinating concept. It might *help* you to understand how it works in your lives if you compare it to nature. Plants, flowers, and trees start as tiny seeds. When you look at the seeds, you cannot imagine what will grow from them. However, the potential for transformation exists in every one. Consider this quote from Howard Colby Ives in his book *Portals to Freedom*:

> What is that mystery underlying human life which gives to events and to persons the power of…transformation? If one had never before seen a seed, nor heard of its latent life, how difficult to believe that only the cold earth, the warm sun, the descending showers, and the gardener's care were needed to cause its miraculous transformation into the growing form, the budding beauty, the intoxicating fragrance of the rose! (p. 13)

Nurturing Character and Marriage

Just as seeds have within them the potential of becoming plants or trees, you both have the potential within you to fulfill your character qualities. These include *friendliness*, *helpfulness*, and *trustworthiness*. As a married couple, you water these quality "seeds" both individually and together. You do this through *loving* one another, practicing positive behavior, problem solving, dealing with life's challenges effectively, and being of *service* to others.

You may also choose to water the "seeds" of your qualities and relationship through developing *spirituality* and incorporating *spiritual* practices into your lives. These might include *loving* and worshipping God, reading and studying *spiritual* books, following *spiritual* teachings, praying, meditating, or participating in a *spiritual* or religious congregation or community.

A parallel of this seed image from nature exists in your marriage. When you first marry, you know the relationship and family you hope to create, but you have no way of knowing how it will turn out. *Love* and nurturing create your marriage over time. As you *encourage* one another to develop character qualities, both you and your marriage transform.

Marriage is one of the best places to work on character. One of you may struggle to practice a quality, and this tests the other. This then becomes an opportunity for the partner to work on *patience*, *compassion*, or some other appropriate quality in response. This, in turn, *encourages* the spouse to *strengthen* the quality. One of you may be *strong* in a quality that the other desires. The example of seeing the quality in practice can inspire transformation to begin. While character growth is an individual activity, it is also an ongoing, dynamic process between you. The more you practice *unity* in this effort, the more potential there is for transformation.

STAGES OF DEVELOPMENT

Creating a family within your marriage by adding children gives you another view of transformation. Throughout your children's lives, you watch them grow and develop. A baby starts small in the womb of its mother. It grows until it goes through the transforming process of being born into a new and very different world. The child then goes through developmental stages over several years. In the same way, character growth goes through many transitions.

Part of growth for human beings comes through the transformation of ignorance into knowledge. Mothers and fathers have a vital role in the education of children so they develop essential *respect* for others and themselves and have well-developed characters. Parents and then educational institutions play key roles in raising children to be literate, educated, and effective contributors to the world. Adulthood is an opportunity for further expanding knowledge. Part of this process happens within your marriage as you gain new information and insights that cause you to behave and interact in new ways.

While a seed cannot choose what type of soil to be planted in, you can make choices that support your transformation. You can plant yourselves in the soil of knowledge and reason. Yet even in good soil, if the soil is dark and dry, the seed will not grow. You need sunlight and water for your seed to grow—*spiritual* insights. Sometimes there are rocks and weeds in your soil—faults and issues that get in your way. If your seed is to transform into a rose bush, you need a Gardener to *help* cultivate you. The Gardener (God) provides *spiritual* guidance for your seed.

A rose bush transforms from a seed, in good soil, with sunlight and water, with the *care* of the Gardener. So will you transform, with knowledge and reason, with *spiritual* insights, and with guidance. This step-by-step view can *help* you to understand the consequences of your behavior and interactions. It will *help* you to be empowered to make better life choices.

Part of your transformation process includes each of you discovering your own character qualities and how to make improvements in them as needed. Often these kinds of insights can be immediately transformational in their effect on your lives and marriage.

DEALING WITH REALITY

All of this might sound positive and wonderful, but you may be skeptical because your marriage seems less than ideal. One of you might have a problem with anger. The other does not handle household *responsibilities* well. You take each other for granted, and you forget to be *courteous* or *helpful* to one another. You may be finding parenting is more of a challenge than you imagined. Intimacy of all kinds is frequently missing. Sometimes the possibility of divorce comes up.

No matter how difficult your circumstances, however, transformation can happen. And, one of the key ways you develop it is through effectively practicing character qualities.

You may react to this idea by thinking that if only the one you are married to would work on his or her character, life would be great! One of you may feel hesitant to grow too much unless your spouse willingly addresses issues too. Nevertheless, even if only one of you practices positive behavior, without the *cooperation* of your spouse, it will support positive growth in your marriage. It may also inspire him/her to make efforts as well. The more difficult your circumstances may be, the more benefit you will see in taking personal initiative to practice and grow, even if you are the only one doing so.

Dan Popov, Ph.D., of Wellspring International Foundation, talks about the importance of change as part of planning for a sustainable life. Here is what he says:

> Your choices matter, so make a commitment and choose a new path, even if you are uncertain about where it will lead you. Be aware—if the path is familiar, it is not a new one. Only if you give your effort your full 100% commitment, will you be able to assess its value effectively later on. Involve others by telling them of your commitment and asking for their assistance—show them how it can benefit both of you. Call on the spiritual power of prayer and allow yourself to be guided forward.

> Your commitment and choice to take a new path in your life will likely result in four to six weeks of turmoil; it will call for conscious awareness and regular effort before it begins to feel right. At the first difficulty along the path, you may be tempted to retreat to a more familiar path, but persevere, be determined, and hold your commitment with integrity. Guidance, confirmation, and support come when you are in action. Observe what is happening and be honest with yourself. Growth is positive change. Be patient, flexible, and graceful—change will come— little by little, day by day.

In this often fast-paced world, you may have learned to expect instant gratification for your efforts, and sometimes this does occur with character work. Character and marriage, however, are long-term projects and will require ongoing time and attention.

As you experience your everyday lives, think about the broader picture. As each individual relationship moves forward in a positive direction, there will be an effect on others. A marriage that reflects its happiness and success out to others profoundly affects children, parents, friends, and strangers alike. The ultimate transformation is a planet filled with marriages and families that are happy, lasting, and based on effective practice of character qualities. This transformation will take time, but the potential is there in the seed that you as a married couple plant, water, nourish, and cultivate.

❧❧❧

"Marriage may be compared to a plant that requires daily nurture, daily attention, daily care, and cultivation. It will not develop of its own accord; only as effort and will are exerted will it grow and mature. For a marriage to succeed, both husband and wife must be committed to its success. They must build an enduring love relationship that is centered in the heart of their consciousness. Their relationship must be nurtured with the water of loyalty and love."
~ Margaret Ruhe, Some Thoughts on Marriage, p. 4

2 ~ 24 Karat Gold Nuggets: Digging Deep into Character

Your marriage is the union of two distinct people coming together to form one couple. However, even in a marriage, you are each individuals with ultimate responsibility for your own characters. Understanding how character works within your marriage requires a mirror. You begin by taking a close look at yourselves as individuals.

Character might be something you both know about, or it may be a new concept. Simply, it is:

- Your moral compass or ethical strength
- The sum of all the qualities you developed throughout your lives as you made choices about how to act
- The essence of who you are as human beings

The character qualities you have constantly shape and guide your thoughts, attitudes, behavior, and interactions with others. Transformation and maturity come through increasing your effective practice of them, and discovering and *strengthening* others that are weak.

For instance, are you *honest? Enthusiastic? Loyal?* Do you practice qualities like these effectively? Or do you only use them when someone is paying attention to you? If you practice a quality in an effective way, it guides your behavior, whether someone else is observing you or not. These qualities influence how you act toward one another and, therefore, your marriage.

DEVELOPING CHARACTER

By the time you were both in your late teens, your characters were quite solidly formed, and they are likely to stay fairly consistent throughout the rest of your lives. You will have many opportunities to make adjustments in how you practice the qualities, however. Part of the purpose of *Pure Gold* is to assist you in making these adjustments, particularly when doing so would make a difference in your relationship and with your families. When each of you consciously chooses to make changes and assist one another in the process, it contributes to a lasting marriage. No one can change either of you against your own will. On the other hand, if you desire to make better choices to improve your lives, no one can stand in your way.

You were actually born with the *capacity* to develop all possible character qualities. Throughout your childhoods, your parents then began to form your characters with their messages of "this is the right thing to do" and "that is a wrong thing to do." You continued building your characters through new experiences and learning from the choices you made.

Consider how parents *encourage* their child to *help* others by setting the table for dinner, watching younger siblings, or doing yard work for an elderly neighbor. As their child becomes an adult, the quality of *helpfulness* will probably be a dominant strength in his/her everyday life. In the story below, the qualities that Melissa and Todd learned from their parents affect their marriage:

> Whether it is Melissa encouraging Todd to be *courageous* or Todd supporting Melissa to be *honest*, they find they are drawing on one another's character qualities in their marriage. As a child, Melissa's parents *encouraged* her to be *courageous* in trying new activities, foods, and experiences. However, she also developed the habit of trying some adventures in high school without telling them. Her habit of secrecy is now affecting her marriage, as she hides things from Todd, like shopping receipts or outings with friends.
>
> Todd's parents divorced after his mother grew tired of his father's cheating and dishonesty. For years, she withdrew and trained Todd to be cautious about new relationships. One thing he learned from his mother's experience was that it is very important to be *honest*. Now, in his own marriage, Todd successfully *encourages* Melissa to be open and *honest* about purchases and other issues in their marriage. Melissa *encourages* Todd to be *courageous* in building a marriage with her. She also *helps* him to practice *courage* by trying new foods and activities.

You are probably aware you have character qualities like *courage* and *honesty* similar to Melissa and Todd, but you may not have stopped to think about the wide range of qualities you both might have.

MANY CHARACTER QUALITIES

If you check most of the world's religious scriptures from the last few thousand years, you will discover that they mention hundreds of character qualities, sometimes called virtues or traits. Part 1 of *Pure Gold helps* you to understand the importance of them and how to practice them in your lives. Part 2 assists you to understand and consult about many of the qualities in depth. This will *help* you determine how they apply to your lives and what changes you can choose to make. Below are the qualities that will appear throughout *Pure Gold*—the golden nuggets of character:

Acceptance	Faithfulness	Peacefulness
Assertiveness	Flexibility	Perseverance
Beauty	Forgiveness	Purity
Caring	Friendliness	Purposefulness
Chastity	Generosity	Respect
Commitment	Gentleness	Responsibility
Compassion	Helpfulness	Self-Discipline
Confidence	Honesty	Service
Contentment	Humility	Sincerity
Cooperation	Idealism	Spirituality
Courage	Integrity	Strength
Courtesy	Joyfulness	Tactfulness
Creativity	Justice	Thankfulness
Detachment	Kindness	Thoughtfulness
Discernment	Love	Trustworthiness
Encouragement	Loyalty	Truthfulness
Enthusiasm	Mercy	Unity
Equality	Moderation	Wisdom
Excellence	Patience	

Each of these qualities is important to your individual lives and to your marriage. With understanding, the willingness to act, and practice, you can develop them and learn to use them effectively.

ASSESSING YOUR CHARACTERS

Sometimes, buried in the tasks of everyday living, you might forget that part of life's purpose is for each of you to grow and improve. To be part of this growth process, you need to know where you are starting. What choices have you made in developing your characters? Who are you today? While your parents initially had more control over how your characters developed, you are now *responsible* for continuing the development process and choosing what you will do next.

The Power of Choices

Each choice you make affects your qualities, and your qualities affect your choices. When you use a quality consistently and well, it becomes part of who you are, and one of your **dominant** qualities. On the other hand, if you do not use a quality, it will become weak and will not be available to you when you need it. Each character quality is like a tool in your toolbox. You learn how to use the tools through ongoing practice and develop the skillful use of them. Failure to use the most effective tool/quality at the appropriate time leads to problems and conflicts between the two of you and also with others.

How effectively are you using the tools of your character qualities? Are the qualities you are using benefiting one another and yourselves? When friends and family members look at each of you, what do they see? Consider asking them for input.

Self-Honesty

Understanding your qualities is a search for *truth*. The Buddhist teachings about marriage pair *truth* together with a lasting marriage:

The greatest happiness which a mortal man can imagine is the bond of marriage that ties together two loving hearts. But there is a greater happiness still: it is the embrace of truth. Death will separate husband and wife, but death will never affect him who has espoused the truth. Therefore be married unto the truth and live with the truth in holy wedlock. (*The Gospel of Buddha*, LXXXI:7-8)

Often you may find it is easier to see challenges in others than within yourselves. Self-*honesty* can be very difficult. It may be easier instead for each of you to make excuses and blame others for why you are the way you are or why you do what you do.

If one or both of you regularly blame other people or circumstances for outcomes you cause, this is a warning sign of immaturity. It indicates that you are unable or unwilling to take *responsibility* for your character growth or life. It is vital to transform this pattern for your own good and that of your marriage. Addressing character issues and *honestly accepting* how you both speak and act opens up the possibility for you to grow and change in many new and positive directions. Like Melissa and Todd in the earlier story, this will benefit your marriage.

When you first started to consider a serious relationship with one another, you put your best self forward for the other to see. Certainly, you meant to do that *sincerely* and not simply to conceal who you really are. Yet people often tend to become careless and overly comfortable in how they act with the people they are closest to. It may be time for you to reclaim that early time in your relationship when you were putting your best self forward. It is worth it to do this *sincerely* because it is *respectful* to be your best self, and not to gain a reward for good behavior from your spouse.

Justification, blind spots, lying to yourself, denial, perfectionism, and just general lack of awareness can all get in your way. Would you drive a car blindfolded? Would you climb up a mountain without learning the proper techniques? Would you ride a road bike without the proper safety equipment? Of course not—the risks would be too high. Yet, you may be approaching the *care* and maintenance of your characters in exactly this manner. It takes reflection, self-observation, and feedback from others to sort out your issues and make new choices. Then, you will both need to reassess yourselves regularly as you develop your qualities and learn how to use them *wisely*.

© 2005 Catherine F. Hosack

Asking Questions

Asking yourselves direct questions can assist you to see if you are behaving in ways that are beneficial. How do others respond when you believe you are acting in a positive way? For instance, here is a set of questions you might ask yourself if you have a concern about whether you are being *truthful* effectively:

- When communicating *truthfully*, am I *careful* to stick to the facts and not make up details?
- Am I *careful* to avoid causing hurt, injury, or insult to others with my words?
- When I am *truthful*, do I sometimes forget to be *tactful* as well and hurt others' feelings?
- Do I search for the *truth* when working to solve problems?

Here is another example, this time about *friendliness*:

- Am I being *friendly* toward everyone on an *equal* basis?
- Do I sometimes use my *friendliness* in a self-centered way to impress someone?

- Have I been in a situation where I was *friendly* to everyone but stayed away from someone who was unfamiliar?

Mutual Assistance

Henri learns about his *friendliness* with the assistance of his wife, Collette:

> Henri is charming and outgoing at work, and he and his wife, Collette, regularly host friends for meals in their home. However, when at restaurants, Henri is often cool and curt to the servers. He believes there is no point in being *friendly* to people he sees only briefly. This attitude concerns Collette, but she is uncertain about raising it with him, because he is generally so *friendly*. One day, however, when Henri ignores a server's attempts to be *friendly*, Collette decides it is time to say something. Colette asks him if he noticed that the waitress appeared unhappy in response to him and was then less *friendly* to the next customers. He has never thought of this before, but Colette's comment raises his awareness and prompts him to reconsider his attitude.

This interaction is a signal for Henri to pay attention. If he does not adjust this aspect of his character, it could have ripple effects throughout his life and marriage. Will he continue to receive *excellent service* at restaurants? Will people begin to doubt the *sincerity* of his *friendliness*? Think about how his attitude might have a negative effect on how his children learn to treat people.

You may be reluctant to ask one another, other family members, or a friend to give you explicit feedback on your behavior. However, it is an act of *trust* and *respect* to invite perspectives from others without getting defensive or arguing in response. With mutual sharing in your relationship, you have the opportunity to influence and support one another, something that is vital in maintaining your marriage. This process of gaining feedback from one another about your characters can then be an ongoing practice. You are one another's helpmate and "coach." [See Chapter 6 for more about this topic.]

HANDLING WHAT YOU FIND

As you assess yourselves, note the following:

- The very effective qualities you have that positively affect one another and other people, including your children
- The weak qualities or ones that you seem to lack
- The qualities you have that you use unwisely at times and that negatively affect one another and other people, including your children; for example, have you ever been overly *helpful*?!

If you are not effectively practicing some of the qualities, or if you use some of them unwisely, working through Part 2 of *Pure Gold* will support you in further developing them. *Thankfully*, there are usually multiple chances to keep improving!

Balanced Perspective

You are not a teacher in school giving yourself a grade, nor an employer doing a performance appraisal to see if you deserve a raise in salary. It is important not to use your assessment to be self-critical and overly hard on yourselves. It is equally important to avoid being overly proud of how well you are doing. Assessing yourselves is simply an opportunity to look at how you are doing compared to practicing the qualities in the best way. The goal is to be *detached* enough to *discern* a *respectful* perspective of yourselves that will support you in striving for character *excellence*. The *Tablets of Bahá'u'lláh* indicate the importance of this goal:

> The light of a good character surpasseth the light of the sun and the radiance thereof. Whoso attaineth unto it is accounted as a jewel among men. The glory and the upliftment of the world... depend upon it. (p. 36)

Ongoing Assessment

Achieving character *excellence* takes practice and *perseverance*. Once you know your strengths and areas for growth, you can establish routines of character self-assessment. For instance, you might set behavior goals at the beginning of each day. Then, at the end of each day, you might ask yourselves:

- How well did I practice character qualities today?
- When was I very effective in practicing them?
- What could I have done better?
- What will I do differently next time?

You can also ask for feedback from one another, checking to see if something you did benefited or hurt one another or your children. If anything you did caused harm, this would indicate that you might need to *strengthen* a quality or use it differently. It is also likely an opportunity for you to apologize *sincerely* and make amends to the one who was hurt.

Your lives are full of *responsibilities*, so doing the work of character development may seem overwhelming at times. You will start to notice, however, that you are more *peaceful* and harmonious in your relationship if you monitor your actions and keep your relationship "cleaned up." When either of you have done something that results in the other being frustrated or annoyed, your ability to function smoothly is negatively affected.

When you realize that you have made a mistake or behaved poorly, you can:

- Promise to change your behavior the next time
- Determine if there are any apologies or amends to make
- Take the necessary actions to restore *unity* between you

Over time, you will discover that your marriage gives you many opportunities to shape and form your character qualities. You do not do most of your character development in isolation from others. Often your best "teachers" are the other people in your life. As French novelist Stendhal wrote in his book *On Love,* "One can acquire everything in solitude except character."

VITAL QUALITIES IN MARRIAGE

As you gradually expand your understanding of character qualities, you will discover which ones are vital to focus on and *strengthen* in one another and which ones will require less of your attention. You will also choose together which ones are most applicable for different circumstances throughout your marriage. There are several qualities, however, that will especially support you in having a lasting marriage.

The first of these vital qualities is *truthfulness*, and then its close companion, *trustworthiness*. *Truthfulness* builds *trust* in one another's words and actions. *Trustworthiness* lets one another know that you will do exactly as you say you will do—you will keep your promises. These qualities are essential for building a firm foundation of *integrity* in your communications and interactions with one another.

Closely linked to these qualities is *faithfulness*. Marriage creates a union between your bodies, minds, hearts, and souls. Interactions you have with others that tempt you away from your *faithfulness* to one another erode the foundation of your lives together. When you are a positive example of this quality, it also supports your children's ability to maintain a successful marriage.

Justice, which includes treating one another with *respect* and appropriate boundaries, also supports the *integrity* and *equality* of your marriage. These qualities all protect you from dominating one another and empower you to create a *strong* partnership.

All of the qualities will affect how you share your thoughts and feelings with one another. Consider two important ones, however. *Generosity* assists you to express yourselves fully to one another, spend quality time together, and freely give attention to one another. You can then pair this with *responsibility*, which supports boundaries and guidelines as to how, where, and when you communicate. See how one couple works out ways to manage their communications:

> Jonathan and Shannon have been married for fifteen years. Each evening, they eat together with their children. Then they settle

their children with quiet activities and spend time sharing the events of their days with one another and having any necessary frank discussions. They find a quiet corner of their home where they can still hear their children but be by themselves. They have to use their bedroom occasionally for privacy, but usually they prefer to leave it as a place focused on sexual intimacy and affirming their *love* for one another.

The children have learned that giving their parents this time alone benefits them. Jonathan and Shannon are calmer and more able to give the children focused time afterward. The couple learned early on in their marriage that Shannon becomes irritable and negative when she is hungry, so they now know to wait and have time to share after a meal. Often they use this time to say a prayer together as well, because they find their discussion is usually more *generous*, open, and heartfelt when they do.

They end each discussion by calling the children in for hugs and for *encouraging* them with positive feedback about their quiet behavior. Jonathan and Shannon have determined that during this couple time, the children will never hear angry voices or arguments.

Finally, a vital quality for marriage is *love*. It is the most powerful form of attraction that comes from the Creator's boundless *Love* and infuses into all of Creation. You may always feel a level of *love* for one another, but the intensity of your feelings changes with time and circumstances. Whatever you are feeling, it is still important to treat one another in a *kind* and *loving* way.

If you ever feel concern that the level of *love* you are expressing to one another is too low, it will *help* to "re-visit" your positive memories from the past and take conscious actions in the present to rekindle your feelings. You may find it *helpful* to focus on activities that *strengthen* your friendship. *Love* will provide the power to sustain your marriage. Always remember, the best way to receive *love* is to give it away freely. The day that you feel like your spouse is the least deserving of your *love*, is the day that he/she will need it the most.

℠ↄↃ

"Love is patient, love is kind. It does not envy, it does not boast, it is not proud. It is not rude, it is not self-seeking, it is not easily angered, it keeps no record of wrongs. ...Love never fails..."
~ *The Bible* (New International Version) 1 Corinthians 13:4, 5, 8

℠ↄↃ

"Do all the good you can
By all the means you can
In all the ways you can
In all the places you can
To all the people you can
As long as ever you can."
~ John Wesley, *God's BIG Book of Virtues*, page 11

3 ~ The Gold Standard: Affirming Your Friendship

True friendship is a firm foundation for marriage that will see you through its joys and challenges. You will have many opportunities to deepen and develop it as your marriage progresses. It *strengthens* when you confide in one another, parent together, support one another through difficulties, share joys, and participate in fun and relaxation. Marriage is very much about companionship and is in many ways one long conversation and relationship with a close friend. Ideally, you will be closer to your spouse than to any other human being.

FRIENDSHIP IN YOUR MARRIAGE

More than thirty years of marriage research done with couples at the University of Washington in Seattle, proves that "happy marriages are based on a deep friendship." Emeritus professor and Gottman Institute co-founder John Gottman, Ph.D., and co-author Nan Silver of *The Seven Principles for Making Marriage Work,* define friendship as "a mutual respect for and enjoyment of each other's company." (p. 19) They also say, "These couples tend to know each other intimately— they are well versed in each other's likes, dislikes, personality quirks, hopes, and dreams. They have an abiding regard for each other and express this fondness not just in the big ways but in little ways day in and day out." (pp. 19-20)

This example highlights a couple who are long-time friends and spouses:

> Chen and Debbie enjoyed themselves as friends before they got married. Appreciating their friendship continues to sustain them throughout their marriage. They laugh over crazy things that sometimes happen. They talk throughout their evening meal, sorting out what they each need to do before bedtime, so they can determine which one of them will shop for groceries that evening. They have a lively disagreement about how to address a problem in their community. Then they consult about how to surprise their daughter with a party for her fortieth birthday. They

remind one another of the meeting the following week with their retirement advisor. Finally, Chen asks Debbie to go with him to a concert on the weekend. They clean up the table and dishes together.

Chen and Debbie's friendship is an important part of their marriage. They genuinely enjoy being with one another. They have developed an important practice in their marriage—spending time together in shared activities. Your financial situation will affect some of your choices, but the key is doing activities together that you both willingly participate in. At times, you may do something that one enjoys more than the other, but the next time you can switch. As often as possible, choose what you mutually enjoy and what will enrich your friendship and conversation.

"This is a special night and we'd like everything to be as romantic as possible. On our pizza, could you group the anchovies into couples?"

Your friendship also provides a safe place to influence one another's character qualities. Intimate friends can talk freely with one another and provide support in *generous* and *loving* ways. Friendship will *help* you be *honest* with one another as needed, without fear that your words will negatively affect your relationship as a result.

The opposite of this friendship model for your marriage relationship is the battle-ready one. If you are working against one another and trying to establish who is right and who is wrong, your marriage will be difficult to sustain! To start to turn this situation around, determine in your hearts to be one another's very best friend and treat each other this way.

QUALITIES OF FRIENDSHIP

How do you describe friendship? What aspects are present in your marriage? Perhaps your relationship includes these:

- *Honesty* and sharing; good communication
- Spontaneous fun and laughter
- *Acceptance*; ability to be oneself
- Support and empathy during difficulties
- *Enthusiasm* about achievements
- *Loving, spiritual* connection
- *Encouragement*
- *Loyalty*
- Important sharing is kept private
- Reliability; *trustworthiness*
- Common life experiences and memories
- Shared goals
- Enjoyment of the same things
- Opportunities to learn together
- Ability to disagree *peacefully* and constructively
- *Service* to others together
- Reconnect easily even after being apart
- Motivational feedback/nudging that influences the other to go forward

How do you want to deepen your friendship?

CHARACTER FRIENDSHIP

The list in the previous section includes many threads of character qualities—*caring, truthfulness, faithfulness, enthusiasm, loyalty*, and more. Friendship within your marriage includes appreciating one another's best qualities and assisting one another to make adjustments as needed.

Author and researcher Blaine J. Fowers Ph.D. writes about "character friendship" as the ideal and lasting friendship (as described by Aristotle):

> ...it is based on the friends' recognition of each other's good character and on the shared pursuit of worthy goals. ... They are brought together because they recognize each other's good qualities—the character strengths that make it possible for them to seek the good together. ... Character friends work together as a team or a partnership to achieve their shared goals. ... Mutual happiness is a by-product of shared commitment and teamwork.... (*Beyond the Myth of Marital Happiness*, "Virtue of Friendship" section, pp. 125, 128)

Work together to practice your character qualities in ways that benefit one another. Practicing mutual *courtesy*, *generosity*, *kindness*, *respect*, and more will deepen your appreciation for one another. It will also deepen your friendship and contribute to making your marriage last.

ॐﲻ

"...marriage is the commitment of the two parties one to the other, and their mutual attachment of mind and heart. ... Their purpose must be this: to become loving companions and comrades and at one with each other for time and eternity...."

~ Selections from the Writings of 'Abdu'l-Bahá, p. 118

ॐﲻ

"And let there be no purpose in friendship save the deepening of the spirit."

~ Kahlil Gibran, The Prophet, p. 59

4 ~ Golden Treasure: Taking Time to Talk

Sometimes communications with one another will go smoothly. At other times, you may think you are speaking different languages. When this happens, you may end up in conflict with one another. It takes *equal* partnership, practice, and skill building for you to be effective consistently in resolving issues without fighting. It requires taking the time needed to be certain you really do understand the other's point of view. One way to support full and effective communication between you is known as **consultation**.

Consultation is a communication skill that can bring your marriage to a new and higher level of maturity and functioning. As most marriages do, you may still have a few unresolved issues in yours. Yet, fighting and conflict do not need to be part of the culture of your relationship. Consultation gives you a viable alternative that is worthwhile to practice.

Skill-Building Opportunity

To increase your skill level, there are activities in the Appendices. Complete Appendix A, "Communication Skill: Consultation in Marriage" and Appendix B, "Communication Skill: Agreed Consultation Practices" together. It may *help* to read all of Chapter 4 first, however.

Describing Consultation

Consultation is a form of full and equal discussion between you, usually aimed at arriving at a decision about something. You focus on a common goal—what is best to do. In Part 2, you will consult together about how you use particular qualities in your marriage. Effective consultation requires you to draw fully on the best of your character qualities, especially *truthfulness, detachment, respect, humility, patience,* and *courtesy.*

You will use consultation to explore your thoughts, feelings, and goals. It will assist you in clarifying situations, resolving disagreements, and making decisions about actions to take. It assists you in sharing your points of view and finding solutions that work, without blaming, arguing, or telling one another what to do.

© 1997 Randy Glasbergen. www.glasbergen.com

GLASBERGEN

"You always complain that I don't know how to show my emotions, so I made these signs."

In his book, *Consultation: A Universal Lamp of Guidance*, John Kolstoe says: "When the intent is to enlighten, understand a truth, or gain a better perspective, and this is done with an attitude of sharing, of promoting love and harmony, it is consultation. Otherwise it is merely conversation." (p. 34)

Khalil Khavari, Ph.D. and Sue Williston Khavari, M.A. describe the value of consultation in this way:

> Consultation trains everyone in thinking logically; becoming more articulate; listening more effectively to others and noticing feelings and emotions; discovering creative solutions; including ethical considerations in decision-making; learning to be candid, yet courteous; respecting others, their preferences, and views; and practicing the principles of the new paradigm [for marriage]— equality, cooperation, and unity. (*Together Forever*, p. 160)

As you develop skill in consulting, your communications will become smoother, and there will be more synergy and *creativity* in your decision-making. Consultation frees you from using strictly linear thinking and makes the best use of both of your styles of working through issues. As you raise ideas, solutions that neither of you conceived of start to unfold and develop.

SUPPORTING EFFECTIVENESS

Your consultations will increase in effectiveness with time and practice. There are, however, a number of ways you can support the likelihood of having a positive experience and outcome.

Full Expression

You have *equal* voices in consultation, and it is vital for you both to express what is on your minds and hearts freely. Withholding your input or dominating the conversation will negatively affect the outcome. If one of you tends to be more dominant in speaking, you will need to use *self-discipline* to give the other an opportunity to speak. The less dominant of you may also need to practice *assertiveness*. Free expression happens when you are both willing to listen *patiently* to one another and not interrupt. Chapter 5 explores listening in depth.

Being both frank and *loving* supports the effectiveness of your consultation. This means that you are being *honest* with one another, but not in ways that hurt. Your *respect* and *caring* for one another as you speak will assist you to focus on determining the *truth* and making effective decisions. If either of you gives or takes offense with what one another says, you will get sidetracked into negative emotions and stop focusing on your goal.

Pure Motives

It is also important to ensure the *purity* of your motives and intentions. If either of you has a hidden agenda—an unspoken goal—or you want to manipulate one another, the consultation is on a weak foundation from the very start. Share with one another if you need support in being *detached* from a specific outcome.

Also, be very aware if you developed the habit of manipulation, particularly toward those of the opposite gender, before you married.

Consultation is not a method to get your own way. You will be *wise* to support one another in changing this pattern, or it will have a consistent negative effect on your relationship.

Detachment

One distinguishing feature of consultation is once you have expressed a thought or idea, it is no longer "yours." For instance, if Eric expresses an opinion about something, he might feel that he has to stick with that opinion, even if his wife, Janice, says something that causes him to re-think it. In consultation, he can let go of his original opinion and allow himself to move forward with his wife. As a couple, they can then build on what is emerging as a great idea.

It is as if there is a central pot where all the input goes, and the pot belongs to both of you. This image supports you in being *detached*, and you can let go of your original point of view as you each share facts and feelings. *Detachment* also assists you to *accept* an outcome that might not be exactly what you wanted.

Supporting Unified Decisions

Once you have made a decision together, you must both fully support it in attitude, action, and words, or you will never know whether it was an effective decision. In other words, if you come to an agreement, but one of you is not *sincere* and mentally or physically works against the decision, you can never know why it failed. The outcome could have been due to the quality of the decision or to the disunity between you.

Remember that making decisions as a twosome is different from group consultation, because there is no such thing as a majority vote. When you consult as a couple, even when it is difficult, the goal is to come to a *unified* decision. Having only two of you challenges you to reach mutual agreement wherever possible. This may require multiple consultation sessions on the same topic, especially if the matter is very important.

Involving Others

At times, you may also need to ask for input or assistance from family, friends, a religious or *spiritual* leader or council, *trusted* mentors, or others. Consult together about whom you will *trust* to *help* you and whether you will meet with them as a couple or individually.

Be *very* cautious about one of you consulting alone with someone of the opposite gender when the person is not related to you. This can be *true* even when the person is providing a professional or religious consultation or *service*. Sometimes your emotional state could lead you to unwise expectations, comparisons, or involvement with the person. If this happens, it is likely to harm your marriage.

Other Attitudes and Skills

The Khavari's recommend to couples a list of nine attitudes and skills that they see as particularly *helpful* for effective consultation:

1. Mutual respect and fellowship
2. Unselfishness and honesty
3. Willingness to speak
4. Listening
5. Patience
6. Speaking effectively
7. Harnessing egotism
8. Creativity
9. Non-offensiveness

(*Together Forever*, p. 161-62)

You may instinctively move ahead into doing what you want. *Humility*, *patience*, and *self-discipline* will assist you to slow down and engage in consultation instead. These qualities can be valuable during consultation as well, because couple decision-making can take longer. The outcome, however, will be far better and more *respectful* of your marriage.

CONSULTATION TOPICS

Any area of your lives can become a consultation topic. You can share your goals, as well as *encourage* and support one another. You can make decisions about having or raising children, your careers, and how you spend or save money. You can determine your priorities and where you will put your energy. This can often be a *joyful* activity as you clarify your directions in life and *create* new opportunities.

When scheduling an event or activity, you will need to compare your schedules and consult about what timing works for both of you. You need to assess whether the activity is essential or negotiable. When you consider being involved in a time-consuming activity, it will be *wise* to first consult about your current commitments and the effect of the new activity on your family.

SKILL-BUILDING OPPORTUNITY

See Appendix C, "Consultation Practice: Service and Time Commitments," which will guide you through consulting about and prioritizing your activity choices.

As your relationship matures and your *trust* in one another grows, you will develop clear areas where you can *confidently* take action without consulting. These are likely to be relatively minor, however, such as what food to buy at the store or inviting a friend over for a meal.

Consultation will certainly be important when you have any major decision to make that involves spending a significant amount of money, the future of your family, or roles and *responsibilities*. Money, particularly, can be a difficult topic. You may each have different ideas of how you should handle it based on your previous life experiences. Consultation will assist you with *peaceful* and mutual decisions for spending, saving, budgeting, investing, and so on.

You will need to determine if the culture of your marriage includes appropriate thriftiness and *generosity*. What are your priorities? How much will you spend on an activity? Are you conserving your resources for what is most important? One of your decisions will be the amount of money you each can spend separately without consultation, or what decisions require mutual input. Defining this clearly will prevent conflict and upset emotions between you. These guidelines will also vary depending on your circumstances, and you may need to adjust them accordingly over time.

```
┌─────────────────────────────────────────────────────────┐
│              SKILL-BUILDING OPPORTUNITY                   │
│   See Appendix D, "Consultation Practice: Your History    │
│   with Money," which will guide you through understanding │
│   how your past affects your current money decisions.     │
└─────────────────────────────────────────────────────────┘
```

SUPPORTIVE STRUCTURES AND PRACTICES

Your consultations will often benefit by including some consistent practices. These will support the quality of your decisions, your interactions with one another, and how and where you consult.

Guiding Principles

One way to achieve consistency and *integrity* in your decisions is to have guiding principles for your relationship and consultations. These will serve as a priority checklist for issues that come up. They can provide a basis for evaluating new ideas, problems, or issues. The guiding principles, once in place, become the measuring stick to determine if your relationship is on track. You may be *flexible* and deviate from these guidelines at times, but only for very good reasons and after serious consultation.

As an example, you may rank a decision according to whether it respects God first, marriage second, children third, work fourth, and so on. Alternatively, you may wish to make a list of your highest values in your marriage and use it as your guideline. An example might include:

- Turn to *spiritual* sources for guidance
- Deal with issues that arise as soon as possible
- Act with *integrity* in all things, particularly in our finances, our work, and our *service* commitments
- Treat one another and all family members with *love, respect,* and *equality*
- Be *generous* with our money and time

Using agreed principles assists you to keep focused on what is most important to you as you make the decisions that arise during consultations.

Privacy

Often you will consult openly in front of your children. It is an excellent skill to model for them. However, you will need to *discern* what is appropriate, as some consultations require privacy. Even if privacy is not necessary, the setting could make all the difference in the outcome. It is best to avoid interruptions, moments of high stress, and consulting in the middle of crying children, dinner burning on the stove, or exhaustion!

© 2005 Catherine F. Hosack

Prayer

Some couples find it *helpful* to pray together before consulting so they are able to start their discussion on a *spiritual* note. Some pause to pray if the consultation becomes difficult or before making a final decision. If you are uncomfortable praying together, and this does not improve with practice, you could start with a moment of agreed-upon silence or soft music. Types and forms of prayer vary across religions and cultures, and you may have to try a number of different methods to find what works for you.

Formality

Often your consultations will be very informal, simply part of the flow of your everyday lives. Other times, it might support you to use more structure, especially if the topic is very complex or serious. These steps may then prove to be useful:

- Pray for the consultation to be effective and the decision to be *wise* and *unified*
- Identify and state the problem or issue precisely so that there is a common focal point
- Gather and review the facts from all relevant sources
- Identify and agree upon any principles or character qualities that are relevant to the matter
- Have a frank and *loving* discussion and apply the principles and qualities to the facts
- Turn to God throughout for guidance by praying and meditating
- Make a decision based on the principles, guidance, and all the input
- Carry out the decision wholeheartedly and in *unity*, *trusting* in a positive outcome
- Reflect upon and evaluate the decision at agreed-upon stages, change direction as needed, and assess the outcome

Helpful Practices to Stay Connected

If you have concerns that a conflict might arise, or you need support in handling an issue *peacefully*, you may wish to try these practices:

- Sit and face one another; perhaps hold hands
- Pause to pray
- Maintain an openness to learn
- Share perceptions and be willing to have your opinions be influenced
- Focus on the present issue
- *Detach* from issues that are not pertinent
- Strive to agree, not to figure out who is "right"
- Recognize when emotions are escalating and back off the discussion; reschedule for another time

- Be *courageous*
- Take time to breathe deeply and calm down
- Say "ouch" if something said is hurtful
- Call a timeout/pause break
- Share feelings
- Be empathetic and understanding; try to understand the other's perspective
- Hug at the end

Some of these practices may be comfortable for you and some may never be. However, if you experiment and practice, the number of them that work for you will grow.

Family Meetings

Throughout your marriage, you are likely to develop a number of different methods and structures that support your effectiveness in communicating and resolving issues. Stephen Covey, for instance, *encourages* and explains regular family meetings in his book, *7 Habits of Highly Effective Families*. He sees them as a place for planning, fun, problem solving, and teaching valuable lessons and skills to children. Kolstoe, in his book *Developing Genius*, says:

> "It's useful to have scheduled times for family conferences. This is not the time to lecture the children. It's a time for sharing, for planning, for uplifting and should be full of joy and family closeness. When children are part of the discussion, they learn how to make good decisions. Families are not democracies where all opinions are equal and the majority rules. Parents retain control but are not rigid or dictatorial. As children mature, their contributions have more weight. When discussion is frank and loving, the result is security, confidence, and unity. (p. 69)

When You Are Not Together

At times, you may attempt to consult over the telephone, through email, instant messaging, or some other method. To be successful, ensure that you both agree it is the appropriate time to consult, and the best method, so that you will not be interrupted.

If you cannot see one another's faces, then you may miss subtle indications that your partner is upset, angry, or concerned. This makes it even more important that you verbalize your feelings. If you will only be apart for a short period of time, you may agree to consult again when you are physically together. If you are apart for longer stretches, then you will need to set up structures that make consultation successful.

COMMUNICATION SKILLS IN CONSULTATION

The more developed your communication skills are generally, the more effective your consultations are likely to be. There are communications practices throughout *Pure Gold*, including in the Appendices. The following sections include some for you to practice as well.

Encouraging and Listening

As you consult, you may find that using the following phrases *encourage* one another and support your effectiveness and the outcome:

- That is a good idea!
- I see what you mean.
- That is an interesting way of looking at it.
- We are looking at this issue from two different angles.
- That is a unique perspective!
- I would like to reflect on that.
- Let me see if I understand.
- I think I need a bit more explanation.
- Perhaps we could take a break and come back to this later.
- Could we pray, and then talk about it some more?
- What are the *spiritual* principles that apply to this situation?
- It seems as if it would be good to get some more facts.

- I am confused—can you please explain it again?
- Please, *help* me to understand.
- That was *helpful* to me!
- You may be right. It is possible that I may be wrong.

These phrases show that you are listening to one another, an important skill that contributes to effective consultation. It may also be *helpful* to use active or reflective listening, where you paraphrase back to the other what you heard. Remember to summarize, not use the exact words. Listening *helps* you to understand what your spouse is thinking and feeling. Chapter 5 will explore listening in depth.

"I" Statements

Another useful communication tool is "I" statements, when you speak for yourself, not "you" statements that are accusations. When you experience very negative emotions, feel annoyed or irritated by behaviors or situations, or wish to communicate feelings or needs, you will find using "I" statements reduces the likelihood of conflict. Below is a detailed description of these and a variation of the technique as written about by psychologist Marshall B. Rosenberg, author of *Nonviolent Communication: A Language of Compassion*.

The purpose of an "I" statement is to make a clear, clean statement of your experience of an event in a way that the other person is most likely to hear it without feeling defensive. The premise of these statements is that feelings are unique to each of you and that you give up your personal power when you say others can "make" you feel something. Example: "You make me angry."

The following is an example of an "I" statement that occurs between a couple who has left their home for a camping trip. They had agreed ahead of time on the *responsibilities* each would handle to be prepared for setting up the campsite.

> "When the agreement we had is not kept, and the things that I need are not available to me, I feel frustrated because I cannot set up our campsite properly. What I would like is to have what I need to complete my tasks."

The following is the format used in the above statement:

a. "When _____." This is a neutral description of a behavior or event.

b. "I feel _____." This is an accurate statement of your feelings without blame or accusation.

c. "Because I_____." This describes the impact on you of the behavior or event.

d. "What I would like is _____" This is a suggested remedy without expectations being placed on the other person.

An "I" statement is quite different from a "you" statement, which includes an accusation. For example, the following "you" statement is full of blame, the desire to punish, a character attack, and expectations. [See Chapter 7 for more about character attacks.]

> "You are always forgetting the things you promise to bring on our vacation, and I am angry because you have spoiled the whole trip. You have to be more *thoughtful* in the future."

More subtle than a "you" statement and equally ineffective is the blaming "I" statement. The following statement is still full of accusations and expectations.

> "When you forget the things you said you would bring, I feel angry with you, because I cannot have a good time, and I would like you to stop forgetting."

It will take some practice for you to be skilled at "I" statements, but it is valuable to learn, as it reduces conflict and assists you to resolve issues *peacefully*. The listener is far more likely to have a neutral or positive response to a straight and well-worded "I" statement.

When Agreement is Difficult

Timeout/Pause

When you are communicating about challenging issues, you might need to pause and reflect or calm down for a few minutes, hours, or days. This timeout is especially important if anger is escalating in either or both of you. Pausing allows you to assess the character qualities you are using with one another and how best to proceed with your discussion. It often prevents you from saying hurtful words that you will regret.

Researchers like Gottman are discovering that when there are escalating emotions or conflict in a discussion, men physically and mentally become "flooded" very quickly. They cannot continue participating in the discussion in a meaningful way. Heart rates and blood pressure rise quickly, and men then need to withdraw to calm down. It can happen to women too, but it usually takes more conflict and is less common. In any case, it is important in a discussion between a couple that you both have mechanisms—like pausing—or verbal or physical reminders that assist you to de-escalate and stay calm in the consultation. Otherwise, it is unlikely to be effective.

Agree ahead of time to call for a timeout in the consultation if needed. If you pause, ensure that you agree when you will start up again and who has the *responsibility* for initiating it. If a pause results in one of you leaving the house, be *courteous* and *respectful* and provide the information of where you are going and how long you will be gone. It is also *wise* to agree on which of you will reinitiate consultation and when, and then do it without reminding!

When you resume consulting, you may wish to try a different approach. According to Kavelin Popov, "Sometimes when you find yourselves at a stalemate (no pun intended) what is needed is to companion one another or listen more deeply to get to the heart of the matter." [See Chapter 5 for more about "spiritual companioning™."]

"Did you know that beauty is just a state of mind? For example, if you said I was beautiful, I wouldn't mind."

Mixing the Past and Present

Various actions can sabotage the effectiveness of your consultation. For instance, mixing the past with the present can confuse the current consultation. Try to be aware when you are bringing old incidents and emotions into the discussion and straying from the current facts and feelings. This happens for George and Ginger:

> George and Ginger have been married for 20 years but still have challenges consulting at times. They begin to talk about what to do with money George's aunt recently gave them. Ginger suggests they split the money and use it for something each has always wanted. George gets upset and immediately brings up that she wasted the money her mother gave them as an anniversary gift five years before. Ginger retorts that her spending habits are just fine. The consultation dissolves with both of them angry.

George has not *forgiven* Ginger for how she handled money previously, and this still presents a problem for him. Ginger is immediately defensive instead of exploring the issue with him, so the consultation ends with neither the past nor the present issues resolved. They will need to work on *forgiveness* before they can resume consulting. When they do resume, it will assist them to agree to leave the past alone and focus on the present issue.

Other actions can also disrupt a consultation. You will likely find it difficult to reach a decision smoothly if you do any of these behaviors:

- Interrupt
- Force your viewpoint on the other
- Deliberately bring up the other's hurtful "hot button" issues
- Imply or state that one of you is right and that the other is wrong
- Have a competitive win-lose attitude
- Insult or blame one another
- Be sarcastic
- Conceal key information
- Be forceful or dominating in words or tone
- Walk away (unless there is danger of violence)
- Answer the telephone and carry on a conversation
- Refuse to validate the other's point of view or feelings
- Point a finger or use other aggressive gestures or overly dramatic postures
- Dictate by saying, "you should," "you must," "you have to," or "you can't"
- Threaten anyone verbally, emotionally, physically, or sexually
- Threaten divorce

If any of these negative actions are occurring regularly, it is probably best to suspend the consultation. You may find it practical to ask yourselves the question, "Do we need to set new boundaries for ourselves and learn better methods of problem solving?" If you have reached an impasse in coming together reasonably, you may also be *wise* to get some outside assistance with resolving the matter.

Kolstoe shares some of the other behaviors that can sidetrack a consultation:

> Since its purpose is to find a solution, consultation should not be used just to gain sympathy or to dump on someone. It's not consultation when talking degenerates into a gripe session

or gossip or complaining. These activities merely rehash the problem, making it worse. Rather than letting the anger out, this sort of dwelling on the unpleasant things of life causes delay, magnifies the hurt, and interferes with long-term healing. ... In consultation, the intensity of suffering is diluted while the solution is developing. (*Developing Genius*, p. 201)

Preserving the Relationship

Even when it is difficult to work through an issue, it is important to maintain a positive attitude. Remembering that preserving the quality of your relationship is vital, will *help* you communicate in a *loving* way. You need to reflect and be clear about the implications of not reaching harmonious agreement. You will tend to be happier and more satisfied with the outcome of the consultation if you have reached a mutual conclusion.

When a matter is very serious, you may also make a decision but agree to wait for a while before taking any action. This allows you to reflect, pray, and then re-visit the decision to confirm whether it is still the right choice.

Deferring to One Another

Even when you handle the consultation process well, there may be times when you find that you cannot find a solution on which you both agree. Then, one of you may choose to defer the decision to the other and support that position. **Note:** This is not effective if it becomes "giving in" resentfully and then undermining the other's actions. If you defer (and this may be after repeated attempts at reaching a decision), it will need to be *sincere* for the outcome to work.

Your attitudes will be more positive if you *accept* that you are making a conscious decision to defer and *accept* the decision as "ours." The decision is then a mutual *commitment* you both can support wholeheartedly. You may find it *wise* to re-consult after some time has passed to update one another on the issue. You may decide to do something different at that point.

You will also need to monitor whether you are deferring often, which could be a signal that you are not spending adequate time in consultation. It could also be a sign that you may not be *respecting* the *equality* in your relationship if one of you is always the one deferring to the other.

ONGOING DEVELOPMENT

A positive practice is to assess your communication and/or consultation some time after it has occurred. Look for specific examples that showed how you were able to support one another, and evaluate any missteps that happened. Do not assume that things went well, but rather specifically ask one another.

Through these assessments, you will learn when you listened well and when you did not, when you *respected* your partner's thoughts and emotions and when you did not. For example, did you throw something from the past into the discussion that made the other upset or angry? Did you remember to acknowledge one another's character qualities? Did you mean to make the other angry? Did you share fully and frankly? Did you raise your voice in a threatening manner or shout?

If your behavior was inappropriate, it is *helpful* (and potentially surprising to your partner) if you stop to apologize and note that you have just fallen into a pattern or response you want to change. Your *wisdom* will grow if, both in the middle and following an incident, you take the time to reflect and identify lessons learned and ways to do things better next time.

If you are having difficulty communicating or consulting, create a regular, daily time to share with one another how you think your communication flowed that day, what went well, and what did not. If consulting is new to you or seems difficult, try choosing several easy issues and practice your consulting skills. Remember to share your successes, as well as the failures. This daily analysis will *help* your relationship and your skills gradually improve.

ജ്യൂഗ്യ

"Consultation requires the disciplined use of communication skills. The germ of an idea needs to develop through changes resulting from each contribution. The ideal is to produce the best possible results that can be obtained from the minds, the backgrounds, the feelings, and hearts of those participating. Consultation has a purpose; talking, listening, and communication are the skills which can move an idea toward that objective. Yet no matter how well-developed these skills are, they do not result in consultation if they do not contribute toward the goal."

~ John E. Kolstoe, *Consultation: A Universal Lamp of Guidance,* p. 39

"Effective consultation can never take place if one person belittles, minimizes, or glosses over something which is of great importance to someone else."

~ ibid, p. 104

"Through consultation the issue can be clarified because someone else is likely to see the problem differently."

~ ibid, p. 105

5 ~ A Gold Key: Learning by Listening

Truly listening to one another creates a powerful, intimate bond between you. It is one of the keys to developing your friendship, marital intimacy, and character qualities. Life can become hectic, especially if you have young children and both of you work outside the home. When you are going multiple directions, it may often feel as if you communicate briefly, and only what is necessary, to keep your household moving.

Effective communication requires that you slow down, fully express yourselves, and hear one another's thoughts and feelings. It means *truly* listening to the words one another says and the emotions and needs behind the words. Even when it is difficult or inconvenient, friends take the time to listen to one another.

"Flamingos have thin thighs, but they don't seem any happier than you."

How to Listen

You were born with the ability to listen, so it may seem strange to you that this chapter is saying you need to learn how to do it. Just hearing someone's words is not the same as effective listening, however. The process is more complex.

Below are a set of "Listening Commitments" that outline for you how you need to listen to one another. They are from *The Conscious Heart* (pp. 262-263) by Kathlyn Hendricks, Ph.D. and her husband Gay Hendricks, Ph.D. (www.hendricks.com). As you read through these, think about which ones would be particularly useful for you to use with one another:

- I commit to listening carefully enough that I can restate the content of what you have said without adding my point of view to it.
- I commit to listening to the feelings embedded in your communication.
- I commit to listening in such a way that our mutual creativity is facilitated.
- I commit to speaking and listening to myself and you free of criticism. (Criticism is defined as "finding fault, censuring, disapproving.")
- I commit to speaking and listening to myself and you free of evaluating either of us. (Evaluating is defined as "appraising, determining the worth of.")
- I commit to speaking and listening to myself and you free of judging either of us as right or wrong, good or bad, smart or stupid.
- I commit to speaking and listening to myself and you free of comparing us to each other or to anyone else. (Comparing is defined as "bringing things together to ascertain their differences and similarities.")
- I commit to speaking and listening to myself and you free from controlling the feelings, energies, or actions of either of us. (Controlling is defined as "curbing, restraining, holding back, having authority over, directing, or commanding.")
- I commit to speaking and listening to myself and you with appreciation. (Appreciation is defined in two senses: "sensitive awareness" and "focus on positive qualities and attributes.")

If there are any of these that are particularly *helpful* to you as a focus, you may wish to write it down and put it near where you usually have discussions.

CONSCIOUS LISTENING

The Hendricks' recommend couples try out these three levels of conscious listening (*The Conscious Heart*, pp. 267-272):

Level One:
Listen for content—Be able to give a concise and accurate summary of what you have heard the speaker say.

Level Two:
Listen for the emotions—Be able to hear the emotion under the words of the speaker.

Level Three:
Listen for the speaker's wants and needs—Be able to hear beneath the words and the emotions for what the speaker is really asking for and needing.

The sections that follow will explore each of these levels in more depth.

Level One: Listen for Content

In this first level of listening, your primary goal is simply to make sure that you understand the words one another is speaking. The listener will do this by briefly paraphrasing what the other has said. It is important not to repeat the words exactly, as this becomes irritating to the speaker very quickly.

It is unlikely that you would want to use this method of listening on a regular basis. However, it can be very valuable when one of you is upset or has a particularly sensitive or deeply emotional issue to express. It can slow down your interaction and ensure that you hear the concerns.

Suggested Structure:

PART A:

The person who is upset and has the concern speaks first.

1. You start speaking and share your concerns and feelings.
2. Your spouse paraphrases what you said. You then confirm that the summary of what your spouse said was accurate (or you correct it).
3. You make a second statement with additional information.
4. Pause for your spouse to paraphrase again. You confirm again that the summary of what your spouse said was accurate (or you correct it).

PART B:

1. Your spouse shares what happened or their point of view about what led to the concern.
2. You paraphrase back to your spouse what he/she said. Your spouse confirms that your summary was accurate (or corrects it).
3. Your spouse makes a second statement.
4. You paraphrase it again. Your spouse confirms that you accurately understand his/her statement (or he/she corrects it).
5. Your spouse apologizes for his/her part in creating the concern.
6. The two of you consult about how to prevent the situation from happening again.

Example:

PART A:

May arrives in her car in the parking lot of Joel's office. She is one hour late to pick him up for a doctor's appointment. He is scheduled for a heart stress-test due to recent chest pains.

Joel: May, I cannot believe you are so late! I've been waiting for over an hour. I had to call the doctor's office to let them know. Of all the days to be late!

May takes a deep relaxing breath, pauses to make sure Joel is done speaking, and then summarizes what Joel said.

May: Joel, I can tell you are upset. You have been waiting a long time for me, and you had to make excuses to the doctor's office.

Joel: It seems like you just do not understand how high my stress level is right now. I'm really worried about what they are going to find with this test.

May: You think I do not *care* about you and your health.

Joel: That's right. It seems that way.

PART B:

May: I had a flat tire on the way here. Unfortunately, I forgot to charge my cell phone properly last night, and it did not work when I tried to call you.

Joel: So, the car problems interfered with you getting here, and you wanted to let me know, but you couldn't.

May: I'm so sorry. I really do *care* about your heart problems. I'm worried too, and I am very upset that I added to your stress. Will you *forgive* me?

Joel: Yes, of course. I'm sorry for yelling at you. Let's get going to the doctor's office. When we are done there, maybe we should stop and get you a cell phone charger that works in the car. We've been intending to, and we just haven't taken the time.

May: Great idea!

After you have gone through these steps, you would be *wise* to ask if there is anything left to say, discuss how it worked for you both, and determine if this is a tool that you want to keep practicing.

Level Two: Listen for the Emotions

Effective listening requires you each to be silent and *carefully* pay attention to the words the other is saying. Note that you can rearrange the letters of "listen" to form the word "silent." If you are focused on actively listening to one another, your feedback and response will indicate you clearly understand the communication.

To be most effective, however, you must listen empathetically with your ears *and* with your heart. Listening within a close relationship means hearing the emotions behind the words and "hearing" what the person has not said. Observe Elsie in this story:

> Devon sighs, leans over, and places his head in his hands. Elsie sits nearby, helplessly watching her husband and unsure what to say to him. She can see his frustration and stress and *encourages* him to tell her what is going on. Now, pacing back and forth across the living room, Devon starts swearing and yelling about his company and about the managers not *caring* about the workers. Elsie "hears" he is angry.

> Devon paces around the room and then plops back in his chair. Elsie can see by his face that he is devastated about something. He finally shares that his company laid him off his job without notice. Elsie "hears" his fear for their family and how much this situation is shaking his *confidence*.

Having an empathetic listener supports you in expressing yourselves fully. Sometimes by listening this way, you sense what emotions are going on in the other earlier than he/she does. Mind-reading or making assumptions can still be hazardous in this situation, however. You still need to ask direct questions to check out what you are "hearing" with one another.

[You may find it *helpful* to read the chapter, "Habit 5: Seek First to Understand…Then to Be Understood" in Stephen R. Covey's book, *The 7 Habits of Highly Effective Families*.]

Level Three requires even more focused attention. In this practice, you work to *discern* what one another wants and needs through encouraging full expression and listening very *carefully*. One way to facilitate this is using "spiritual companioning™."

Kavelin Popov, author of *The Family Virtues Guide* and *A Pace of Grace* (www.paceofgrace.net), names "The Art of Spiritual Companioning™" as one of the core life-skill strategies for *creating* relationships grounded in the virtues of *love* and *trust*. She says:

> Spiritual companioning requires the awareness that we cannot keep each other happy but we can keep each other company. We can only walk beside one another in the journey of life. We cannot control one another nor do the spiritual work of the other in our relationships. The purpose of spiritual companioning is to help one another empty our cups and get to the heart of the matter. We do this by asking cup-emptying questions starting with "what," "when," and "how"— never "why," which puts each other on the defensive.
>
> If your spouse is upset about you coming home late without warning, and says, "Where were you? I was really worried!," be prepared to explain, and also to ask a companioning question such as, "What were you worried about?" For all you know, he or she pictured you lying on the highway after an accident. Companioning is a way to meet our loved ones right where they are and allows them to reveal their deepest concerns. It leads to making *true* amends, such as a promise to call if you will be delayed again.
>
> Whatever your spouse says, you can show compassionate curiosity in return, even if it sounds like an accusation. Ideally, we would always use tact when sharing our feelings, but sometimes that just doesn't happen. We need to be ready to listen even when it isn't easy. Asking questions that relate to whatever your

partner says, such as, "What do I do that feels belittling to you?" or "When do you lose trust in me?" requires both compassion and detachment to deeply hear the meaning your spouse assigns to what you do and say, or what you don't do and don't say. When you listen to one another with a companioning approach, it allows you to get to the pearl of truth at the bottom of the cup. The listener then asks, "What would help you to feel my love?" or "What would it take for you to trust me again?"

Companioning always ends with Virtues acknowledgments:

- "You were so honest in telling me what really troubles you."
- "I appreciate your courage to look at your deepest feelings."
- "Thank you for your forgiveness and being willing to make a fresh start."

When a couple takes turns companioning and hears one another fully, without the typical parallel conversation where no one is *truly* heard, *beautiful* openings of *trust* and intimacy can occur. [**Note:** See Kavelin Popov's books for more details on the steps of spiritual companioning.]

LISTENING CHALLENGES

You may notice at times that you are having misunderstandings and challenges in your communications with one another. This is a signal to look at how you are listening. The following sections will give you some of the ways you might be interfering with your effectiveness.

Mind-Reading

One pitfall that often happens with couples is that they believe they can or should be able to read one another's mind. Being in a close relationship with someone often gives you greater sensitivity to one another's thoughts and emotions, and sometimes you *can* guess quite accurately what the other is thinking. However, it is unwise to make assumptions about what the other person thinks, feels, needs, or wants without directly asking and listening. Often, attempting to "listen" to one another without direct communication causes misunderstandings that disrupt your relationship.

You may also believe you should not have to ask for what you want or need, and you do not really want something if you have to ask for it, anyway. This thinking will trap you in a cycle of unhappiness, because it is not possible to figure out all one another's needs effectively and reliably without interactive communication. It is best to express your needs to one another, listen, and respond.

Planning a Response

Often within relationships, one of you may be better at listening than the other. Women often multitask and either miss parts of the conversation or give the appearance of not listening. You may need to slow one another down at times to ensure listening is occurring. Men often jump into being problem solvers. You may need to listen, learn, and understand what your wife is saying rather than trying to identify a problem and solve it. Let one another know if you just need someone to listen rather than to develop an immediate solution.

Jenita and her husband, Alan, have consulted and mutually decided Jenita would be a fulltime mother for their three children. Most days she copes well with their ups and downs. Today, however, has been exhausting. She is tense and on the verge of tears as her husband, Alan, walks in the door from work. Their daughter Polly has a temperature, son Calvin thinks the walls are his personal art canvas, and the baby is fussy. To top it off, the toilet overflowed, the dinner burned, and the neighbor yelled at her because their dog kept barking out in the yard. "Just hold me for a minute," she begs Alan as she hugs him hello. "I just need a break from the insanity." Alan listens to all that has gone wrong, and when she calms down, asks what he can do to *help*.

Most people tend to focus on what they will respond to the speaker instead of simply listening to what the person is saying. Alan exercised *self-discipline* and did not jump into the middle of Jenita's outpouring with comments and ideas for solutions. Once Jenita is calmer, they can problem-solve together. If your mind is planning your response, you cannot listen effectively. The Hendricks say in *The Conscious Heart* (pp. 265-266), that the response planning tends to fall into the following categories:

- To judge or evaluate
- To criticize
- To influence or control
- To compare
- To fix

When you *truly* listen to one another instead of impatiently waiting to respond, it enhances *trust* and *unity* between you. Being listened to *helps* you to feel *respected*, validated, and appreciated. It boosts your *confidence* and increases your feelings of *love* for one another. Conscious listening also contributes to your ability to be effective in problem solving together. This then reduces or prevents conflict between you.

Culture and Gender

Cultural or gender-related influences may affect your communication patterns. Some cultures, for instance, teach that it is important *not* to be *honest* or direct in communication, if there is any chance that it will upset the listener. It is the custom in some cultures for people to share loudly and often with each other as an expression of *love,* assuming everyone should listen but not be bothered by negative comments.

Some families and cultures teach male children not to express themselves, but instead to stay quiet, listen, and let females do the communicating. Others teach male dominance and that females should be demure and silent. This is a complex and broad subject, and one that may or may not be an issue for you as a couple. If it is, then studying—and getting exposure to—each other's cultures, as well as reading books about gender differences, may support you in communicating effectively.

Physical or mental disabilities could also affect your ability to communicate or listen to one another. Any kind of hearing loss may cause inaccurate listening and misunderstandings. Some medicines could affect your abilities. Mental illnesses or serious problems from the past could also be a factor, and you will be *wise* to seek professional counseling individually and/or together. Signs of mental impairment might include excessive and unreasonable anger, paranoia, depression, very high levels of anxiety, suicide threats, or repeated abusive and damaging comments. You may need training or guidance in how to listen to one another in all these special circumstances in effective ways.

The more you understand about one another's culture or communication challenges, the more likely you are to be successful at influencing and supporting one another with character development. [See Chapter 6 for more on this topic.]

଼ଡ଼ଔଃ

"Everyone has so much on their minds. The burden seems heavy and must be unloaded regularly. But there are few people who are willing to be loving listeners. Make sure that you are the best and the most willing uncritical listener that your spouse could possibly find. Don't let the bartender do it, don't leave it to strangers. Not even friends should take your place."

~ Khalil A. Khavari and Sue Williston Khavari, *Together Forever*, p. 75

ಬಿ೦ಅ

"Lord, make me an instrument of Your peace
Where there is hatred, let me sow love
Where there is injury, pardon
Where there is doubt, faith
Where there is despair, hope
Where there is darkness, light,
And where there is sadness, joy.

"O Divine Master, grant that I may not so much seek
To be consoled as to console
To be understood as to understand
To be loved as to love.
For it is in giving that we receive
It is in pardoning that we are pardoned
And it is in dying that we are born to eternal life. Amen."

~ St. Francis of Assissi

6 ~ Refined Gold: Influencing and Supporting One Another

Being responsible for and working on one's own character and behavior is a challenging task. Often, you can support, assist, and influence one another, as well as inspire mutual relationship growth and change. Some of the ways you can accomplish this are:

- Choosing a quality to practice each day or for some other time period
- Speaking freely to one another about character qualities
- Sharing positive responses when you each use qualities effectively
- Suggesting particular qualities to one another when they are needed
- Offering guidance to one another when you face circumstances that have been challenging in the past
- Reinforcing one another's *commitment* to make *wise* choices
- Providing *gentle* feedback about any behavior that concerns you
- Responding with appreciation to one another for assistance offered
- Notifying one another when there is a desire for personal change and support with it
- Inspiring one another to *persevere*
- Asking one another for *help*

All these and more will *encourage* growth in both of you.

THE VALUE OF INFLUENCE

Gottman and Silver report, "…men who allow their wives to influence them have happier marriages and are less likely to divorce than men who resist their wives' influence." (*The Seven Principles for Making Marriage Work*, p. 100) They focus on men because the Gottman research team has found that women generally already take their husbands' opinions and feelings into account, but men are less likely to. A United States Center for Disease Control report issued in December 2004 also indicates that married couples are generally healthier because they mutually influence one another toward healthy habits. The report points to an exception, which is that male weight tends to be somewhat higher in married couples. As you become *stronger* in practicing *equality* in your marriage, partnership and mutual influence will grow, and any gender imbalances will lessen or disappear. Your relationship and friendship will then be more satisfying to you both.

Being open to feedback and allowing your spouse—or anyone else—to influence your growth in positive directions requires a foundation of *trust*, *love*, and *respect* between you. It also requires agreement and willingness to be partners in this way. Keep your feedback toward one another *gentle* and positive. That way it will not have a negative effect on your relationship or escalate into criticism or attacks. In doing so, you will likely find common ground on areas that are working well and what needs to change and how. In deciding whether to change, you will find it beneficial to assess the positive and negative effects of all your choices.

REFINING CHARACTER

All interactions and feedback between you can cause a shift in your relationship and your effective practice of the qualities. In a marriage, the two of you are intimate helpmates. Since one of the key purposes of life is for you to refine your characters, one of the vital tasks you have in marriage is supporting and empowering that development process in one another.

You can compare refining your character to taking a raw gem from a mine, polishing it, and cutting it until it sparkles and shines as a *beautiful* jewel. In the context of your relationship, this "polishing and cutting" process might be difficult and uncomfortable at times, but ultimately rewarding.

Some of the polishing process happens between you, but there is always an element of individual work. One of you gets some feedback from the other that something you did was less than stellar, or some mess happened because you did not practice a quality effectively. You know if you do not pay attention to your behavior, there will be ongoing negative consequences.

There are a number of actions you can take as individuals that will end up influencing and supporting you as a couple. The sections that follow provide some details.

Become Willing to Act

You may need to start the transformation process by overcoming denial and becoming willing to acknowledge there is a problem. Once you understand where you are not using a character quality effectively, you then need to be willing to do something to go forward.

Some issues might be minor ones, such as not holding a door open for someone at times. Others can be more serious, such as lying or stealing. Set your goal to become willing to address even the hardest issues. Then take small steps forward, which will assist you to *strengthen* your will. You may find that even the toughest issue was not as difficult to address as you thought it might be at first.

Self-Reflect/Pray/Meditate

If you have little or no experience in these reflective practices, you can start very simply. Prayer and meditation may just mean taking some quiet time alone to think and reflect upon issues that need your attention. You may find it *helpful* to use the specific character quality information in Part 2 as a focus.

This quiet time may be where you determine what your attitude and choices will be. It may also be an opportunity to create your plan for the best way to interact with close family and friends.

If you have more experience, praying and meditating may be turning to a *loving* Creator to become involved in your life and growth. This can be a time for seeking to see your character and behavior more clearly. Reflection will *help* you to understand where you went wrong, what you might have done differently, and what you might do in the future.

Write in a Journal

There are many ways to maintain a journal in support of character refinement. You might write down daily what is happening in your life, your feelings, and the reactions you have. This can give you additional insights about what you need to transform in your life. You may wish to have one page for each quality you are working on and make notes about your progress. Another method many people find useful is to write down a prayer for assistance, pause to pray, and then write down what you feel the answer is to your request. Choose a *wise* person (or God) to write to and ask for *help* whenever you are stuck. You will be amazed by what answers you get.

Clear Your Conscience

You may feel some guilt, shame, or remorse over actions you took that did not work out well and resulted in someone being hurt or upset. These are good indicators that there are better actions to take. Sensing these emotions is very similar to pausing to feel where pain is located in your body. Clearing your conscience begins with finding out where it hurts and why.

Take a close look at yourself to see who you are hurting. It is possible you are only hurting yourself, but highly unlikely. You need to be clear how your actions are affecting others. You are then ready to *accept responsibility* for your actions and identify where you need to make amends, ask *forgiveness*, or adjust an attitude or behavior. Once you have done your best to address the issue, try not to dwell on what happened, and let it go, so you are not stuck in negative thinking instead of taking positive action.

Practice Forgiveness

Marriage researchers Howard Markman, Scott Stanley, and Susan Blumberg define *forgiveness* as the "decision to give up your perceived or actual right to get even with, or hold in debt, someone who has wronged you." (*Fighting for Your Marriage*, p. 303)

Forgiveness involves *accepting* the fact that you may have harmed someone else and your own self as well. It frees you to move forward in life. Holding grudges instead, or keeping a ball of anger inside, freezes you in the past mentally and emotionally and can even make you physically ill. *Forgiveness* allows *love* back into your relationship and makes it possible for you to both heal from the effects of what happened. It *helps* rebuild *trust*.

You will handle tests, difficulties, and disagreements in your relationship with prayer, consultation, *patience*, and *courage*. To maintain *love* and *unity* in your marriage, however, requires that you *detach* and let go of blame, resentments, and hard feelings.

When you have done something that hurt the other, the quicker you address the issue, the more likely you are to maintain *integrity* and *unity* between you. Three important practices related to immediate *forgiveness* can support your marriage:

1. Spontaneously admit when you have been wrong in something, or that you have not used a character quality effectively.
2. Ask for *forgiveness* or pardon from the other.
3. *Forgive* promptly in return.

Sometimes *forgiveness* can be more difficult for you and may take more work. *Fighting for Your Marriage* (pp. 316-319) lists these suggested steps as *helpful* in achieving *forgiveness*:

1. Schedule a couple meeting for discussing the specific issue related to forgiveness.
2. Set the agenda to work on the issue in question (identify the problem or harmful event).
3. Fully explore the pain and concerns related to this issue for both of you.
4. The offender asks for forgiveness.
5. The offended agrees to forgive.
6. If applicable, the offender makes a positive commitment to change recurrent patterns or attitudes that give offense.
7. Expect it to take time.

If either of you bring the past back up in a negative way with one another, it is a signal that you may have unresolved issues, and *forgiveness* needs to be addressed once again.

Make Amends/Reparation

It takes *humility* and *courage* to admit when you are wrong and to do what you can to handle the situation in a way that does not cause more harm. Making amends often includes an apology, but it is important to focus on a behavior change, not just words. You may need to consult with the person most affected to see what he/she believes needs to happen to resolve the situation.

Obviously, if the issue is that you stole money, you will likely have to pay it back. Sometimes, however, what you owe to a person may involve much more than money. It may take hard work to prove your *loyalty* and *trustworthiness*. In essence, you are asking with your efforts for an opportunity to start over. There is also the type of wrongdoing that is so severe that it would be best for you to make amends by simply staying away from that person, such as if you have threatened someone's life or well-being. Whatever you do, however, it must be *sincere* and come from an *honest* feeling of regret about what happened.

Deal with Tests and Difficulties

One way your character develops is through facing, handling, and growing from the tests and crises that are part of life. For instance, if you face a difficult decision about what to do with a family problem, you can use character qualities to handle it, and *strengthen* your ability to use the quality in the process. Think about how heat is used to mold and shape metal or glass into *beautiful* objects. In the same way, the heat and fire of challenges can support you in molding your character.

You may be tempted to bury or resist the pain that occurs when you are struggling with a character issue or some other problem. Pain, however, is a *helpful* indicator that you *truly* need to *detach*, *accept* your part is what is happening, and deal with the source of the challenge.

Appreciate Time and Wisdom

Truly understanding your mistakes, their impact, and healing from them takes time. Your *wisdom* and understanding, as well as your skill in handling your character quality development, will grow. If you feel as though you need to speed the process up a bit, look for guidance from people who have experience and *wisdom* and are willing to share it. Consider people who have demonstrated the degree of character growth that you are seeking, and ask them if they would be willing to give you some advice or insights.

Lighten-Up

Humor and laughter at your mistakes is often natural and appropriate. Sometimes you just might be taking yourself too seriously. If you can find what was funny in what happened, you may have more clarity in spotting what direction to go next. You may be able to assist others to laugh along with you. (**Note:** Sarcasm is destructive and is never appropriate humor in a relationship.)

Practice, Practice, Practice

With *courage* and *self-discipline*, you can try again to take actions using particular qualities and learn from the experience each time you do...practice, practice, practice! Whether it is one failure or a dozen failures in a row, you are entitled to make a new and better choice next time. You learn as much, or more, from your mistakes than from your successes. When you were learning to walk, did you give up the first time you fell?

Character refinement is a daily—sometimes hourly—process. The goal is to *persevere* and be better each evening than each morning and improve little by little, day by day. As you grow and develop as individuals, you grow as a couple. How you influence one another, then, is important.

THE INFLUENCING PROCESS

Often there are small things in your marriage that bother you.
You might be irritated at your husband for leaving the cap off the
toothpaste tube. You might be annoyed at your wife for leaving the
toilet seat down all the time. One of you is careless with leaving
dishes in the kitchen sink. The other leaves footprints on the floor.

It could be easy for you to begin to criticize one another for not
being *thoughtful, caring, flexible,* and more. Instead, you might look on
these as practice areas. Will you draw upon *acceptance* of the irritation,
or try to influence appropriate change through consultation? How
can you handle situations so you are not in conflict with one another?

MR. AND MRS. BRICKSTONE WILL SOON FIND OUT THAT
SMALL IRRITATIONS CAN BECOME BIG ONES.

© 2005 Catherine F. Hosack

In the following story, Jack and Marsha are learning the importance
of influencing and supporting one another through a more difficult
situation:

One evening, Jack and his wife Marsha sit drinking coffee at
the kitchen table. Marsha is concerned about something that
happened, and they agree to consult about it. Recently, Jack's
coworker, Isabelle, divorced her husband and moved her elderly
mother into her house. Being *compassionate* and concerned, Jack
listens to her as she works through her anger and fear. However,

being a friend to Isabelle caused strain in his family this week, when he postponed going to the movies with their son twice in order to visit with Isabelle at her home.

Marsha begins the conversation by letting Jack know how much she appreciates his ability to be *helpful* and *compassionate* to others. Marsha assures Jack she *trusts* him. She is concerned, however, that Isabelle may misread his intentions if he continues to be so *compassionate* to her while she is very vulnerable. She also feels it is best for their son to be able to count on Jack's promises and see the importance of *commitment*.

Marsha was alert and *discerning*. To influence Jack, she drew his attention to something that could harm their family. In this situation, Jack must then look at how he is using his qualities. Certainly, Jack is being *compassionate*, but is he being *wise* and *respectful* to his own wife and son? Is he guarding his *integrity*? Is he teaching his son that he is a man of his word? He needs to ask himself if he is secretly attracted to Isabelle, and if it is unwise to spend time alone with her at this point. In support of one another, Marsha and Jack can consult about Isabelle and work together to protect the *integrity* of their family. A key consideration will be what their actions communicate to their young son.

Maintaining Harmony

It will *strengthen* your relationship if you are both open to the possibility of change and willing to engage in ongoing growth. If you see in one another a *sincere* desire to change or improve in a particular way, you may be able to *help* by being in a supportive role. You will find it *wise* to consult together about what is *helpful* to one another. You can then also clarify what feels intrusive instead.

Real life will bring out both the best and the worst of your characters, sometimes making it challenging to maintain harmony. By committing to your relationship, by having willing and *honest* hearts, each of you will find ways to *cooperate* with, influence, and support one another. Remember to be *gentle* and open with each other as you both give and receive support. You are on the same "team," and your *unity* is vitally important.

ৰুৎৎৎ

"Those who are unwilling to adapt and change their behavior or consider compromise a sign of weakness do not understand that there is a world of difference between giving way to another person because we are forced to do so, or because we are threatened, and giving way because we want to, or out of affection. Indeed, such flexibility, far from being a weakness, is a sign of great strength of mind. Between people who love each other, giving is very important. What we think we are losing in power, control, or self-affirmation, we are in fact recovering in maturity, wisdom, and serenity."

~ Mehri Sefidvash, *Coral and Pearls*, p. 10

"Nearly all of us have had the experience of a situation in which there was a lot of tension or people's nerves were frayed and a shared laugh was enough to make the atmosphere warm and joyful again. All too often we underestimate the importance of a smile, an embrace, a kind word, a sincere compliment, or the giving of one's attention. It is precisely the small things that can change difficult moments into special ones."

~ ibid, pp. 11-12

7 ~ The Golden Rule: Sharing the Positive

All the world's religions talk about the Golden Rule—treating others the way you would like to be treated. You will need to put yourselves in the other's place regularly to be able to empathize with character challenges and life circumstances. This will support you in sharing *compassionate* and understanding words with one another.

Using positive words and tone of voice builds *love, respect,* and *confidence* in one another and in the stability of your relationship. It is *wise* to begin this practice from the beginning of your marriage so that it becomes a long-term practice, but it is never too late to start. It can include greeting one another warmly after you have been apart, perhaps hugging or kissing at the same time. Saying, "I *love* you" is also affirming. However, speaking positively about one another's character is especially vital.

Positive affirmations about character also spread to your whole family. If you as partners demonstrate this pattern of using positive language with one another, it is highly likely that any children in your home will speak positively. Remember, parents have a key role in forming their children's characters.

Like many people, you may find it easier to spot someone doing something *wrong* than to spot someone doing something *right*. It takes practice to look consciously for one another's positive actions, but it is very affirming for both of you when you do. The more positive thoughts and words you can generate about one another, the more you are likely to avoid destructive conflict. Most people typically feel a great sense of satisfaction when someone notices the good job they have done or the effort they put into it. You need to be able to count on one another for positive affirmation and *encouragement*, especially on difficult days.

CHARACTER QUALITY LANGUAGE

One of the most powerful and *peaceful* ways to influence one another is to include the specific qualities regularly in your speech: Character

Quality Language. Thinking and speaking positively and *kindly* to and about one another *encourages* you to be your best. Kavelin Popov says:

> Language has great influence to empower or discourage. Self-respect is built when shaming or blaming language is replaced by naming the Virtues, our innate qualities of character. Virtues are used to acknowledge, guide, and correct. The Language of Virtues [Character Quality Language] helps us remember what kind of people we want to be.

Remember that honoring one another's positive qualities can keep a marriage intact and happy.

Look at these two statements:

Good Statement:
> I appreciate that you picked me up directly from work so we could be on time for the concert. I have had such a hectic day! I am so glad you brought an umbrella, too.

Better Statement Using Character Quality Language:
> Thank you for picking me up even though you do not like driving in downtown traffic. It was very *thoughtful* of you...my day was hectic with deadlines, and I could not leave early to meet you at home. I especially appreciate that you were so *caring* in bringing an umbrella to protect me from the rain.

There is nothing wrong with the first interaction, and your spouse would likely feel appreciated. However, the second *affirms* his/her character and shows your appreciation of the qualities in daily life. *Thoughtfulness* and *caring* will be words you use frequently in this practice. Here is another example:

Good Statement:
> It is nice that you did the dishes.

Better Statement Using Character Quality Language:

    Thank you for doing the dishes even though it was my turn.
It was very *thoughtful* of you…my day was difficult. I especially
appreciate that you were so *careful* with the new plates. I broke
one yesterday, and we cannot afford to lose any more.

This example shows some other qualities:

Good Statement:

    Thanks, dear, for listening about my problems at work.
Better Statement Using Character Quality Language:
I feel much more *peaceful* now that we have talked about what I
am going through at work. It means a lot to me that you *sincerely*
listen to me and *care* about me.

There are some aspects of using Character Quality Language to be
aware of as you practice it. When you praise or *encourage* one another,
it loses its effectiveness if it is in the form of a comparison that says,
"You are better than someone else." Your tone of voice and phrasing
can also alter your intended outcome. It is important that there is
not implied criticism beneath the positive comment about how you
did the action; for example, "It was thoughtful of you to *finally* do
the dishes." You must also monitor the *purity* of your motives in
these interactions. If either of you are trying to be manipulative or
controlling, the other will begin to distrust your use of the Language.
The goal is to be *loving*, *honest*, and *sincere*.

Using Character Quality Language may feel unnatural at first, but if
you are *sincere* in using it, you will find it becomes comfortable and
natural. You may notice you automatically become suspicious of one
another's motives when you hear such positive language being used.
Try to *detach* from this reaction, which is likely based on experiences
with other people, and give one another the benefit of assuming you
each have good intentions.

No matter how foreign the Character Quality Language may seem to
you at first, the simple process of learning the names of the qualities

will begin to inspire you to identify them in one another. This will affirm for you what you most appreciate in one another. Who you are is not your clothes, hair, car, or job—who you are is your character. To know one another's character is *true* intimacy. To be known, *loved*, and appreciated for who you actually are, gives you a solid foundation for your marriage.

Using this language regularly can affirm and *encourage* the *strength* and use of the qualities in one another. It is very difficult to effectively discuss and understand thoughts and experiences for which you have no common vocabulary. Character Quality Language gives you just that.

© 2005 Catherine F. Hosack

APPRECIATION, AFFIRMATION, AND ENCOURAGEMENT

The benefits of Character Quality Language live and grow in your words and actions. Let one another know that you appreciate hearing the positive words. You may wish to express specific appreciation by saying something such as, "Thank you for noticing I have been more *patient* lately."

Sandra Gray Bender, Ph.D., writes about this topic in *Recreating Marriage with the Same Old Spouse*:

Some people believe they shouldn't have to thank their spouse, that he or she was fulfilling a responsibility. This belief is usually ineffective in a marriage. Most partners like to be thanked, even for fulfilling their responsibilities. (p. 115)

Appreciation is an expression of pleasure from the speaker's point of view. The message is "I value (like, enjoy) what you did." Appreciation is easy to communicate and rewarding to receive. Appreciation is commonly used by many people, so it is familiar. Appreciation tells another person that his or her deed was noticed and it benefited the speaker. Appreciation can motivate a partner to repeat the behavior because most partners enjoy pleasing their spouse.

An *affirmation* is an expression of empathy and understanding from the receiver's point of view. The message is "You have used a lot of effort (courage, integrity, skill, talent, endurance, for example) in your actions." Affirmations validate a person's motives and efforts, and validation is an important building block of identity. They are a communication of empathy...: "I see your good intentions." Although affirmations are not commonly communicated between spouses, they can be a powerful demonstration of understanding and acceptance. Our identity flourishes in the presence of someone who is affirming. We bond with persons who recognize the best in us and can experience God's presence in the relationship. (pp. 111-112)

As you become skilled in recognizing one another's positive qualities, you may fall into the trap of taking them for granted. Expressing appreciation, and celebrating successes and improvements, need to be an ongoing part of the culture of your marriage.

It will *help* you to influence one another if you also add the quality of *encouragement* to your interactions. *Acceptance* is a gift that frees the other to choose whether to change. *Encouragement*, however, often inspires the other to adjust an attitude, behavior, or character quality. No, do not do this to manipulate one another! In the following story, Annette *encourages* her husband, Chuck:

Chuck argues angrily with his brother, Marcus, about a new job Marcus wants to take in another country. He does not want

Marcus to move so far from him or their parents. Chuck's wife, Annette, *encourages* him to look at all sides of the issue to *help* prevent a family crisis. She wants to support Chuck in a way that will *encourage* resolution of the problem. She sees the importance of having relatives you can count on, and she does not want him hurting the relationship with his brother.

Empathetically, she affirms Chuck's feelings and his point of view. Over the next few days, every time Annette sees Chuck ease up on his negative attitude toward his brother, she tells him how happy she is to see it.

Annette's positive comments *help* Chuck realize how much he values his relationship with his brother. He knows Marcus will come home to *help* their aging parents if they need him.

One day, Chuck barely mumbles under his breath that he should probably give his brother a phone call. Annette *encourages* him to go ahead. She lets him know he is a *forgiving, peaceful,* and *compassionate* person, and she is sure he can act that way in this circumstance. Annette's reminder to Chuck of his qualities *helps* empower him to reconnect with Marcus.

Dr. Gary Chapman, author of a series of books on Love Languages, talks about the importance of *encouragement* and the power it has to release potential in another:

Giving verbal compliments ["You look great today!"] is only one way to express words of affirmation to your spouse. Another…is encouraging words ["I have confidence you will do very well and achieve your goal. Keep going strong!"]. The word *encourage* means "to inspire courage." All of us have areas in which we feel insecure. We lack courage, and that lack of courage often hinders us from accomplishing the positive things that we would like to do. The latent potential within your spouse in his or her areas of insecurity may await your encouraging words. (*The Five Love Languages: How to Express Heartfelt Commitment to Your Mate*, p. 42)

Encouragement requires empathy and seeing the world from your spouse's perspective. We must first learn what is important to our spouse. Only then can we give encouragement. With verbal encouragement, we are trying to communicate, "I know. I care. I am with you. How can I help?" We are trying to show that we believe in him and in his abilities. (ibid, p. 45)

One of the key success criteria of *encouraging* someone is noticing and affirming even the smallest positive action. It means consciously looking for actions you can speak about *sincerely* and positively. Even if you do not do exactly what one another wants, it is important to give positive feedback to the *effort* you each make. This will *encourage* an increase in positive behavior.

Copyright 2004 by Randy Glasbergen.
www.glasbergen.com

"You don't appreciate the nice things I do. Yesterday I burped
'I love you' in Morse Code and you didn't even thank me!"

FIVE LOVE LANGUAGES

Chapman's Five Love Languages are a very effective communication tool. He says that to have a full "love tank," you need to express *love* to one another in the ways that make the receiver feel *loved*. If you are not receiving *love* in the most important way, then you may begin to question whether your spouse *loves* you. This can cause gradual erosion in your relationship. You can use a number of methods to communicate *love*, called "Love Languages," but it is vital that you each use your spouse's most important language to maintain a *strong, loving* marriage. Here are the primary Languages from Chapman's work:

1. **Words of Affirmation:** verbal compliments; words of appreciation; praise; encouragement; kind words; noticing and appreciating the positive actions and qualities of the other

2. **Quality Time:** undivided and focused attention; togetherness (not just being in the same space at the same time, but interacting); uninterrupted time; quality conversation; regard marriage as a relationship, not a problem to be solved; eye contact; listen for feelings/emotions; observe body language; sympathetic listening; self-revealing intimacy; sharing; doing activities together

3. **Receiving Gifts:** something you can hold in your hand; symbol that you were thought about; cost not usually important; visual symbol of love; not just on special occasions; this includes the gift of your presence, especially at important moments

4. **Acts of Service:** do things for the other; housework/yard work; make requests (not demands) of the other; done with loving attitude (not fear, guilt, or resentment); this includes actions that reflect equality and partnership, not role stereotypes

5. **Physical Touch:** loving physical contact; intimate touch; tender hug; back rub/massage; kissing; holding hands; holding while crying/comforting; faithfulness

You will find it *helpful* to identify which are the primary Love Languages for each of you—although it is great if you use them all! You can then discuss ways to keep one another's "love tank" full.

BALANCING TOWARD THE POSITIVE

The overall goal for you in your marriage is to keep the level of positive comments high, and your friendship *strong*. In other words, keep the number of positive feedback comments you make to one another far higher than the number of negative ones. Staying positive includes starting discussions *gently*, making polite requests, and assuming your spouse has good intentions. It also includes keeping the amount of criticism very low.

To honor one another's positive qualities and *help* one another through character challenges, one additional important concept to understand is that none of the qualities stands alone. They all work best when they support and balance one another. For example, if you look at the quality of *contentment*, you would see that it allows you to be *peaceful* about your life together. If you are having difficulty being *content*, and your marriage is unsettled and agitated, the qualities of *acceptance*, *flexibility*, or *patience* could assist you. If you are excessively *content* to the point where you are very passive and unwilling to change, you will probably need to draw on *assertiveness*, *purposefulness*, or *responsibility* to *moderate* or balance your relationship. If you are so *content* you are bored, then *creativity* or *enthusiasm* might assist you.

It may *help* you to understand this concept by comparing it to exercising. When done in *moderation* or balance, you gradually learn how to effectively tone your muscles and master your skills. Practicing excessively, or not enough, however, can cause injury and frustration. The same thing is *true* with your character qualities. When you use any one of the qualities unwisely or too *strongly* without other *moderating* qualities, they can also cause harm to relationships or to yourself.

Consider how Amira learns to balance the quality of *enthusiasm* with *contentment* and *purposefulness*:

> Amira and Dawson recently married. Amira moved to the town where Dawson lived before their wedding, and she is now job-hunting. She also wants to find a place for them to live that is new for both of them. Amira *enthusiastically* reads the real estate

ads each morning, looking for a new home. Every evening when Dawson comes home from work, she shows him information about another home. She knows if she just keeps looking, she will find the perfect place. At first, Dawson appreciates her *enthusiasm* and willingly goes to look at places. Now, however, he is becoming tired of going from home to home, discussing the perfect place to put the couch. He wants her to focus more attention on her job-hunting.

Dawson is beginning to distrust Amira's *enthusiasm* because it never seems to result in anything productive. One evening, they talk about what is happening, and he shares how much he admires her *enthusiasm*. Then he asks her to consider *moderating* it with being *content* at their current place for a few more months.

He also shares with her that he wants to be able to *trust* her judgment, and asks her to spend time *sincerely* thinking about what is really important in a new place. He asks her to be *purposeful* in consulting with him about what both of them want to enjoy in a new home. He also shares with her that he would be more comfortable buying a home once she has a secure job, and he requests that she *commit* to that goal.

In Amira and Dawson's discussion, they are able to identify how Amira can balance her *enthusiasm* with a number of other qualities. *Encouraging* her to use these qualities enables Dawson to give Amira feedback without being critical of her character, and Amira has specific ways she can make adjustments.

Generally, the more you learn about the best uses for each of the character qualities, and how they *moderate* and assist one another, the more opportunities you will find to practice them in your life. Part 2 will give you more examples of how the qualities work together.

ೂೂೞ

"A good character is in the sight of God…and the possessors of insight, the most excellent and praiseworthy of all things, but always on condition that its center of emanation should be reason and knowledge and its base should be true moderation."
~ 'Abdu'l-Bahá, *The Secret of Divine Civilization*, p. 60

„★‟

"The emotional relations between spouses are extremely fluid and can change from moment to moment. A smile or a loving glance at the right time can evaporate ill-feeling in an instant. …

"Just as important is active approval. No one—no matter how accomplished—is ever beyond the need for approval and recognition. Approval is as vital as air. So, be on the look out for fanning the relationship by genuine approval."
~ Khalil A. Khavari and Sue Williston Khavari, *Together Forever*, pp. 207-208

8 ~ A Gold Star: Giving and Responding to Feedback

As you learn about character qualities, it will become obvious that developing your characters is a process, not a fixed destination. Remember, each choice you make affects your progress. As an individual, you can set and act on goals that focus on the qualities you most want to develop.

As discussed in Chapter 6, you may use a variety of methods to assist you, such as daily self-assessment, journal writing, prayer, focus and effort, and learning from your experiences. Within your marriage, however, you have the additional method of *accepting* and requesting feedback from one another. Yes, you can *request* it, not just *give* it!

"Here! Do Me!"

COMPLAINTS AND CRITICISMS

Chapter 7 addressed giving positive and affirming comments to one another. Chapter 8 will now assist you when you need to raise a concern or share troubled feelings with one another. No matter how great your marriage relationship is, and no matter how hard you try to stay in a positive mode, sometimes you will have complaints about one another. Gottman and Silver put it this way:

> You will always have some complaints about the person you live with. But there's a world of difference between a complaint and a criticism. A complaint only addresses the specific action at which

your spouse failed. A criticism is more global—it adds on some negative words about your mate's character or personality. (*The Seven Principles for Making Marriage Work*, p. 27)

Watch out though…if you are not *careful*, you could slip into "complaining" about your spouse's character and justify it! And another warning—it is not a good idea to complain about your spouse to others. This can be considered backbiting and may lead to destructive gossip. You may need to draw on the qualities of *loyalty* and *self-discipline* to assist you to keep quiet.

Backbiting and Gossip

You may be unfamiliar with the term "backbiting," which is speaking in a negative, spiteful, derogatory, or defamatory way about someone who is not present. The intent is destructive, and it creates disunity between people. Backbiting negatively affects the heart and soul of the speaker and listener. It also harms the person being spoken about. The words may be *true*, but the harm is great enough that this does not justify backbiting.

Gossip occurs when fact or fiction spreads from one person to another, often with the intent to hurt the person being talked about. You will need to *discern* your motives for sharing with someone outside your marriage. At times, you will also need to assess whether it is *wise* to share information about someone else with one another. If gossip begins to happen about your marriage or regularly within your marriage, relationships will suffer. The faster you can stop this habit, the better.

Setting and Timing for Delivering Feedback

A fundamental quality that is very useful within the context of providing one another with feedback is *cooperation*. Within your marriage, you will often need to raise concerns with one another. It is important to pay attention to how, when, and where you deliver it. The way you handle complaints or feedback with one another makes all the difference in your relationship.

You may find influencing one another is a smooth and easy skill to learn. However, you may find that it takes *commitment* to engage in some trial and error before it becomes natural. Probably some *patience* will *help*, too! Brent and Rachael are working through this process early on in their marriage:

> Whenever Brent tries to share feedback with Rachael about improving her organization skills, she quickly responds with a negative comment about him. Brent notices that whenever Rachael gives him feedback, she not only says the point once, but she keeps coaching him repeatedly until it becomes nagging and irritating. Often, he yells and argues with her in response. Both of them tend to give one another feedback at the point in which they are most upset or annoyed with one another.

There are some key areas where Brent and Rachael are off track. Obviously, they *care* about one another, or they would not be trying to give one another feedback. However, their methods are causing conflict in their marriage. Here are actions to better support them:

- Ensure the feedback is welcome, and the other is willing to listen
- Include positive Character Quality Language [See Chapter 7.]
- Listen *carefully* to the feedback without retaliating
- Give feedback and allow the other to process it without harassing him/her
- Consult calmly about solutions, instead of escalating into conflict
- Choose a time to discuss an issue when it is possible to do so without attacking one another
- Agree that one issue is settled before another issue is brought up
- Do not accumulate issues and dump them on one another all at one time

Here is how the couple turns in a more positive direction:

> Brent and Rachael start to notice the troublesome patterns in their marriage. To move their relationship forward, they consult and agree that they will not give feedback to one another when

they are upset. They agree to say, "Let's talk about this when we are calm" and to say nothing more about it until later. They also agree to listen more effectively to one another, and increase their focus on the qualities they appreciate in one another. With *cooperation* and practice, Brent and Rachael learn to support one another by giving healthy feedback without escalating into negative behavior.

ENSURE A POSITIVE OUTCOME

It is a very important step to ask your spouse if he/she is open and willing to receive comments. There is no point in talking if the other is not able to listen. The feedback process will also work best if you as the giver speak *lovingly*, and you are conscious about not burdening the other's heart with too much at once.

Giving feedback also works best if you consciously choose appropriate times, such as when you are both rested and not distracted. You and your spouse are more likely to have problems communicating if you are:

- In emotional or physical pain
- Overly hungry or tired
- At certain stages of hormonal cycles
- Angry or upset about something
- Feeling lonely or sad

The following are some of many ways you can practice responsible self-*care*:

- Ask someone to listen to your feelings
- Rest or exercise as needed
- Eat a healthy meal
- Visit a friend or family member
- Pause before reacting and ask for time apart to calm down
- Pray or meditate
- Take a walk in nature

Once you are in a calmer state of mind and ready to give one another feedback, it is *wise* to remind yourselves of how important *love* is in the process. Actually, it is a good idea even when you are still upset! Consider this quotation about character in marriage and the importance of being *loving* from Rúhíyyih Rabbani in her book, *Prescription for Living (Revised)*:

> Your union cannot produce more than you two contribute to it. If you are full of imperfections, intolerant, impatient, exacting, dictatorial, suspicious, short-tempered, selfish, do not imagine that these characteristics are going to make your marriage happy or that by changing your partner a new union will be more successful! Marriage, like all our other relationships in life, is a process which, among other things, serves to grind the sharp edges off us. The grinding often hurts, the adjustment to another person's character is difficult at first, that is why love is needed here more than in any other relationship. Love, being essentially a divine force, binds; it leaps like a spark the gaps between people's thoughts and conflicting desires, between perhaps widely different temperaments. (pp. 87-88)

You may find it works best if you pause before giving feedback and remind yourselves of what you especially *love* about one another. Remember if all you give one another is negative feedback, you will begin to resist talking with one another. Therefore, each time you provide feedback that might be challenging, start and end with giving positive and reaffirming feedback, and acknowledge one another's best character qualities.

WHEN YOU TRIGGER EMOTIONS

Sharing feedback with one another can often trigger emotions that you will need to process and share. Historically, women have been better at expressing their emotions to the men in their lives, but men are increasingly learning to do this skill well. Your communications are undergoing dynamic changes, and it will take time to learn how to interact most effectively.

© 2003 by Randy Glasbergen.
www.glasbergen.com

—GLASBERGEN—

"I do so share my deepest emotions with you!
Hungry and tired are my deepest emotions."

Strong or Confused Reactions

If your emotional reaction to feedback is very *strong* or confused,
you may need time to think about the feedback before responding.
Perhaps one or both of you need a period of prayer and reflection,
to go for a walk, or to wait a day to talk about it.

Watch how this happens with Malia and Josh:

Malia *loves* to be *helpful* to others, which is a positive character
quality. However, sometimes she impulsively *helps* her husband,
Josh, and is puzzled when he becomes irritated and annoyed with
her. One day she and Josh are doing some yard work at their
home. He is on the ladder cutting tree branches with an electric
trimmer. She decides to be *helpful* without asking him and starts
moving around the base of the ladder gathering up the fallen
branches.

Unfortunately, Malia bumps up against the ladder, distracting
Josh, and causing him to cut the electrical cord with the trimmer.
This trips the power off to their home, and he nearly falls from
the ladder. Josh quickly becomes agitated and yells at Malia.
She snaps back, "I was only trying to *help*!" Later that day, after
they calm down and are able to talk about the situation, Josh's

feedback assists Malia to realize that she needs to add the qualities of *discernment* and *respect* to her interactions. This will *help* her to ensure that people want and need *help* before she begins to act.

Pushback or Attacking Response

Part of Josh's feedback to Malia is a direct request that she assess how she is being *helpful*. In this case, Malia is open to looking at her actions. However, when one of you raises an issue or makes an assertive request as part of your feedback, the other might respond with an unexpectedly negative message in return. This kind of "pushback" defensive reaction or attacking response can stop or sidetrack the original concern under discussion. The one raising the issue can use the following steps to handle the situation:

1. Make a statement that reflects or summarizes the content and feelings of the reaction message, with special emphasis on the other's feelings. Do this as many times as is needed in response to statements the other makes until feelings calm down. [**Note:** You began to learn this paraphrasing skill in Chapter 4, Level One of Consciously Listening, pages 48-50.]
2. Do not get sidetracked into discussing the content of the pushback/reaction message.
3. Treat the other with *respect*; do not use judgmental words.
4. Re-assert the original message when appropriate.

Here is what it might look like:

> **Hallie:** I need to know that I can count on you to go with me to my medical appointments. I am afraid the treatments will make me dizzy, and I will not be able to drive home. I feel anxious when I am not sure whether you will go with me.
>
> **Kevin:** You *never* understand how difficult it is for me to leave work! [Pushback/Attacking/Reactive/Defensive statement]
>
> **Hallie:** You are concerned it could be a problem for you at work if you go with me.

Kevin: I will never be able to keep up with my work if I take time off every week.

Hallie: You are afraid you will get too far behind on your assignments if you are gone.

Kevin: I am just not sure how to make it work. (He is calming down)

Hallie: It is very important to me that you go with me to the doctor, and I am asking that you work it out with your manager. I feel worried when I am going to the doctor for these treatments, and I would really appreciate it if you are able to come with me. (Hallie re-states her original request.)

Kevin: I now understand how important this is to you. I will talk to my manager tomorrow.

Once Kevin knows that Hallie has heard his concerns, he is more willing to move into problem solving. If Hallie starts reacting to and discussing Kevin's pushback message, she could start to criticize him for not *caring* about her, try to manage his job situation for him, and more. The emotions for both would escalate. Instead, Hallie is paraphrasing and reflecting Kevin's message and feelings back to him. This validates them and moves the discussion forward without conflict.

Preventing Conflict

Discussions like Hallie and Kevin's work best when there is *equality* and *respect* in your relationship. If one of you is used to getting the other to agree to what you want, or one of you attempts to dominate the other unfairly, you will probably create conflict that damages your marriage. The following guidelines will assist you to prevent feedback from escalating into conflict:

- Be aware of the rights you each have
- Choose your words *carefully*, avoiding critical or derogatory comments
- Make requests and not demands

- Stay calm
- Be prepared to listen to and understand the response
- Repeat the request if necessary and appropriate
- Use *assertiveness* appropriately, not as a manipulative tool to get everything you want, ignoring the other's needs

Processing the Emotions

If you notice that feedback triggers *strong* emotions, and you become upset, it will be *wise* to give yourselves some time to reflect and consult to sort through the reasons why. Here are some steps to consider:

- *Accept* that you are upset
- Recognize that the upset feelings are yours, and do not blame others for them
- Assess whether the current situation is reminding you of a negative interaction with someone else in the past
- Determine if one or both of you did not keep a *commitment* or broke a promise
- *Discern* whether either of you had expectations that were not fulfilled
- Assess all the related communications to see if there was anything that was not communicated and should have been
- Assess whether your timing or tone of voice were inappropriate

It will take practice to be skillful at communication generally, and feedback in particular, that assists both of you and does not leave you with hurt feelings or conflict.

Ways to Influence

You will find it *helpful* to discuss the boundaries and methods of giving feedback and influencing one another, so they are effective and not hurtful. Sometimes just agreeing on a simple signal like saying "ouch" can be light and playful, but very effective if the feedback is overly negative. Consider this approach that the Khavari's recommend:

> The marriage relationship must above all else be a relationship of true friends—honest acceptance of the person as a package of the good, the bad, and the average. Improving each other should be a secondary aim and done with extreme care, gentleness, and subtlety—making sure that the relationship doesn't degenerate into that of parent-child, teacher-pupil, angel-mortal. You must keep it at the level of total love, acceptance, and parity. Then you can improve together as a team. (*Together Forever*, p. 186)

Tone of Voice

One skill that will contribute to your ability to "coach" one another *gently* and communicate effectively is using a positive and appropriate tone of voice. Your tone is a powerful non-verbal cue beyond the words that you say. If you pay attention, you will notice that if there is a different message in them both, you tend to believe what people say with their tones of voice more than with their actual words. The tone that you use, therefore, will affect every communication you have.

Note: Your cultures or accents can affect the "tone" of your words. The rhythm of your comments, the accents on syllables, and voice inflection can convey "meaning" to the other, perhaps resulting in a misunderstanding. As you talk with one another about what different tones of voice mean, you can explore whether cultural factors are affecting your communications and interpretations.

SKILL-BUILDING OPPORTUNITY

See Appendix E, "Communication Skill: Tone of Voice," which gives you specific phrases to practice.

Humor

You may also be able to use humor with one another. Sometimes *gentle* and *friendly* teasing or reminding one another of something funny that happened related to character could be effective. Be cautious about how you each deliver and respond to humor, however, as sometimes teasing can result in hurt feelings.

It is unkind to tease one another in a belittling way and then say, "I was only kidding!" Remember, as well, that it is especially *wise* to avoid using sarcastic humor, which underneath you really intend to be destructive. If one of you is sarcastic to the other, you may wish to make a direct request that it stop.

MAKING REQUESTS

Often you will make requests of one another in your relationship as part of a general willingness to *help* one another. Sometimes, however, you will make them when something negatively affects your relationship and concerns you. You have the option to stay quiet and simply *detach* and let it go, *accepting* or *forgiving* the action. Alternatively, you can make a direct request to your partner to consider making some better choices.

While it is unwise to *demand* that your spouse make a change in an attitude, behavior, or the use of a character quality, there may be times when a request is reasonable and appropriate. This method *helps* you to influence one another in a positive way rather than attacking one another.

It is important to be aware that when you make a request of one another, there is an array of choices for your responses. If the request is *sincere* and not manipulative, and the tone of voice and choice of words is appropriate, you will probably respond with a degree of openness and *acceptance* of the request and feedback.

Alternatively, you could respond by becoming angry, upset, declining the request, negotiating for a solution, and more. Before you make a request of one another, you may find it *helpful* and *wise* to think through whether you are prepared to handle whatever the response is to your request. In any case, consultation will assist you to find a solution.

The following scenario illustrates a couple handling an issue with a request:

> Robert walks into the bedroom to find Catherine's dirty clothes lying in a heap on their bedroom floor. She is very *purposeful*, has a lot on her mind, and tends to stay focused. She does not pause to put her clothes in the laundry basket at the end of each day. He has tried yelling at her about the mess, telling her she is not being *thoughtful* and is acting like a slob, which has hurt her feelings but not influenced her to change her actions. He decides to make a request this time instead, and he chooses to include Character Quality Language that acknowledges her *purposefulness*.
>
> He begins by addressing their last interaction. "I know the last time I brought up the issue of you leaving your dirty clothes on the floor, I called you names and told you that you were not being *thoughtful*. I am sorry I was so unkind. I see now how *purposeful* you are and that it is difficult for you to stop long enough to put your dirty clothes in the basket when you have so much on your mind. I am asking you, though, to take a minute, please, to put them there when you take them off. It would *help* us to *purposefully* create a more orderly and intimate atmosphere in the bedroom. It would also be less work for me on laundry day."

Of course, when Catherine agrees and follows through with Robert's request, he will use Character Quality Language and honor her for her *purposefulness* and her *forgiveness* for his earlier harsh words! [See Chapter 7.] Note that his request positively affirms one of her character qualities and includes valid and *purposeful* reasons for her to make a change in her actions.

Character Attacks

When Robert yells at Catherine, he attacks her character by telling her that she is inconsiderate and not *thoughtful* about the impact of her actions. Character attacks are highly destructive to marriages. Gottman and Silver say you are unlikely to stay together, or have a happy marriage, if these attacks are a regular habit. Character criticism tends to set up contempt between you, and it leads to an eventual shutdown in communications, a sign that your marriage is in serious trouble. They say in *The Seven Principles for Making Marriage Work*:

> By simply reminding yourself of your spouse's positive qualities—even as you grapple with each other's flaws—you can prevent a happy marriage from deteriorating. (p. 65)

> All spiritual views of life are consistent with loving and honoring your spouse. (p. 102)

SKILL-BUILDING OPPORTUNITY

See Appendix F, "Communication Skill: Making Requests," which will assist you in making requests effectively.

STOPPING CHARACTER ATTACKS

If you notice a pattern of conflict in your relationship, it may be a warning to look for whether character attacks are occurring. Alisha and Frank are just learning how destructive an attack can be on their marriage:

> Alisha and Frank decide to try playing tennis together. Alisha, a new player to the sport, admires the way Frank, who is a seasoned pro, plays the game so well. However, she becomes frustrated when Frank plays beyond her ability and rushes through the game. At first, Alisha tries to keep up, but she quickly loses interest in playing when she constantly feels stressed and overwhelmed. She stomps off the court and yells at Frank that she cannot believe how inconsiderate and impatient he always is! [character attack]

> Frank quickly defends himself as they begin to argue. Recognizing that the argument is escalating, they stop and agree to cool off for a few minutes. Alisha walks around a nearby park

and reflects on the words she used. She begins to realize she could have been *kinder* and more *tactful*. Frank lies down on the grass under a tree and reflects. Although he is unhappy about how Alisha communicated with him, he realizes that he could have been more *patient* and *courteous* to Alisha as a beginning player.

After their *peaceful* moments apart, Alisha and Frank both apologize, talk through what happened, and *commit* to behavior that is more positive. They also take time to share the qualities they appreciate about the other, such as Alisha's *enthusiasm* to learn a new sport and Frank's *commitment* to play the game well. They begin a new game at a *moderate* pace and have an experience that is more *peaceful* for both of them. Practicing this shift in behavior and language over time *strengthens* the qualities in their characters.

Note that the words Alisha and Frank used with one another started out negative, attacking, and defensive. Alisha uses the word "always" when she is attacking Frank, which makes the attack on his character even *stronger*. Their shift in language from character attack to character affirmation during their next game will be a vital change in direction for the relationship.

Another phrase that might cause conflict in your marriage could be "You never do X." "Always" and "never" are words that will usually trigger one of you to get upset, because it is unlikely that either is *true*. "Often" or "rarely" might be more accurate, although these could also prompt a defensive reaction.

As you learn to give feedback, respond to it, and progress by influencing one another's qualities, your goal is to stay positive as much as possible. You may find it *helpful* to follow these steps, some of which Alisha and Frank are learning to use:

- Engage in self-awareness and self-assessment
- Practice *detachment* from emotional reactions

- Remind yourself of the damage that character attacks cause
- *Discern* when change is needed, and consult about the issue or take action
- Keep your relationship "cleaned up" with apologies and amends
- Practice the qualities to increase their effectiveness

MOTIVES

When you give feedback to one another, take time to assess whether to change and why. It is great to want to create a more *peaceful* and happier relationship. However, it is also important to make sure you are consciously choosing to change and *sincerely* responding to one another. It will not work if you are actually unhappy about changing.

You both need to be certain it is best for your marriage to work on the aspect of growth that you are discussing. It is unwise to change or pretend to change just to get some kind of reward such as, hugs, smiles, sex, or approval. It is also understandable, but unwise, to expect the other, in turn, to change or do something in response to a change one of you makes. If manipulation and control are a significant part of the dynamics between you, the result is likely to be disunity, distrust, and disaster. Your positive choices, along with *excellent* motives, will support your marriage best.

Note: If you are concerned about something very serious, or if you think you may be over-reacting to something minor, you may wish to seek *help* from a counselor or *spiritual* advisor. Often a dispassionate observer can spot the dynamics of what is going on in your life better than you can.

⁖я⁃

"A trap we all fall into is to hurt the most those we love the most— we fail to respect them. We continue to correct what we consider to be their mistakes, we criticize their decisions, we try to change their attitudes, and we argue about matters of form. Of course, there is nothing wrong in expecting the best from those we love, but to try to improve our partner by continually making negative comments about him or criticizing him is certainly not the best way to help him better himself or to show him respect. ...

"Respect means wanting the other person to grow and develop into what he is and can be. Respect automatically excludes exploitation and selfish expectations. To have respect for a person we love means having the desire that he should grow and develop according to his own wishes and his own capabilities, and not just because this is useful for us."

~ Mehri Sefidvash, *Coral and Pearls*, pp. 26-27

9 ~ Gold Rings: Interacting Qualities

Learning how to practice qualities effectively is an important step in maintaining your relationship. This chapter, then, delves deeper into the complexities of how you might use—or misuse—a character quality. When you consistently use a quality effectively, it will have a positive impact on you and those around you. If the quality is weak, used to excess, or applied unwisely for the circumstances, it may cause harm or conflict. Your qualities affect each interaction you have.

MISUSING CHARACTER QUALITIES

The concept of misusing qualities—using them inappropriately—may be new for you, and it can take on a number of different forms. This chapter will explore a few of them.

If either of you are misusing a quality, it may mean one of two things, both of which are important:

- You already know how to use the quality effectively, but you are applying it inappropriately for the circumstances or choosing to use it in a way that causes hurt or conflict
- You have a *strong* inclination to use this quality; however, you have not yet learned to use the quality in an appropriate way

As you learn to identify which qualities you are misusing, you will accomplish two worthwhile objectives. The first objective is that you will be able to transform how you use the quality so that it reverts to being beneficial to yourselves and others. You will be able to use it effectively with practice.

The second objective may come to you as a pleasant surprise. By identifying a misused quality, you may discover that you have great potential for a quality that you simply did not know you had. For instance, it is very easy to spot when someone is a faultfinder. The occasional tendency to be a faultfinder may not be too significant.

However, when a person does it all the time, he or she can be very difficult to be around. Everything is open for comment, from the news to burnt potatoes. Faultfinding can be a significant challenge within a relationship.

The surprise for you may be in discovering that faultfinding is actually misused *discernment*. If you look *carefully* at this quality, you can see that it empowers you to see clearly and deeply into all matters and make *wise* decisions based on what you discover. If you are a faultfinder, you take what you see and become critical about it. You may be misusing a solid quality like this, and not even know you could be using it in a very effective way.

Whenever you are engaged in negative behavior, or you are aware that something you are doing is causing conflict, you can look at the "Identifying and Balancing Misuses" for each quality in Part 2 of this book to determine which one connects to your behavior. Once you spot the negative misuse, then you can trace it back to discover the positive use instead. You then have a guide to learning how to practice the quality effectively. Your strength in using the quality will grow faster and easier than it would be if you were very weak in the quality altogether. You already have a *strong* inclination toward using the quality effectively.

Misuse Causes Conflict

Misuse of a quality is usually due to selfishness, ego, pride, anger, disrespect, fear, anxiety, hate, or some other negative emotion. These feelings may cause you to overreact toward one another and end up in conflict rather than consulting through an issue *peacefully*. If you can identify when one of you is misusing a quality, and influence a shift back to using it effectively, you can often find a positive way to avoid a conflict.

Here is an example of a couple realizing they are not practicing a quality effectively:

> Tanya and Yoshi have been married for a few months. They are very *friendly* with others, often hosting people at their home.

However, Yoshi notices that sometimes Tanya seems to be easy to fool or cheat, and her friends are able to pressure her to do things. Tanya, in turn, notices Yoshi enjoys being popular and increases this by being *friendlier* to certain people than to others. Sometimes, he is so preoccupied with seeking attention, he loses track of who his real friends are.

Tanya and Yoshi begin regularly arguing about each other's behavior, and the conflict has begun threatening their marriage. Tanya is beginning to withdraw emotionally, and Yoshi is staying away from home more in the evenings. After a particularly difficult day, Tanya decides that their marriage is too important to continue going this way. She suggests to Yoshi that they discuss their issues calmly.

Through consultation, Tanya and Yoshi both begin to see that they are misusing the character quality of *friendliness*. This insight allows them to begin balancing their behavior. They start to support one another in reclaiming *friendliness* as a positive quality. As the conflict over the issue decreases, they gently remind one another to be *careful* not to slip into old patterns. As they learn how to best use their *friendliness*, they discover there are many people who really need and appreciate it.

Tanya and Yoshi are effective in influencing one another in ways that benefit them personally and their marriage. They shift away from misusing a quality.

BALANCING OR MODERATING QUALITIES

Balancing or *moderating* a quality is one way to transform a quality misuse into effective use. For example, one of you is *strong* in practicing *courage*, but this has turned into harmful, reckless, and risky behavior. Balancing the behavior by adding *caring* and *respect* will *help* change the recklessness back into genuine *courage*.

Moderation is a quality that can benefit all areas of your life together. You need to be somewhat cautious in how you apply it to character qualities, however. *Moderating* a quality, in this context, does not mean practicing a quality at a level of mediocrity or "doing it half-way" instead of whole-heartedly. This would be a misuse of *moderation*. Your goal is to be *excellent* in practicing qualities, through making *wise* choices.

© 2005 Catherine F. Hosack

Moderating truthfulness, for instance, does not mean that lying is *acceptable* at certain times. Lying, telling half-truths, or withholding vital information will create anger, resentment, and disharmony in any relationship. *Moderating* this quality means that there may be circumstances in which telling all of the *truth* that you know, all the details, is not *tactful*, timely, or *wise*.

Here is a very common example. Every *wise* man in the world has learned there are times and places for direct *truthfulness* and other times when you need to modify it with *tactfulness*. Consider a situation when your wife is dressed up for an evening out. She asks, "Honey, do you think this dress makes me look fat?" At that moment, telling the *truth*, the whole *truth*, and nothing but the *truth* might cause a serious conflict and hurt feelings. Simply responding, "You look *beautiful* tonight," or "I really like the blue dress on you better" might be the *wise*, *tactful*, and *truthful* response!

You will find it assists you to draw on *sensitivity* and *discernment* to assess your qualities and interactions and see how to practice *moderation* in every situation. How *moderation* applies varies according to the circumstances. Choices shift depending on the needs of the situation you are in, so what might look *moderate* at one time is not *moderate* the next one. You need to look at your interactions and complete circumstances and be *flexible*.

Consider how this applies to Karin and her husband, Simon:

Karin, a very *creative* graphic designer, works all over the world *helping* clients develop effective and inspiring marketing materials. Her innate ability to spot what is not working in what a client is doing and to *create* new designs for them makes her a highly valued employee. Her *enthusiasm* in communicating her designs to her customers is part of why she is in demand across the globe.

This evening, Karin and her husband Simon attend a *spiritual* study session where the facilitator asks each participant to create some kind of artistic representation of a story she just read. As Simon begins working on his project, Karin notices the colors he is using and thinks they are completely wrong with each other. She immediately goes into high gear with Simon as though he were a million dollar client of hers. She *enthusiastically* tells him how he should use a new color scheme with reds and yellows and replace gray with black. Simon pauses for a moment, looks at his artwork, and stops. He is angry with Karin for her aggressiveness and lack of *respect* for his own *creative* expression and needs.

In this scenario, it would have been *wise* for Karin to be sensitive. She needed to *discern* that it was not appropriate for her to use her *enthusiasm* in a personal situation in the same way she does at work. She especially would have been *wise* to ask Simon if he was open to her input. Below is a replay of the scenario with Simon responding differently. In this case, he recognizes Karin's misuse of *enthusiasm* and *helpfulness*. It might go like this:

Simon listens to Karin's suggestions about his project. He smiles teasingly at his wife and says, "Honey, I *love* how *enthusiastic* you are. And I know you want to be *helpful*. I just need to do this project my way. Thank you for *caring*."

Simon's response in this instance is more likely to preserve his relationship with his wife and *help* her to see her misuse of qualities. She will find his *loving* feedback *helps* her to act differently in the future. In a consultation together about this issue, Karin would be *wise* to specifically ask Simon to be watchful and let her know if he sees her misusing or about to misuse her *enthusiasm*.

MISUSING DOMINANT QUALITIES

When you misuse your dominant qualities—the ones you know and use well—it typically results in conflict between you and others. When you can identify the dominant quality that you are misusing, it reduces conflict in your close relationships. Consider how Francisco misuses his qualities with his wife, Bonita:

> Bonita is in the way of the television while passing out snacks to her husband, Francisco, and his friends. She walks in front of them in the middle of the most important ball game of the year, and they miss seeing the winning play. He yells at her to get out of the way and then argues with her in front of his friends. She walks away, obviously upset.
>
> Francisco thinks to himself that he was being *assertive* and *truthful*, two of his most dominant character strengths, and is annoyed that Bonita is hurt. He dismisses her feelings by telling his friends she is over-sensitive. After one of his friends comments that he might end up kicked out of the bedroom and left to sleep on the couch, Francisco swallows his pride and follows Bonita into the kitchen to discuss what happened.

What might support Francisco in similar circumstances, is *moderating assertiveness* with *respectfulness*, and *truthfulness* with *tactfulness*. *Assertiveness* and *truthfulness* are very dominant qualities for him, which he knows how to use consistently and effectively. He is also at high risk at certain times to misuse them. When he and Bonita talk in the kitchen, she lets him know how much she appreciates his *truthfulness*. She then shares with him that his misuse of it hurt her feelings.

This feedback can *help* Francisco avoid conflicts by adjusting how he uses the qualities and how he balances them with other qualities. The couple also agrees that they will consult before the next game about the best ways for Bonita to be hospitable to Francisco's friends.

Sometimes, as with Francisco and Bonita, a conflict might arise between you in front of other people. This can be more difficult to cope with than when you are alone, although it can also *help* you stay calmer! When this occurs, here are some possible ways to handle it:

- Breathe deeply and focus on *detachment*
- Acknowledge to yourself that there is an issue
- *Accept* that it might not be possible to deal with it at the moment
- Try to focus on what is happening and whom you are with
- If possible, request to the other the opportunity to discuss it later
- If appropriate, find a quiet location and deal with it swiftly

If you need to handle the issue further, then when you are no longer with others, consult about it until it is resolved.

Misusing Creative Imagination

One way your minds can get you into trouble, and you may need to assist one another, is when one of you misuses *creative* imagination. You may have a lively imagination—many people do. Unfortunately, you may also be very skilled in imagining scenarios happening with your spouse that have no basis in reality. When you do this, you may also interact with one another as if what you imagined is actually *true*.

Often what you imagine comes from your fears or some experience in the past and has no direct connection to the current situation. This type of imagining can be a sure way of causing conflict in your relationship. Observe how this occurs for Vicki and Richard in the brief drama below:

> Vicki glances out the front window one last time before turning off the living room lights and heading for bed. She does not understand where her husband Richard is and why he is not answering his cell phone. It is very unlike him not to call if he is late at the office or goes out with his friends, which was very

different than with her first husband. Richard comes home late that night and slips into bed without waking her.

Entering the kitchen the next morning, Richard quickly kisses Vicki, saying his car battery is dead, asks her to get it charged, and says he needs to borrow her car for the day. He rushes out the door, leaving Vicki standing alone and in her bathrobe, wondering what is going on.

After recharging the battery, she gets into Richard's car later to go to work. In the back seat of the car is a bikini bathing suit that she knows is not hers or their daughter's. Shocked and upset, she begins questioning what is going wrong in her marriage. Should she stay with a man who is so secretive and apparently cheating on her, just as her ex-husband did?

Later that evening, as Richard enters the house, she begins crying, yelling, and accusing him of being unfaithful with another woman [character attack]. Richard listens to her and is not sure whether to laugh, cry, or get angry. He tells Vicki that his boss pulled him into a major planning session the previous evening, and he apologizes for turning off his phone and not taking time to call her. He explains that he rushed out in the morning to continue the meeting. Then he reminds her that he picked up their daughter and one of her friends after swimming practice earlier in the week, and tells her that the friend dropped her suit.

Similarly to Vicki and Richard, you may immediately try to make sense of a situation when something happens, you imagine what significance it has, and try to sort out its impact on you and others. That is not necessarily a bad thing, except when you carry it to excess, or let your imagination run wild.

You might notice how often you start imagining all kinds of things when one of you does not respond, has a strange facial expression, does not call, and so on. Often, then, you are likely to have a negative interaction with one another the next time you speak that may include a character attack. What is important to be aware of is that your interaction may be largely based on what you imagined, not on what was actually going on.

To turn this destructive pattern around, the first skill to build is awareness of this automatic imagination process that goes on in your head. Secondly, you need to develop the ability to interrupt your thoughts before they cause you to act in a way that damages your relationship. Then you need to develop the ability to respond based on the facts of the current situation—what really happened—instead. It will support your efforts to do the following:

- *Discern* which character qualities apply
- Assume the other person has good intentions
- Practice what calms you down (meditation, music, building project, prayer, play a sport, walking, cleaning...)
- Wait to communicate until you can do it in a positive way
- Consciously put the past behind you and focus on the present
- Engage in consultation to fact-find, share feelings, and problem-solve with what could have prevented the situation

All these steps will contribute to a higher level of harmony between you.

SKILL-BUILDING OPPORTUNITY

See Appendix G, "Communication Skill: Stop Misusing Creative Imagination," which will assist you in having clear communications without confusing them with imagined scenarios.

THE MISSING QUALITY

At times, one of you may do something that concerns the other. In response, you may believe that you have discovered what quality your spouse may be missing. You decide he/she should be doing the exact opposite of what is happening. For example, you might see your husband as irresponsible because he forgets to clean the floors a few times when it needs to be done. You do not like this, and you start letting him know that you want him to be *responsible*.

There is a more effective and *peaceful* alternative. Consider how this happens for Layla and Mike:

> Layla and Mike walk from the parking lot into the conference building. She has to get the sound system tested, handouts ready, and refreshments set up before she welcomes the keynote speakers. Mike is carrying boxes of nametags and folders, because he is *responsible* for setting up registration. She rushes ahead of him, letting the door shut in his face, and causing him to drop his boxes. When he catches up with her, he criticizes her for always being impatient. "Can you try being *patient* once in awhile?" he asks in frustration.

> Not only does Layla's impatience cause her stress, but it is also very difficult for Mike. His frequent comments on the issue to Layla in a variety of circumstances make her feel misunderstood, unappreciated, and belittled. Everything he tries to do to get her to become *patient* fails. Not only that, but also little by little, Layla feels that Mike is trying to change her and erase who she really is. Either she then yells at Mike, or she acts coldly toward him when he tells her to be *patient*. They both become increasingly unhappy.

You can fill in the blanks and change the story to apply to the two of you. What are you asking one another to become the complete opposite of? Like Mike, do you see impatience and ask for *patience*? Often, when you think you have found a "bad quality" in your spouse, such as Mike did with Layla, a different interpretation might reduce conflict between you. What Mike fails to see is that he cannot *help* Layla become *patient* by criticizing her impatience, just the opposite of what he would like to see. By looking at the whole situation, he can see impatience is actually the misuse of her dominant character quality of *excellence*. She always wants to get things done in the best possible way and done efficiently.

When Mike acknowledges Layla for her high standards and her goal to be *excellent* in all that she does, she can respond to him positively. He is seeing her *true* and best self. He addresses how she is, not how she is not. Additionally, Layla also may begin to see that when she misuses *excellence*, she starts to become impatient. *Moderating excellence* with a quality like *contentment* or *cooperation* can *help* her be more *patient* and work better with others. When Mike *encourages* her to avoid misusing *excellence* by focusing on *respect* for others first, he is not attacking her impatient attitude, but is supporting her in using one of her best qualities effectively.

DECISIONS FOLLOW EVENTS

At times, when some significant negative event occurs in your life, you might use a quality excessively to prevent that negative event or something similar to it from recurring. You might behave—often unconsciously—as if practicing the quality will produce an automatic positive result for you. Consider how this happens for Sheela:

> Once again, Sheela can smell alcohol on her young husband's breath. Instead of getting angry, she smiles and greets him with a hug. She is positive that if she stays with Colin, she can get him *help*. Her friends want her to leave him since he repeatedly slaps her and treats her poorly. She can see her marriage is destructive, but she is determined to be *strong, forgiving,* and *loyal*.

> As a young child, Sheela watched her alcoholic father walk out the front door, get into his old beat-up car, and never return. For a while, Sheela comforted her mother as she struggled with loneliness. Then life began to change when her mother brought home man after man. Maybe one man would be around for a month or so, but each one would eventually disappear, just like her father. Sheela fears if she does not *care* for Colin, or if she confronts his drinking problem, he too will leave her.

Sheela is misusing *strength, loyalty,* and *forgiveness,* even to the point of allowing her husband to harm her. She is not holding him accountable for his actions. She desperately does not want her childhood history to repeat itself. Her situation changes when she begins to use *courage* and *assertiveness* and reaches out to a support group for assistance.

RESPONDING TO MISUSES

These examples show many ways to misuse qualities and cause disunity or conflict between you. It can be effective for you to pre-identify behaviors in which either of you tend to misuse a quality. You can agree that when these situations arise, you will be open to supportive suggestions from one another. This *helps* to protect your *unity*.

As an example, here are some consultation points between a couple that could happen before a husband visits his father in a nursing home. He often gets upset at the staff, wanting his father to receive more attention. They share:

- The concerns on their minds
- How to be *assertive* with the staff but empathetic to their workload
- The qualities that could assist the husband with the staff (maybe *acceptance, patience, or courtesy*)
- The consequences of losing his temper
- How to increase the staff's involvement with the father

This type of consultation will *help* you to identify your own specific trouble areas, so you can be supportive to one another.

Remember, to *help* you think of one another as your ally and not an accuser, start with the positive. It is vital to recognize one another's best and dominant positive qualities before you share your perception that there was a misuse. It shows *respect* first, followed by your constructive input. Most people quickly stop listening to someone who offers only negative feedback without first acknowledging their good qualities. It is *wise* to also end with sharing the positive qualities of one another.

The more extensively you understand character qualities, the more nuances and layers you will start to observe. It can be easy at times to interact with one another about character as you simply practice a quality effectively. However, at other times, the complexity may be very challenging. This is one of the great gifts of marriage—you can *help* one another as spouses in many ways. Philosopher George Santayana once wrote, "Character is the basis of happiness…." (*The Life of Reason*, p. 223)

—GLASBERGEN—

"How can you say I'm not romantic? Yesterday I almost thought about maybe buying you some flowers!"

ଞଔଓଷ

"It takes two people to make a successful marriage and reciprocity is at the heart of it. If only one of you is doing the good things, with little reciprocation from the other, resentment develops and trouble starts. So return her kindness. She will be encouraged and is much more likely to do it again."

~ Khalil A. Khavari and Sue Williston Khavari, *Together Forever*, p. 99

"The best index to a person's character is (a) how he treats people who can't do him any good, and (b) how he treats people who can't fight back."

~ Abigail Van Buren, "Dear Abby" newspaper column, May 16, 1974

10 ~ Solid Gold: Building Intimacy

Intimacy is an indispensable aspect of life in a happy marriage. It is a special feeling of closeness between you that comes from sharing aspects of yourselves and your lives that no one else does. It develops from your own unique experiences together and the quality of your friendship.

You may think of intimacy as primarily physical or sexual. However, *true* intimacy is a mental, emotional, and *spiritual* bonding between you as well.

Some people have never known *true* intimacy in their marriage. If this includes you, it will take time to create it. Some people fear and resist it, or they think it is boring and stale when they know someone very well. The opportunity in it, however, is to be happy that someone intimately knows you and *loves* both the best parts of you and your quirks.

With intimacy, there is comfort in being able to count on your spouse as your life partner. You can have *confidence* in one another's ability to meet or support the needs you both have. You can start a sentence, and the other can finish it. You know what makes each other laugh. You can read a book and know that the other will *love* it. Intimacy deepens and enriches your friendship and marriage and is a key ingredient in maintaining your bond.

VULNERABILITY

To have an intimate relationship with one another requires the qualities of *trust* and *confidence*. You can feel very vulnerable as you share information and experiences. You must be *loyal* and protect one another by not using your personal knowledge in a hurtful way. This is private between you, not public for airing as "funny" stories without one another's permission. You hold one another's hearts, and sharing something that is embarrassing or exposes one another's tender areas, hurts your marriage.

If you use your spouse's challenges and failures in a way that is harmful, it will reduce or destroy intimacy between you. Conversely, it will build intimacy when you handle delicate situations with *love*, *caring*, and *compassion*. Therapist and author of *Coral and Pearls*, Mehri Sefidvash, writes:

> If we have a relationship based on love, we can be open and honest with our partner without fear of being judged and knowing that support will be extended to us. We are sure that our partner is our best friend and will, whatever happens, always help us. Where there is love in our relationship, we can allow ourselves certain liberties: the liberty to get angry now and again, or even to lose control without fearing that a permanent scar will be left; the liberty to be imperfect; the liberty to make a fool of ourselves without losing the respect of our partner; the liberty to change and to grow and also to make mistakes without fearing that we will be abandoned at our moment of greatest need or that we may be subjected to a barrage of recriminations and judgments, the worst of which is undoubtedly "I told you so!"
>
> We need support particularly when the worst side of our character is exposed to our partner. It is just at this time that the acceptance and affection of our partner become the mainstays of our life. To preserve our personal dignity, we all need to feel the warmth and approval of someone we love and respect. (pp. 41-42)

Do you have this in your marriage? What would it take for you to *create* it?

Part of what may assist you to expand your intimacy, is assessing your level of *trust* in one another, and building it higher. If you are struggling with *trust* or need to re-build it after an incident, you may find it *helpful* to practice it in small ways that build *confidence*. If you can make and keep promises consistently with one another, this will make a big difference. You may also need to seek professional counseling.

Intimacy does not mean being so enmeshed with one another that you lose your separate identities. Sometimes in an unhealthy marriage, a couple can also have a very unbalanced relationship, where one is very dependent on the other without good reasons. *True* intimacy requires partnership and *equality*.

INTIMACY THROUGH COMMUNICATION

One way intimacy grows between you is through having open lines of communication. It builds as you share your thoughts and feelings about what is happening in each of your lives and in your marriage. It comes from a pattern of successfully consulting with one another and the *trust* and *confidence* that results as you resolve issues *peacefully*.

If one of you is an introvert and the other an extrovert, you may find it challenging at times to handle an imbalance of communication between you. It will take extra effort to ensure that there are enough pauses and *encouragement* for the introvert to speak, and enough *self-discipline* on the part of the extrovert to stop filling up all the speaking time.

One way that you build intimacy is by sharing about your character qualities *honestly* and *sincerely* with one another. You probably know the very best about each other. You are also more familiar with one another's challenges with refining character qualities than you are with even close family members or best friends.

You know your wife loses her *patience* when coworkers do not *help* her, or when the children make a mess in the kitchen. You know your husband loses his *enthusiasm* when someone makes negative comments about his cooking or latest project. As mentioned earlier, you are also more likely to let one another significantly influence your character qualities than you let others. You are *true* partners in the process. In the following scenario, Helga and Gunther struggle with their communication and activities after retirement:

> For several weeks, Helga watches her husband Gunther drink cups of coffee and assemble model airplanes in their basement. He often shows her his latest plane, happy with his new hobby. She is glad he is busy, and she makes constant suggestions to him for improvements. She says how much better it would be if he could use red paint instead of blue or use the more expensive varnish. Gunther gradually stops showing her his work. Helga complains to him that he is creating a mess and smell in the house with the models. After a while, Gunther stops doing the models completely.

> One day as Gunther sits at the kitchen table and sips his coffee, Helga asks him why he is not working on his models. He replies that he became discouraged at never being able to make an airplane that seemed to be good enough. He said she was always pointing out ways he could make the plane better and complaining.

Realizing her negative words interfered with his *confidence* and *enthusiasm* in building the models, Helga apologizes and promises not to do it again. She *encourages* him to continue with his new hobby, which he does. They agree to build a workshop for him in the back yard, so the mess is not in the house.

In every marriage, there are times when you may cause difficulties for one another, just as Helga did with Gunther. Perhaps you even feel justified in your actions. The more you hang onto being "right" and labeling your spouse as "wrong," however, the greater the distance in your relationship. Intimacy cannot exist when you are in that mindset. Unless one of you is behaving unjustly or doing serious harm to the other, rarely does it end up making a difference that you were right, but only that you come together again in *unity*.

Long-Distance Connection

There are times for most couples when you are apart. Moves, business travel, family illness, visiting relatives, and more will physically separate you. A foundation of friendship and intimacy will assist you to keep in touch through the telephone, email, or other means that work for you.

Before you leave one another, reaffirm your relationship and *commitment* to be in communication. Create an agreement for how often and when you will be in touch with one another. You will also need to know how to reach one another for emergencies. It may be *helpful* for you to spend some extra time together deepening all layers of intimacy between you before you are apart as well.

You might think it is easier to wait until you are back together to share what is going on in your lives, but whenever possible, it is better to keep up-to-date. You can start to feel distant from one another, otherwise. One other way to maintain closeness over the telephone is to pray together before hanging up. This may feel strange to you at first, but it will be easier with practice.

PHYSICAL CLOSENESS

You are also more physically intimate with your spouse than with any other person. You know she is self-conscious about the mole on her shoulder. You know he is dreading going gray. You know she dreams of running every morning, but she never does more than walk down the road. You know he snores sometimes while he sleeps. You *encourage* one another's physical well-being through good diet and exercise. Sometimes you are healthy, and sometimes not. You see one another at your physical best and at your worst.

© 2005 Catherine F. Hosack

Intimacy also grows between you with shared patterns and habits in your home and life. One starts a task and the other finishes it. You diaper the baby together and play with her toes. You sit on the steps watching the sunset. One holds the nails while the other hammers (Ouch, that one might hurt!). One brushes down the horses while the other cleans stalls. You both sit with the children and read bedtime stories. One cooks and the other does the dishes. Intimacy comes from working together on what needs to be done in your lives.

Physical intimacy includes sex and touch, of course, but Chapter 11 will address this topic separately.

SHARED EXPERIENCES

Sharing all the experiences of marriage, including the challenges and tragedies that happen in life, can *create* deep intimacy if you allow it. You know what makes one another cry, get angry, grieve, and rejoice. When difficulties happen, you know what each of you will handle well or poorly, and where you need to support and compensate for one another. Intimacy builds your ability to respond instinctively to meet one another's emotional needs with listening, hugs, *encouragement*, or prayer.

Intimacy can also happen between you through increasing your connection to *spirituality*. Again, this develops through shared experience. If it is not part of your lives, you may wish to experiment with including it. *Spiritual* intimacy usually begins with having the same or similar beliefs and values. Perhaps you worship or pray together. You might read scripture or study it together as part of the pattern of your married life. You might have children together and be responsible for their *spiritual* education. Marriage can be more than a physical union. It can also be a union of your souls.

SKILL-BUILDING OPPORTUNITY

See Appendix H, "Communication Skills: Humor and Fun," which will *help* you deepen your intimacy, understanding, and practice in these areas.

Note: In Part 2, in the "Consult and Take Action" sections, you will find a consistent question about how each quality can enhance intimacy. You may find it *helpful* to re-read Chapters 10 and 11 if you find it difficult to answer the questions.

ಬಿಌ

"The barriers to intimate connection crumble away when there are feelings of trust, safety, and respect. This attitude creates the grounding from which equality flows very naturally. As we recognize the triggers that stimulate old patterns of self-protection, we can address and systematically disarm them, both internally and in dialogue with our partner.

"Like a skilled technician who steps cautiously into a minefield to deactivate the bombs, it takes great courage to do this tedious and dangerous work. Our reward is the joy that comes in playing and dancing together with abandon and delight, as equals."
~ Linda and Charlie Bloom, *101 Things I Wish I Knew When I Got Married*, p. 69

11 ~ A Golden Gift: Uncovering Sexual Oneness

You might think it is a bit strange to connect character qualities with sex, but in fact, it is a very natural fit. They affect every part of your relationship, including lovemaking. Becoming aware of and gradually integrating the qualities into your marriage can transform the intimacy of your sex life. When you practice them during lovemaking, your sexual life together can increasingly become a great source of *love* and *unity* for both of you.

Your marriage is a special and very natural place for sexual expression. Together you have the freedom to explore how it can build *unity* and *love* between you. When your sensuous touch and sexual acts have mutual *equality* and *respect* at their foundation, they *strengthen* your marriage bond.

Moderation and *detachment* apply, however. The media has distorted sex in many ways, portraying it as almost exclusively important in a couple's life. Often articles, books, and movies elevate sex higher than any other aspect of relationships, turning it into a virtual spectator sport.

It is increasingly common for couples to begin with sex, live together or jump quickly into marriage, and never get to know one another with *true* intimacy. After the initial physical intensity lessens, they discover they have little in common, and divorce a short time later. This process has failed to produce happiness.

Misled by this false standard, you might be in a marriage where there is sexual attraction, but you do not know each other very well. However, it is not too late to build your relationship into one that can last. The key is in understanding and *encouraging* one another's character qualities in all aspects of your lives, including during sexual intimacy.

Sexual intercourse, and all that accompanies it, is the most physically intimate aspect of your marriage. It creates an intense experience of oneness between you that can contribute to all aspects of your relationship. The intimacy that you build through sharing other experiences also enhances the oneness you experience in bed. Intimacy in lovemaking is not just a physical connection between you; it is also a joining of your hearts and souls. The Khavari's say, "lovemaking is the shared play of two equal partners." (*Together Forever* p. 89)

The Real Reason The Ice Caps Are Melting.

CHARACTER QUALITIES AND SEX

You can enhance your sexual intimacy through sharing your thoughts and requests with one another and using the character qualities to *help* you. You might draw on *confidence, assertiveness,* and *creativity* in deciding how and when you want your lovemaking to happen and what you both need. If you are experiencing a lull in your sex life, you might draw on *enthusiasm* or *creativity* for a boost.

You might apply some qualities easily and quickly. Others might require more discussion. Cleanliness (*purity*), for instance, is likely to be important to both of you, but you may have different standards for it. You will need to agree on what personal hygiene actions you will take before sexual intimacy. Together you can also be *flexible* and agree to set aside assumptions you may have about what the other appreciates or limitations you may have put on your participation. You can explore what interferes with having a full and satisfying sexual life in your marriage that builds oneness between you and what to do about it.

If you spend time thinking about it, you can actually apply virtually every quality in a positive way to enhance your sexual intimacy. Think of *generosity*, *thoughtfulness*, and *flexibility*. Then think of *gentleness*, *patience*, and *respect*. Each of these and more can guide your attitude and actions as you touch one another and join your bodies together. The intent is that your sexual experiences build from your intimacy, and your intimacy enhances your sexual experience of oneness.

Quality Misuses Related to Sex

Misuse of qualities can also be a concern with sex. For example, a misuse of *faithfulness* could look like extreme possessiveness or jealousy of one another. A misuse of *self-discipline* might have you withdraw touch from one another completely.

Society is experiencing an epidemic of infidelity in marriage. However, pairing character qualities such as *commitment* and *faithfulness* with sex can transform it into a special, intimate gift for your marriage. *Creativity* is a positive quality to enhance your sexual intimacy within your marriage. If you choose to be unfaithful and seek sexual fulfillment from someone other than your spouse, you would need to misuse your *creativity* to avoid being caught.

Misused *forgiveness* is also a chief culprit in sexual impropriety. You may incorrectly assume that there will be no consequences if you are unfaithful, or you agree to not be concerned if both of you break your vows. These misuses will damage your marriage and hurt your families.

CARE IN TOUCHING

Gentleness is often a quality you both appreciate from one another, especially if one of you is *stronger* than the other. Sometimes there are circumstances where it is even more important, however. Touch from another person that is intended to be pleasurable can instead be uncomfortable or scary depending upon experiences you have had. If you have ever experienced abuse, such as inappropriate touch, rape, or incest, it might be very difficult for you to *trust* that it will be safe to let someone touch you intimately. You may be *wise* to communicate to the other what happened and what interpretations you made about it. Be *patient* and *loving* with one another as you work through healing. Be conscious, however, that your spouse may only wish to know about it briefly, or alternatively may wish to know more than you want to share. It is important to find a comfortable balance for what you share between you.

Any remaining pain from unsafe touch can produce tension, resistance, or suspicion of the motives of anyone who tries to touch you sexually, even when it is your *trusted* spouse. If this is *true* for you, establishing all the other areas of intimacy as shared in Chapter 10 is especially important. As you can imagine, it is much easier to become sensuously and sexually vulnerable to someone who is *truly* your best friend and *trusted* life companion. The *strength* of your communication skills and your relationship will support you both in sharing what you need and in responding to one another's requests.

Sometimes part of the solution to *creating* a safe and *trusting* environment when there has been past abuse can be simple. For instance, you can take turns initiating touch, or make light available during lovemaking so you can clearly see your spouse. You may develop signals for one another when you need activity to slow down, become *gentler*, or stop altogether. If past negative experiences are affecting your sex life, you will need to explore with one another how to build *trust* and intimacy between you, and you may need to seek professional counseling. **Note:** If there has ever been sexual coercion or abuse between the two of you, professional assistance for both of you is especially important.

HAVING CHILDREN

Sex, of course, often leads to conceiving children. Pregnancy and parenthood affect your lovemaking and marriage, and they can often present you with challenges. Your responses to one another during pregnancy change, as do your perceptions of what is attractive.

After birth, mothers who are experiencing constant touch from their babies or young children may find it difficult to switch into the intense touching that comes with being a sexual partner to their spouse. Of course, exhaustion and finding time together are also challenges to handle! You might need to take advantage of the baby's naptime for togetherness.

Sometimes a new mother may feel less attractive to her husband because of pregnancy weight gain. Carol Ummel Lindquist, Ph.D., author of *Happily Married with Kids*, advises husbands to reassure their wives verbally that they are attractive. She *encourages* reassuring touch through cuddling or massage that works as either a substitute or lead-in for sexual encounters. (p.190)

James and Lindsay find a way to make their relationship a priority, even though they are new parents:

James and Lindsay *love* having a baby. James enjoys watching their son Daniel smile, and he teaches him to make funny faces. Lindsay likes the bond she shares with Daniel as he nurses. But one aspect of parenthood they are struggling with is physical exhaustion, which not only affects their sleep but their intimacy as well.

Lindsay decides it is time to renew their *commitment* to one another. She drops Daniel off with her mother and surprises James by using *creativity* to set up a full day together. They walk in the park, eat a slow, *peaceful* lunch at their favorite restaurant, and have time for playful activities in their bedroom. They incorporate *cooperation*, *enthusiasm*, *gentleness*, and *love* into their intimate reconnection time. Together, they *strengthen* one another and rejuvenate themselves to spend happy quality time with Daniel later that evening.

Having children will challenge your marriage in many ways. It is important to remember that one of the greatest gifts you give your children is maintaining a *peaceful*, *unified*, and successful marriage.

DISCERNING STANDARDS

For couples at any stage of their marriage, one of the most vital contributions you will each make to sex within your marriage is practicing the quality of *chastity*. People often associate this concept with abstinence before marriage and do not think about it in relation to marriage. However, *chastity* includes the quality of *faithfulness*—only having sex with one another. This avoids any comparisons or feelings of competition with someone else. *Chastity* also *encourages* you to rely on one another for your stimulation and not on media (videos, magazines, and more) that involve you in seeing sexual images of people other than your spouse.

The media can also cause challenges by giving you unreasonable standards of performance and attractiveness to achieve. It communicates that sex should always be spectacular, you should both be in top physical condition, and the frequency should be off the top of the charts. This standard might occasionally be realistic, but it is highly unlikely to hold *true* at all times throughout your marriage. Together you will work out the rhythms that meet your mutual needs. Some couples have sex daily, some three times a week, some weekly, some monthly, and others less often. If the frequency drops off significantly, then you will need to understand why and what you will do or not do in response. And, yes, you can consult about what works for both of you!

Sex is an important part of your marriage, but it is only one aspect of it. If you value the broader intimacy that comes from your friendship and *love* as more important, you will be able to use the quality of *wisdom* and better handle the inevitable disruptions to your sex life that come with children, illness, and aging. The friendship will last, but in some circumstances, sex may not. If you have developed a *strong* level of intimacy through your sex life, however, it will support the *strength* of your friendship.

Note: In Part 2, in the "Consult and Take Action" sections, you
will find a consistent question about how each quality can enhance
intimacy. You may find it *helpful* to re-read Chapters 10 and 11 if you
find it difficult to answer the questions.

ഇൗരു

"It is important to acknowledge that God could have arranged the
whole reproduction thing any way He wanted: a hidden button, a
super-secret handshake, or some unique facial exchange that brought
about conception. Really, He could have. But instead, He designed
sex. He must have had a good reason, but what is it? The answer,
in short, is that God wanted sex to be a lot more than just a really
fun thing for wives and husbands to do together. And He wanted
it to be more than an extremely enjoyable way to populate the
planet. He had a far loftier goal in mind. God designed marital sex
to be an encounter with the divine. Sexual intimacy, with all of its
overwhelming emotions and heart-pounding sensations, was never
intended to be experienced solely in the emotional and physical
realms. Rather, it is to be a spiritual, even mystical, experience in
which two bodies become one. God is present in a very real way
every time this happens.

"Sex really is holy. It's a sacred place shared in the intimacy of
marriage."

~ Tim Alan Gardner, *Sacred Sex, A Spiritual Celebration of Oneness in Marriage*, pp. 4-5

12 ~ The Gold Medal: Creating a Lasting Union

Hopefully you are beginning to understand why it is so important to spend time paying attention to your character qualities. Behavior based on these qualities is one of the greatest sources for happiness in your lives. A well-developed character *helps* you influence others in a positive way, often through your example.

Practicing your character qualities to the best of your ability supports and *strengthens* the unity of your marriage. Many faiths also believe there is a *spiritual* life to look forward to after physical death, and your character qualities will be as important to your happiness and well-being there as your physical hands, eyes, and feet are here.

Staying in Action

Marriage is often challenging, and the relationship between you will change as you go through all its stages, particularly having and raising children. The more you practice the qualities effectively, and bind your hearts together as friends and *equal* partners, the greater will be your ability to stay together happily.

Living life with a high standard of character is often difficult. It takes repeated practice, reflection on progress, setting goals, and consistent striving. It requires *commitment* and dedication based on the conviction that developing yourself and your marriage in this way is worthwhile.

25 YEARS
SAME
LOCATION

BBBrown

Challenges may occur when an imbalance exists between the two of you. Perhaps one of you is working on a quality that the other does not demonstrate. If you *persevere* and practice the quality consistently, however, your spouse's heart may shift, and his or her understanding may grow. This could prompt him/her to practice the behavior as well.

You may also disagree about which quality is applicable in a particular circumstance. For example, one of you may be *patient* in waiting for something to happen, and the other may think *assertive* action makes more sense. You should consult with one another about the two approaches and come to an agreement about which to choose. You can also experiment to see what works and learn from it. At times, you may simply need to *trust* your spouse's intuition about what is best. Consider how this worked out with Aruna, Rashid, and their daughter, Aditi:

> Ever since Aditi could read and write, her father Rashid talked of her attending the college where he graduated. He believes the law program there would be a great opportunity for his eldest daughter. Her mother, Aruna, is concerned the large campus in a major city might overwhelm Aditi, making adjusting to college more difficult. Aditi suggests they visit three different campuses to *help* make the decision.

> Throughout the visits, Rashid points out how graduates from his college receive higher paying jobs or obtain jobs more quickly after graduation. However, after they visit all the schools and see Aditi's reaction to them, Rashid realizes his wife is right about what is best for Aditi. Aruna feels the larger school would so overwhelm Aditi that her grades would suffer. As a family, they agree where she should go to school.

As you develop character qualities, you will notice that while they require internal effort and *commitment*, they grow best through interactions with others. Your marriage is a great place to practice and *encourage* character growth and development. The more you interact with one another, the more you will use these qualities. Be *creative* with how you learn them together!

A Spiritual Connection

You may find it *helpful* to support yourselves and your marriage by *creating* or nurturing a *spiritual* connection between you. Marriage Therapist Paul Coleman, Psy.D., in his book, *The 30 Secrets of Happily Married Couples* (pp. 139-142), indicates that decades of research demonstrate that people highly involved in religion usually have the happiest marriages. He attributes this to religion *helping* people make sense of their lives and providing meaning and values. He also *encourages* couples to pray together. Even if you are not involved in a specific religion, you are likely to draw closer to one another through your choice of *spiritual* practices.

> Steven works in a local factory, and his wife, Marie, is juggling her part-time job as she *cares* for their three children. Medical problems with their youngest child add stress to their lives. Yesterday, the factory went out of business, putting Steven out of work. When the alarm sounds this morning, they hug before getting out of bed. They sit on the edge of the bed together, hold hands, and pray together that God will *help* them. Steven will search the newspaper and Internet today for a new job. Marie will go to her manager and ask to work more hours. Seeing Steven and Marie's firm commitment to each other *helps* their children adjust to the changes and keeps the family close.

Ways you may build a *spiritual* connection with one another could include going on retreats, spending time in nature, finding ways to be of *service* to one another and to the community, studying and discussing *spiritual* topics, and doing *loving* acts for one another. In doing activities such as these, you begin *accepting* and understanding your similarities and differences, and blending them together in *unity*. This *unity* is vitally important for your marriage, and it is achievable whether the differences are racial, religious, age, or any number of other factors. Being open-minded and *respectful* will assist you to maintain harmony.

You are not and never will be the same people. Your goal in marriage, however, is to explore and maintain the ways you can work together in harmony. When you achieve a high level of harmony in your marriage, you have a greater capacity for addressing the many dimensions of your life, such as family, work, and community *service*. Others will also be attracted to your *love*, and your union will bring happiness to them as well as to yourselves.

Pure Gold assists you to know one another very well and to *create* positive character-based behaviors, attitudes, and communication patterns in your marriage. These contribute to harmony in your relationship.

**"Looks aren't everything. It's what's inside you
that really matters. A biology teacher told me that."**

The in-depth study and consultation you will do together about the character qualities in Part 2 will *help* you maintain your friendship and achieve the gold medal of a happy, lasting marriage.

                ຂ໐ເຮ

"In exasperating situations, we must find the time to pause and reflect if we are not afterwards to regret our words and actions. The Golden Rule, 'Do unto others what you would have them do unto you' or 'Do not do to others that which you do not wish done to yourself' is a useful guideline for action. By putting ourselves in our partner's shoes now and again, by trying to discover what he or she feels, we can come to realize many things about our partner, we learn to respect him [or her] more fully, and we open our hearts to new levels of understanding, compassion, tenderness, and intimacy. In many circumstances where tension is great and emotions are running high, knowing how to say 'I'm sorry' can reduce tension and make the other person more inclined to recognize his or her own mistakes."

~ Mehri Sefidvash, *Coral and Pearls*, pp. 27-28

ഇൗ

"Virtue is sometimes associated with perfectionism. When it comes to human beings, to be perfect does not mean to be flawless. It means to be whole and complete. Part of the completeness of being spiritually alive and aware is to accept our flaws, our mistakes, and our failings as teachable opportunities which can bring us new learning. It is in working with the virtues which we have over- or underdeveloped that we find the energy for new growth. Life is not about being perfect. It is about perfecting or cultivating our virtues. Perfection is the process of bringing our gifts to fruition."

~ Linda Kavelin Popov, *The Family Virtues Guide*, p. 3

Part 2

Encouraging Character Qualities

Character Qualities

Acceptance
Assertiveness
Beauty
Caring
Chastity
Commitment
Compassion
Confidence
Contentment
Cooperation
Courage
Courtesy
Creativity
Detachment
Discernment
Encouragement
Enthusiasm
Equality
Excellence
Faithfulness
Flexibility
Forgiveness
Friendliness
Generosity
Gentleness
Helpfulness
Honesty
Humility

Idealism
Integrity
Joyfulness
Justice
Kindness
Love
Loyalty
Mercy
Moderation
Patience
Peacefulness
Perseverance
Purity
Purposefulness
Respect
Responsibility
Self-Discipline
Service
Sincerity
Spirituality
Strength
Tactfulness
Thankfulness
Thoughtfulness
Trustworthiness
Truthfulness
Unity
Wisdom

Part 2: Character Qualities

INTRODUCTION AND INSTRUCTIONS

Part 1 taught you the importance of character qualities. The more you understand these qualities, and the more you put them into practice, the happier and more lasting your marriage will be.

Part 1 laid the groundwork for Part 2. You may find it helpful to refer back to it from time to time as you go through Part 2. Part 1 introduced you to several different aspects of character. It also began your training in many communication skills. Part 2 will give you an *excellent* opportunity to practice them, especially consultation.

Part 2 guides you step-by-step through 56 character qualities. You will be able to apply each quality to your own selves and to your marriage, learning about them and practicing them together.

Part 2 is designed for couples to study openly and honestly together as a team. However, each of you will also benefit from taking private time to study the qualities.

You will further explore intimacy as part of each quality in Part 2. As you discuss and consult together, refer to Chapters 10 and 11 from Part 1 for additional help with intimacy issues.

A word of caution to you: Through this consultation process, you will discover things about yourselves and one another! Do not say, "Ah ha! This is just the way *you* are!" Rather say, "Ah ha! This is just the way *I* am!" Practice *courtesy* and *respect* with one another. This is not your big opportunity to start pointing fingers at one another. Do not belittle, insult, demean, or criticize one another! This is intended to build your marriage up, not be an opportunity to tear it down!

Remember, character development is a lifelong journey, not a fixed destination. The more you pay attention to your character development, the deeper and faster your progress will be.

Both of you and your marriage will grow when you follow this simple process:

- Gain knowledge and understanding
- Consciously choose to change
- Begin to act in a new way
- Reflect on your actions and their impact
- Decide whether to act differently next time

SUGGESTIONS FOR USING PART 2 EFFECTIVELY

Read and study it **when** it works best for you:

- Daily
- Weekly
- Monthly
- Annually

Chose **how** you use it:

- Read a brief portion each day as a focus for practice
- Discuss one quality in depth at a time
- Explore several qualities together

Read and study it **where** it is most convenient:

- Home
- Vacation
- Vehicle
- Business travel
- Mountain
- Beach
- Prairie
- Farm
- City
- Village
- Tent
- Hut
- Cabin
- Almost anywhere!

Read and study it in the way that it works best for you.

Structure

Each quality has three separate sections. To assist you in your journey, here are some suggestions for each:

1. **Expand Our Insights**—Read, reflect, and discuss! Begin with the *spiritual* quotation at the top of the page. Next, you will see the highest *ideals* of the quality explained. Lastly, there is an insightful quotation at the bottom of that section.

2. **Consult and Take Action**
   a. Read and consult about questions 1 and 2, and how each question applies to you:
      o Determine and decide what new choices you will make to strengthen or balance your qualities. Make a plan to carry them out better next time.
      o *Commit* to remove any character choices that have not worked in the past. Consult together about what support you may need to be successful.
   b. Then, continue with the remaining discussion questions. These will *help* you discover how you are currently practicing the quality in your marriage and what new choices you might make.

3. **Strengthen Our Relationship**
   a. Read each suggestion for practicing the quality.
   b. Consult about and choose which ones you will do.
   c. Discuss what additional actions you will take.

Use *Pure Gold* as your easy reference guide to assess your behavior and choices regularly. You will discover that it is a valuable tool to keep handy everywhere you go. You will learn to understand yourself, one another, and others better than you ever thought was possible.

Enjoy your journey together!

ᤒ Acceptance ᤒ

EXPAND OUR INSIGHTS

If it is possible, as far as it depends on you, live at peace with
everyone.
~ Christianity: *The Bible* (New International Version), Romans, 12:18

Accepting one another unconditionally gives us the freedom to be
ourselves physically, mentally, emotionally, and spiritually. We are
free to love one another just as we are, without expecting the other
to change. However, this acceptance often gives us the freedom
to choose to change. As an act of love to one another, acceptance
frees us to grow and develop our skills, capacities, and talents. We
understand that challenges are part of life, and we handle them
without complaint and with humor and grace. Practicing acceptance
assists us in being patient and in forgiving mistakes. Sometimes we
are uncomfortable, frustrated, or upset in response to one another's
actions or words. When we talk about these feelings, we may agree
to be flexible and make changes in our attitudes, speech, or behavior.
Other times, we may simply choose to accept that our points of view
are valid but different.

"To accept" means to tolerate what you regard as an unpleasant
behavior of your partner, probably to understand the deeper meaning
of that behavior, certainly to see it in a larger context, and perhaps
even to appreciate its value and importance in your relationship.
~ Andrew Christensen and Neil S. Jacobson, *Reconcilable Differences*, p. 124

How are we practicing Acceptance ?
What new choices will we make?

CONSULT AND TAKE ACTION

1. Identifying and Strengthening *Acceptance*
   a. Are we critical and judgmental? If so, when? How can *love*, *respect*, or other qualities support *acceptance*?
   b. Do we act as if everything must be exactly according to our standards? If so, when? How can *detachment, flexibility*, or other qualities assist us?
   c. When can *contentment, forgiveness, patience, unity*, or other qualities assist us with strengthening *acceptance*?
2. Identifying and Balancing Misuses of *Acceptance*
   a. Do we wrongly let others treat us poorly? If so, when? How can *honesty, strength*, or other qualities assist us in using *acceptance* effectively?
   b. Are we silent and therefore make it easy for others to behave irresponsibly? If so, when? How can *excellence, responsibility*, or other qualities assist us?
   c. When can using *discernment, wisdom*, or other qualities prevent us from misusing *acceptance*?
3. When is the lack of or misuse of *acceptance* a source of conflict for us? If necessary, how can we restore harmony?
4. Where do we struggle to *accept* one another?
5. What has happened in our lives that we have not *accepted*? Do we feel angry, sad, or some other emotion about it? How can we resolve the matter and completely put it in the past?
6. How can *acceptance* enhance all types of intimacy between us?

STRENGTHEN OUR RELATIONSHIP

- ♥ Identify people in our lives who are different from us, discuss their unique characteristics, and initiate building friendships
- ♥ *Create* a practice, such as a prayer or warm hug, that we can use to bring us closer together after a conflict or serious disagreement
- ♥ Stop a complaint about the other, and practice *acceptance* instead
- ♥ Identify something in the other or in our relationship that is unlikely to change and *accept* it as it is
- ♥ How else are we *committed* to practicing *acceptance*?

✧ Assertiveness ✧

EXPAND OUR INSIGHTS

Man is not intended to see through the eyes of another, hear through another's ears nor comprehend with another's brain. ... Therefore, depend upon your own reason and judgment and adhere to the outcome of your own investigation....

~ Bahá'í Faith: *Promulgation of Universal Peace*, p. 293

Assertiveness is being self-assured and decisive in contributing ideas and opinions, as well as stepping into action. It helps us to be confident in our attitudes, when we speak, or as we respond to situations. When we are assertive, we think for ourselves, and we use positive energy to express ourselves clearly. We make direct requests of one another when we have needs or preferences of all kinds. Assertiveness helps us to set appropriate and respectful boundaries that guide us in treating one another in positive ways. We also use assertiveness to defend our actions and ourselves appropriately. Assertiveness helps us to be responsible for taking care of ourselves, being accountable for our words and actions, and engaged in character growth. We take leadership as appropriate in activities that contribute to our family and community. We also directly engage in ensuring our marriage is vibrant and ever growing.

This above all: to thine own self be true, and it must follow as the night the day, thou canst not then be false to any man.

~ William Shakespeare, *Hamlet*, Act I, scene iii

How are we practicing Assertiveness?
What new choices will we make?

CONSULT AND TAKE ACTION

1. Identifying and Strengthening *Assertiveness*
   a. Do we fail to act to prevent one another or others from treating us with disrespect? If so, when? How can *equality*, *justice*, or other qualities support *assertiveness*?
   b. Do we keep quiet inappropriately? If so, when? How can *confidence*, *courage*, or other qualities assist us?
   c. Do we set appropriate boundaries? If so, when? How can *responsibility*, *strength*, or other qualities assist us?
   d. When can *encouragement*, *perseverance*, *purposefulness*, *truthfulness*, or other qualities assist us with strengthening *assertiveness*?
2. Identifying and Balancing Misuses of *Assertiveness*
   a. Do we behave in bold, aggressive, or pushy ways? If so, when? How can *humility*, *respect*, or other qualities assist us in using *assertiveness* effectively?
   b. Do we use words or a tone of voice that are rude or offensive, just to get our way? If so, when? How can *courtesy*, *tactfulness*, or other qualities assist us?
   c. When can using *acceptance*, *compassion*, *discernment*, *flexibility*, *unity*, or other qualities reduce our misuse of *assertiveness*?
3. When is the lack of or misuse of *assertiveness* a source of conflict for us? If necessary, how can we restore harmony?
4. How well do we express our own ideas, opinions, and requests? How do we respond to these expressions from one another?
5. How can we tell if one of us is being aggressive instead of *assertive*?
6. How can *assertiveness* enhance all types of intimacy between us?

STRENGTHEN OUR RELATIONSHIP

- ♥ *Assertively* request the other to assist with an unmet need
- ♥ Pre-plan what to say when we need to share something with one another that might be difficult
- ♥ Acknowledge and *assertively* handle an issue in our home
- ♥ Identify times we have not been *assertive* and discuss why
- ♥ How else are we *committed* to practicing *assertiveness*?

❧ *Beauty* ❧

EXPAND OUR INSIGHTS

By giving away our food, we get more strength, by bestowing clothing on others, we gain more beauty; by donating abodes of purity and truth, we acquire great treasures.

~ Buddhism: *The Gospel of Buddha*, XXIV:4

Beauty is the expression of what is most positive and attractive in one another and our surroundings that gives pleasure to the mind, body, heart, or soul. As we take care of our health and well-being, it increases our beauty. Beauty grows and shines in our marriage through a warm smile, a spontaneous gift, and other expressions of love, caring, and gentleness. We bring beauty of all kinds into our home, creating harmonious order and cleanliness. This creates a beautiful place where we enjoy spending time and welcoming others. The area outside our home is well tended and attractive. We enrich and beautify our lives and ourselves through music, art, literature, dance, science, nature, spiritual activities, clothing, and new ideas. When there is beauty in our lives, it lightens our spirits and brings us happiness.

There is no beautifier of complexion, or form, or behavior, like the wish to scatter joy and not pain around us.

~ Ralph Waldo Emerson, *The Conduct of Life*, "Behavior"

How are we practicing Beauty?
What new choices will we make?

CONSULT AND TAKE ACTION

1. Identifying and Strengthening *Beauty*
   a. Are we careless with our physical appearance or the attractiveness of our home? If so, when? How can *creativity, excellence,* or other qualities support *beauty?*
   b. Are we unappreciative of nature's *beauty?* If so, when? How can *enthusiasm, joyfulness,* or other qualities assist us?
   c. When can *caring, gentleness, purity, respect, spirituality,* or other qualities assist us with strengthening *beauty?*
2. Identifying and Balancing Misuses of *Beauty*
   a. Do we idolize physical *beauty* through lust or pornography? If so, when? How can *chastity, detachment,* or other qualities assist us in using *beauty* effectively?
   b. Are we intolerant of physical imperfections, and mistreat them with unwise diets or excessive exercising? If so, when? How can *acceptance, moderation,* or other qualities assist us?
   c. Do we spend extensive time, money, and effort to adorn or *beautify* our bodies (makeup, jewelry, tattoos)? If so, when? How can *contentment, humility,* or other qualities assist us?
   d. When can using *flexibility, purity, purposefulness,* or other qualities reduce our misuse of *beauty?*
3. When is the lack of or misuse of *beauty* a source of conflict for us? If necessary, how can we restore harmony?
4. Do we treat *beautiful* people better than we do unattractive ones? What value do we place on inner *beauty?*
5. What activities are we doing that prompt us to appreciate *beauty?*
6. How can *beauty* enhance all types of intimacy between us?

STRENGTHEN OUR RELATIONSHIP

♥ Express appreciation for something beautiful in one another
♥ Work together to beautify an area inside or outside our home
♥ Exercise *moderately* and eat healthy food together
♥ Visit a place that offers *beauty,* such as a beach, garden, park, field, mountain, museum, or theater
♥ How else are we *committed* to practicing *beauty?*

❧ *Caring* ❧

EXPAND OUR INSIGHTS

...do good—to parents, kinsfolk, orphans, those in need, neighbors who are near, neighbors who are strangers, the Companion by your side, the way-farer (ye meet)....

~ Islam: *The Qur'án*, 4:36

♥

When we care, we give sincere love, attention, consideration, and assistance to one another in a timely and appropriate way. Doing this shows that we value and honor each other's well-being, needs, preferences, and feelings. We care deeply about one another, looking for ways to bring the other happiness. Keeping our marriage strong and vibrant is a priority in our lives. We do not assume that our actions would truly be caring to the other. Instead, we ask before acting. This helps our actions to be positive and meaningful in ways that we know the other appreciates. We notice when the other is going through a difficult time. We show we care by listening attentively and empathetically, and by giving encouragement and support to one another as needed.

♥

The capacity to care gives life its deepest significance.

~ Attributed to Pablo Casals

How are we practicing Caring?
What new choices will we make?

CONSULT AND TAKE ACTION

1. Identifying and Strengthening *Caring*
   a. Do we ignore one another's obvious or predictable needs and wishes? If so, when? How can *helpfulness, thoughtfulness,* or other qualities support *caring?*
   b. Do we treat one another or our possessions as though they do not matter? If so, when? How can *love, respect,* or other qualities assist us?
   c. When can *compassion, generosity, idealism, kindness, sincerity, service, unity,* or other qualities assist us with strengthening *caring?*
2. Identifying and Balancing Misuses of *Caring*
   a. Do we meddle, hover over-protectively, or attempt to manage too much of one another's lives? If so, when? How can *discernment, justice,* or other qualities assist us in using *caring* effectively?
   b. Are we *creating* an unhealthy dependence between us or communicating that the other is not capable? If so, when? How can *detachment, responsibility,* or other qualities assist us?
   c. When can using *assertiveness, equality, peacefulness, spirituality,* or other qualities reduce our misuse of *caring?*
3. When is the lack of or misuse of *caring* a source of conflict for us? If necessary, how can we restore harmony?
4. How do we show our *care* and appreciation for one another?
5. What would be an inappropriate amount of taking *care* of one another? What would we do if it was becoming a problem?
6. How can *caring* enhance all types of intimacy between us?

STRENGTHEN OUR RELATIONSHIP

♥ Write and share *caring* and supportive notes expressing appreciation for one another
♥ Prepare a special meal for one another or someone we *love*
♥ Assess and re-balance where we are neglecting self-*care*
♥ Choose a *caring* act for the other to do; provide feedback to one another about how it worked, and guidance for improvement
♥ How else are we *committed* to practicing *caring?*

✎ *Chastity* ✎

EXPAND OUR INSIGHTS

One speck of chastity is greater than a hundred thousand years of worship and a sea of knowledge.
> ~ Bahá'í Faith: Bahá'u'lláh, *quoted in an unpublished letter*, November 2003

Chastity is a respectful and reverent gift of purity to one another. It allows us to have full, enjoyable, and appropriate sexual expression with one another exclusively and within our marriage. We protect our relationship and family through faithfulness to one another. We are moderate and modest in our speech, clothing, and movements, so we do not attract inappropriate attention and attraction from others. Chastity moderates and restrains our excessive sexual thoughts, preoccupation, and actions. We consult and share as we strive to balance respect for one another's needs with the freedom to decline intimate requests for appropriate reasons. Appropriate privacy in our marriage is important, and we avoid gossiping with others about the intimate aspects of our lives. We seek what supports our spiritual, mental, and physical strength to help us make wise choices. Our entertainment and fun choices respect our best as human beings. Chastity keeps us focused in positive directions that respect one another and the integrity of our marriage.

Chastity is the cement of civilization and progress. Without it there is no stability in society....
> ~ Mary Baker Eddy, *Science and Health*, p. 57

How are we practicing Chastity?
What new choices will we make?

CONSULT AND TAKE ACTION

1. Identifying and Strengthening *Chastity*
   a. Are we sexually seductive, or do we flirt or cross intimate boundaries with others, even just for fun? If so, when? How can *faithfulness, self-discipline,* or other qualities support *chastity*?
   b. Do we focus on our physical attraction to one another and ignore mental, emotional, and *spiritual* qualities? If so, when? How can *respect, spirituality,* or other qualities assist us?
   c. Do we use media (television, books, magazines, Internet) or other devices to excite sexual responses? If so, when? How can *patience, purity,* or other qualities assist us?
   d. When can *beauty, commitment, equality, integrity, loyalty, trustworthiness, strength, unity,* or other qualities assist us with strengthening *chastity*?
2. Identifying and Balancing Misuses of *Chastity*
   a. Do we behave prudishly or rigidly restrained? If so, when? How can *enthusiasm, flexibility,* or other qualities assist us in using *chastity* effectively?
   b. Do we label sexual intimacy as "wrong" and withdraw or suppress it? If so, when? How can *encouragement, forgiveness,* or other qualities assist us?
   c. When can using *generosity, humility, love, joyfulness, mercy, spirituality,* or other qualities reduce our misuse of *chastity*?
3. When is the lack of or misuse of *chastity* a source of conflict for us? If necessary, how can we restore harmony?
4. What do we see as the spiritual aspects of *chastity*?
5. How can *chastity* enhance all types of intimacy between us?

STRENGTHEN OUR RELATIONSHIP

♥ Agree on what is or is not appropriate touch and sexual activity
♥ Agree what intimate information we keep private between us
♥ Discuss what our clothing choices communicate to us and others
♥ *Create* a special communication or action between us for when we wish to have physically or sexually intimate time together
♥ How else are we *committed* to practicing *chastity*?

✺ *Commitment* ✺

EXPAND OUR INSIGHTS

And being not weak in faith…what he had promised, he was able
also to perform.
~ Christianity: *The Bible* (King James Version), Romans, 4:19-21

Commitment is a promise and binding agreement with one another.
We meet agreed expectations and carry out promised actions, which
build our trust in one another. We deeply value our marriage and the
sacred promises we made to one another in our wedding ceremony.
We strive to keep our marriage and family healthy, growing, and
intact. We share our friendship, love, time, and energy with one
another. Commitment also empowers us in our work and community
service to contribute our best efforts. It assists us to be loyal and
faithful to one another, even when it is difficult. We do not take our
commitment for granted. We show our commitment to our marriage
by speaking positively about one another instead of complaining,
backbiting, or criticizing. Commitment is a solid rock upon which we
can build a vibrant, happy, and lasting marriage.

Many of the mistakes couples commonly make stem directly from
the partners' failure to be mindful of their commitment every
day; a marriage can't thrive if the partners see commitment just as
something they promised on their wedding day.
~ Howard J. Markman, Scott M. Stanley, Susan L. Blumberg,
Fighting for Your Marriage, p. 321

How are we practicing Commitment?
What new choices will we make?

CONSULT AND TAKE ACTION

1. Identifying and Strengthening *Commitment*
   a. Do we show a lack of *respect* for our word or promises? If so, when? How can *faithfulness*, *integrity*, or other qualities support *commitment*?
   b. Are we drifting through life without taking action? If so, when? How can *purposefulness*, *responsibility*, or other qualities assist us?
   c. When can *acceptance*, *enthusiasm*, *love*, *loyalty*, *patience*, *perseverance*, *trustworthiness*, *strength*, *unity*, or other qualities assist us with strengthening *commitment*?
2. Identifying and Balancing Misuses of *Commitment*
   a. Are we too inflexible and rigid to renegotiate priorities or promises? If so, when? How can *flexibility*, *wisdom*, or other qualities assist us in using *commitment* effectively?
   b. Do we keep *commitments* no matter what the cost is to health, safety, or relationships? If so, when? How can *discernment*, *respect*, or other qualities assist us?
   c. When can using *equality*, *honesty*, *humility*, *integrity*, *thoughtfulness*, or other qualities reduce our misuse of *commitment*?
3. When is the lack of or misuse of *commitment* a source of conflict for us? If necessary, how can we restore harmony?
4. What vital promises and *commitments* do we make to one another and ourselves? How can we support one another in keeping them?
5. How can *commitment* enhance all types of intimacy between us?

STRENGTHEN OUR RELATIONSHIP

- Share what our wedding vow(s) mean to us
- Each morning, for a week, make and keep a promise to do something for the other
- Write down a goal to do together, the ways to achieve it, and begin acting on our *commitment*
- Have a ceremony and re-create our *commitment* to one another
- How else are we *committed* to practicing *commitment*?

⊱ *Compassion* ⊰

EXPAND OUR INSIGHTS

A man should not hate any living creature. Let him be friendly and compassionate to all.

~ Hinduism: *The Song of God: Bhagavad-Gita,* XII

Compassion is our sympathetic and sincere concern and understanding for others and their difficulties. Compassion helps us sense pain in one another's hearts and lives and in those close to us. This helps us to act in ways that relieve this suffering, sometimes sacrificing our own needs in the process. Compassion allows us to reach out generously to comfort, listen to, or forgive one another and ourselves. We especially appreciate caring words when one of us makes a mistake, is in trouble, or is hurt. In our marriage, we are compassionate in response to one another and ourselves when we express how sorry we are for what we have done. Compassion helps us to be good friends.

Hugging is an instinct, a natural response to feelings of affection, compassion, need, and joy. Hugging is also a science, a simple method of support, healing, and growth, with measurable and remarkable results. In its highest form, hugging is also an art.

~ Kathleen Keating, *The Hug Therapy Book,* introduction

How are we practicing Compassion?
What new choices will we make?

CONSULT AND TAKE ACTION

1. Identifying and Strengthening *Compassion*
   a. Do we not allow ourselves or others time to grieve or adjust to illness, deaths, failures, or traumas? If so, when? How can *kindness*, *love*, or other qualities support *compassion*?
   b. Do we have an uncaring or judgmental attitude about problems, limitations, and issues we, or others who are less fortunate, are experiencing? If so, when? How can *caring*, *thoughtfulness*, or other qualities assist us?
   c. When can *encouragement*, *flexibility*, *forgiveness*, *generosity*, *gentleness*, *helpfulness*, *mercy*, *patience*, *sincerity*, *unity*, or other qualities assist us with strengthening compassion?
2. Identifying and Balancing Misuses of *Compassion*
   a. Do we become overly involved with others' problems? If so, when? How can *discernment*, *responsibility*, or other qualities assist us in using *compassion* effectively?
   b. Do we support and enable others to the point that they are not *responsible* for themselves? If so, when? How can *justice*, *respect*, or other qualities assist us?
   c. Do we extremely or unwisely defend one another from being hurt by others? If so, when? How can *detachment*, *wisdom*, or other qualities assist us?
   d. When can using *self-discipline*, *tactfulness*, *truthfulness*, *unity*, or other qualities reduce our misuse of *compassion*?
3. When is the lack of or misuse of *compassion* a source of conflict for us? If necessary, how can we restore harmony?
4. When do we find *compassion helpful*? Not *helpful*? Why?
5. How can *compassion* enhance all types of intimacy between us?

STRENGTHEN OUR RELATIONSHIP

❤ Hold one another's hand and listen during a difficult time
❤ Visit a grieving or ill friend together
❤ Take time to hug and show we care about a difficult situation
❤ Understand and *forgive* one another for a mistake
❤ How else are we *committed* to practicing *compassion*?

❧ *Confidence* ❧

EXPAND OUR INSIGHTS

...the righteous are as confident as a lion.

~ Judaism: *Tanakh*, Proverbs, 28:1

Confidence is being sure of our capacity to think and act effectively so that others can depend on us. We assertively take initiative and use our talents and gifts to contribute to our family, others, and ourselves. Confidence is a triumph over our doubts and fears, and it supports us in thinking positive and constructive thoughts. We show our confidence in what we believe in and what we think has value. It gives us the emotional security to speak up and be honest with one another and to try new things. We have confidence and trust that we will support one another through both joyful and difficult times during our marriage. We know our marriage will last. We have the strength, wisdom, and judgment to rely on one another and the confidence to ask for help when needed. We have confidence that there will be many sources of guidance and blessings for us throughout our lives.

A marriage based on full confidence, based on complete and unqualified frankness on both sides; they are not keeping anything back; there's no deception underneath it all.

~ Henrik Ibsen, *The Wild Duck*, Act 4

How are we practicing Confidence?
What new choices will we make?

CONSULT AND TAKE ACTION

1. Identifying and Strengthening *Confidence*
   a. Are we afraid to be involved with others and activities? If so, when? How can *courage, friendliness*, or other qualities support *confidence*?
   b. Do we feel that we are less competent than others are? If so, when? How can *excellence, respect*, or other qualities assist us?
   c. When can *commitment, cooperation, encouragement, enthusiasm, purposefulness, patience, perseverance, responsibility, strength*, or other qualities assist us with strengthening *confidence*?
2. Identifying and Balancing Misuses of *Confidence*
   a. Do we become overly sure of ourselves or conceited and bragging? If so, when? How can *detachment, humility*, or other qualities assist us in using *confidence* effectively?
   b. Do we feel so self-assured that we believe our way is always the right one? If so, when? How can *tactfulness, unity*, or other qualities assist us?
   c. When can using *contentment, discernment, gentleness, peacefulness, self-discipline, wisdom*, or other qualities reduce our misuse of *confidence*?
3. When is the lack of or misuse of *confidence* a source of conflict for us? If necessary, how can we restore harmony?
4. When does *confidence* in one another assist us with taking action? How does *confidence* in God or a *spiritual* power help us in our daily lives?
5. When does over-*confidence* create a challenge in our relationship?
6. How can *confidence* enhance all types of intimacy between us?

STRENGTHEN OUR RELATIONSHIP

- ♥ Try something new together and share how we feel about it
- ♥ Identify a *confidence*-growth area for each of us, and request support and *encouragement* from the other
- ♥ *Create* an artistic display of a *confidence*-boosting quote
- ♥ Celebrate the successful completion of a difficult project
- ♥ How else are we *committed* to practicing *confidence*?

✺ *Contentment* ✺

EXPAND OUR INSIGHTS

Let your conversation be without covetousness; and be content with such things as ye have...

~ Christianity: *The Bible* (King James Version), Hebrews 13:5

With contentment, our hearts and minds are tranquil, and there is a peaceful feeling in our marriage, home, and lives. It is a calm acceptance of what we cannot change, including the natural flow of rhythms and cycles in our bodies and family. We do not compare, push, or agitate for life to be different than it is, or become fearful about the future. We calmly choose, instead, to be content with our lives. We slow down and enjoy the moment we are in and appreciate the friendship we have with one another. We are content when we spend our time wisely for purposes and professions that make the best use of our talents and abilities. This means we have goals, dreams, and visions for our lives. However, we are content with the ultimate outcome of our efforts. Contentment can also be present in our lives when we engage in spiritual practices such as prayer or meditation. We are content with our lives and trust we will have what we need to live happy and productive lives.

As you relax your inflexible expectations of yourself, you tend also to relax your expectations of others.

~ Susan M. Campbell, Ph.D., *Beyond the Power Struggle*, p. 86

How are we practicing Contentment?
What new choices will we make?

CONSULT AND TAKE ACTION

1. Identifying and Strengthening *Contentment*
   a. Do we whine and agitate one another for our lives to change? If so, when? How can *acceptance, detachment,* or other qualities support *contentment?*
   b. Do we waste our time anxiously wishing that people or circumstances were different or worrying about the future? If so, when? How can *joyfulness, service,* or other qualities assist us?
   c. When can *flexibility, humility, patience, purposefulness, spirituality, unity,* or other qualities assist us with strengthening *contentment?*
2. Identifying and Balancing Misuses of *Contentment*
   a. Do we withdraw to avoid solving a problem or go along with what we should not? If so, when? How can *assertiveness, honesty,* or other qualities assist us in using *contentment* effectively?
   b. Do we let our lives and minds become stagnant, resisting fresh ideas and change? If so, when? How can *creativity, enthusiasm,* or other qualities assist us?
   c. When can using *courage, idealism, purposefulness, responsibility,* or other qualities reduce our misuse of *contentment?*
3. When is the lack of or misuse of *contentment* a source of conflict for us? If necessary, how can we restore harmony?
4. What demonstrates we are *content,* or instead passively letting life happen? How does *spirituality* or *faith* relate to this for us?
5. How can *contentment* enhance all types of intimacy between us?

STRENGTHEN OUR RELATIONSHIP

- ♥ *Create* an area in our home for daily meditation and prayer
- ♥ Acknowledge a fear we have about our relationship and take steps toward resolving it and becoming *content* about it
- ♥ Identify and *detach* from an issue we are pushing to resolve
- ♥ Choose a day when we do not whine, complain, or express anxiety about the future
- ♥ How else are we *committed* to practicing *contentment?*

✎ *Cooperation* ✎

EXPAND OUR INSIGHTS

...marriage can be a source of well-being, conveying a sense of
security and spiritual happiness. ... For marriage to become a haven
of contentment it requires the cooperation of the marriage partners
themselves, and the assistance of their families....

~ Bahá'í Faith: *Compilation of Compilations, Vol. II*, p. 384

With cooperation, we fully communicate, engage in consultation,
work together in harmony, and support one another. We approach
tasks together with a positive spirit. We deeply appreciate the
cooperation we contribute to our marriage, family, and community.
We share thoughts, ideas, and time, and do not try to force one
another to do something. We support one another's personal goals,
and we work in loving partnership toward our common goals.
With cooperation, we can accomplish more together than we can
separately. Sometimes this means we compromise or adjust our ideas
to accommodate those of the other. Cooperation helps us to find
solutions that work well.

Successful marriage is an art that can only be learned with difficulty.
But it gives pride and satisfaction, like any other expertness that
is hard won.... I would say that the surest measures of a man's or
woman's maturity is the harmony, style, joy, dignity he creates in his
marriage, and the pleasure and inspiration he provides for his spouse.
An immature person may achieve great success in a career but never
in marriage.

~ Benjamin Spock, *Decent and Indecent*

How are we practicing Cooperation?
What new choices will we make?

CONSULT AND TAKE ACTION

1. Identifying and Strengthening *Cooperation*
   a. Do we act too independently and resist assistance from one another? If so, when? How can *equality*, *helpfulness*, or other qualities support *cooperation*?
   b. Do we refuse to work with one another and/or do not consider the other capable of *helping*? If so, when? How can *flexibility*, *patience*, or other qualities assist us?
   c. When can *caring*, *creativity*, *encouragement*, *enthusiasm*, *excellence*, *love*, *peacefulness*, *purposefulness*, *responsibility*, *service*, *unity*, or other qualities assist us with strengthening *cooperation*?

2. Identifying and Balancing Misuses of *Cooperation*
   a. Do we sacrifice our values or principles to work with someone or go along with others against our better judgment? If so, when? How can *chastity*, *strength*, or other qualities assist us in using *cooperation* effectively?
   b. Do we *cooperate* only to gain something from them? If so, when? How can *honesty*, *respect*, or other qualities assist us?
   c. When can using *assertiveness*, *confidence*, *detachment*, *discernment*, *integrity*, *self-discipline*, or other qualities reduce our misuse of *cooperation*?

3. When is the lack of or misuse of *cooperation* a source of conflict for us? If necessary, how can we restore harmony?

4. When do we clearly work better separately? When do we work well together? Are we happy with the balance between both?

5. Where would we like to *cooperate* better with others?

6. How can *cooperation* enhance all types of intimacy between us?

STRENGTHEN OUR RELATIONSHIP

♥ Do a household or outdoor task that requires *cooperation*
♥ Develop a marriage or family "mission statement" that clarifies what is important to us
♥ *Cooperatively* plan a fun family activity
♥ Contribute to a friend or family member's project or activity
♥ How else are we *committed* to practicing *cooperation*?

❧ *Courage* ❧

EXPAND OUR INSIGHTS

...our Lord, brings comfort to the weary and sorrow-laden; he restores peace to those who are broken down under the burden of life. He gives courage to the weak when they would...[gladly] give up self-reliance and hope.

~ Buddhism: *The Gospel of Buddha*, 1:3

♥

Courage is bravely stepping forward to act or defend what we believe is right, even when we stand alone or there is a high personal cost. When we feel afraid in life, courage empowers us to persevere, especially when the going gets tough. We courageously speak what is in our hearts and on our minds. We take risks, exploring new ways to nurture our marriage and our own personal growth. Courage powerfully supports us during parenthood, tragedies, moving to a new home, changing careers, moral or ethical challenges, and all of life's adventures. It helps us start over after disruptions or loss. Sometimes to cope with difficulties, we need to be courageous and ask others for help. Courage can come from prayer, faith, and the steadfast trust that God will be with us and help us as we strive to move forward.

♥

Perfect courage is to do without witnesses what one would be capable of doing with the world looking on.

~ Francois de la Rochefoucauld, *Sentences et Maximes Morales*, no. 216

How are we practicing Courage?
What new choices will we make?

CONSULT AND TAKE ACTION

1. Identifying and Strengthening *Courage*
   a. Do we let fears hold us back? If so, when? How can *confidence*, *purposefulness*, or other qualities support *courage*?
   b. Do we allow one another or others to dominate, use, or abuse us? If so, when? How can *assertiveness*, *justice*, or other qualities assist us?
   c. Do we deny or ignore our values? If so, when? How can *faithfulness*, *loyalty*, or other qualities assist us?
   d. When can *encouragement*, *friendliness*, *idealism*, *strength*, or other qualities assist us with strengthening *courage*?
2. Identifying and Balancing Misuses of *Courage*
   a. Do we act recklessly without consideration for our own or others' welfare? If so, when? How can *caring*, *thoughtfulness*, or other qualities assist us in using *courage* effectively?
   b. Do we speak inappropriately, resulting in negative consequences or conflict? If so, when? How can *respect*, *tactfulness*, or other qualities assist us?
   c. When can using *compassion*, *humility*, *peacefulness*, *self-discipline*, *unity*, *wisdom*, or other qualities reduce our misuse of *courage*?
3. When is the lack of or misuse of *courage* a source of conflict for us? If necessary, how can we restore harmony?
4. What are some *courageous* acts we have done in our lives?
5. How can we tell if either of us needs to practice *courage*? How can we support one another with this?
6. How can *courage* enhance all types of intimacy between us?

STRENGTHEN OUR RELATIONSHIP

- ♥ Identify lessons learned from facing fears and being *courageous*
- ♥ Share passionately from the heart about an issue that is important to us and difficult to talk about; *create* a plan to make a difference with it
- ♥ Do something that we are afraid to do or have postponed doing
- ♥ Nurture a difficult area of our relationship
- ♥ How else are we *committed* to practicing *courage*?

❧ *Courtesy* ❧

EXPAND OUR INSIGHTS

When a (courteous) greeting is offered you, meet it with a greeting
still more courteous, or (at least) of equal courtesy.

~ Islam: *The Qur'án*, 4:86

Courtesy is showing gracious and loving consideration for one
another. It often has us put one another's needs before our own.
We use respectful gestures, polite manners, and kind language to
demonstrate we genuinely value our relationship. One way we are
courteous is using polite expressions, such as "please" and "thank
you." We also stay conscious of our body movements and actions
so we are not accidentally discourteous to one another. Sometimes
when we feel stressed or in a hurry, it is even more important to
remember courtesy. Otherwise, we might hurt one another's feelings
by being short-tempered or giving orders. We make requests instead
of demands. Courtesy provides a loving smoothness to all our
interactions within our marriage.

See ye not Courtesy is the true Alchemy, turning to gold all it touches
and tries?

~ George Meredith, "The Song of Courtesy"

How are we practicing Courtesy?
What new choices will we make?

CONSULT AND TAKE ACTION

1. Identifying and Strengthening *Courtesy*
   a. Do we act rudely toward one another or not use manners? If so, when? How can *respect, thoughtfulness*, or other qualities support *courtesy*?
   b. Do we give orders rather than make polite requests? If so, when? How can *gentleness, humility*, or other qualities assist us?
   c. Do we take one another for granted? If so, when? How can *caring, love*, or other qualities assist us?
   d. When can *compassion, generosity, helpfulness, equality, kindness, patience, service, unity*, or other qualities assist us with strengthening *courtesy*?
2. Identifying and Balancing Misuses of *Courtesy*
   a. Do we inappropriately step back to wait for others to take action, or focus on our self-consciousness in a situation? If so, when? How can *assertiveness, confidence*, or other qualities assist us in using *courtesy* effectively?
   b. Do we act politely to one another with selfish motives or to make ourselves look good? If so, when? How can *honesty, sincerity*, or other qualities assist us?
   c. When can using *cooperation, equality, friendliness, purposefulness, strength*, or other qualities reduce our misuse of *courtesy*?
3. When is the lack of or misuse of *courtesy* a source of conflict for us? If necessary, how can we restore harmony?
4. When is *courtesy* most difficult for us to practice?
5. How can *courtesy* enhance all types of intimacy between us?

STRENGTHEN OUR RELATIONSHIP

❤ Consciously say "please," "thank you," and "you're welcome" for every service we do for one another for a week; continue?

❤ Plan a dinner with guests and use our best manners and *courtesy*

❤ Infuse *courtesy* into our interactions by assisting with exiting a vehicle, holding a door open, or helping the other with an errand

❤ When we are frustrated with one another, interact with *courtesy*

❤ How else are we *committed* to practicing *courtesy*?

❧ *Creativity* ❧

EXPAND OUR INSIGHTS

It behoveth the craftsmen of the world...to exert their highest
endeavor and diligently pursue their professions so that their efforts
may produce that which will manifest the greatest beauty and
perfection before the eyes of all men.

~ Bahá'í Faith: *Selections from the Writings of 'Abdu'l-Bahá*, p. 145

Creativity is having original inspiration and ideas that lead us to
develop new things that have never existed before. Our marriage is
a unique and special relationship that we create together. We freely
use our imaginations to keep our approach to life and our marriage
interesting and invigorating. We create new and wonderful ways to
enhance our love, communication, friendship, and marriage. We
generate creative ideas and make plans to carry them out. We dare
to dream big and discover new ideas, possibilities, and inventions.
Innovative solutions arise in our consultations that address issues in
our lives. Expressing creativity through writing, poetry, music, or art
nourishes our souls. Often we can then share what we have created
with others. We are creative in discovering new ways to express
our thoughts and emotions to one another. We regularly add new
experiences and spice to our lives.

True creativity often starts where language ends.

~ Arthur Koestler, "The Act of Creation," bk. 1, pt. 2, ch. 7

How are we practicing Creativity?
What new choices will we make?

CONSULT AND TAKE ACTION

1. Identifying and Strengthening *Creativity*
   a. Do we limit or avoid new possibilities? If so, when? How can *enthusiasm, joyfulness*, or other qualities support *creativity*?
   b. Do we do something the same way all the time? If so, when? How can *confidence, flexibility*, or other qualities assist us?
   c. Do we cut ourselves off from artistic expressions? If so, when? How can *beauty, spirituality*, or other qualities assist us?
   d. When can *courage, encouragement, love, patience, self-discipline,* or other qualities assist us with strengthening *creativity*?
2. Identifying and Balancing Misuses of *Creativity*
   a. Do we mischievously *create* plans that hurt, injure, or insult others? If so, when? How can *discernment, integrity*, or other qualities assist us in using *creativity* effectively?
   b. Do we desire something so strongly that we invent dishonest ways to achieve it? If so, when? How can *chastity, honesty*, or other qualities assist us?
   c. Do we daydream or make up clever stories to conceal, justify, or exaggerate our behavior? If so, when? How can *detachment, truthfulness*, or other qualities assist us?
   d. When can using *excellence, moderation, purity, purposefulness, responsibility, sincerity, thoughtfulness, wisdom,* or other qualities reduce our misuse of *creativity*?
3. When is the lack of or misuse of *creativity* a source of conflict for us? If necessary, how can we restore harmony?
4. Where are we being *creative* in our lives? Where can we be more?
5. How can *creativity* enhance all types of intimacy between us?

STRENGTHEN OUR RELATIONSHIP

- ♥ *Create* a great "date" or occasion for one another
- ♥ Participate in a musical, expressive, or artistic activity
- ♥ Consult about new directions we would like our relationship to go in, and *create* reminders or actions that support them
- ♥ *Create* a new decoration for our home that demonstrates our *love*
- ♥ How else are we *committed* to practicing *creativity*?

~ *Detachment* ~

EXPAND OUR INSIGHTS

A serene spirit accepts pleasure and pain with an even mind, and is
unmoved by either.

~ Hinduism: *The Song of God: Bhagavad-Gita*, II

Detachment is gently stepping back to gain some emotional distance,
input, and clarity about a situation or one another. It also helps
us assess what is appropriate to be attached to, such as putting
less importance on material possessions. Detachment allows us to
empathize with one another without making the other's feelings our
own. We consider our own thoughts, feelings, and the facts, and then
we choose how to respond and act in situations. This is especially
important when our reactions relate more to the past rather than
to what is happening currently. We do not jump to jealous or angry
conclusions that can damage our marriage. Detachment helps us
accept necessary times apart without letting sadness or loneliness
interfere with our lives. When we interact with people, places,
or things that negatively affect our well-being or our marriage,
detachment helps us lovingly pull back. It also helps us to accept our
weaknesses without constant self-blame, and our strengths without
excessive pride. Sometimes prayer and meditation can assist us to let
go of a problem or of an unexpected outcome. It is putting God's
will above our own.

All emotions are energy that can be used by us in many different
ways. We can train ourselves to use the energy, instead of just feeling
it and reacting unconsciously.

~ Happy Dobbs, *Spiritual Being: A User's Guide*, p. 198

How are we practicing Detachment?
What new choices will we make?

CONSULT AND TAKE ACTION

1. Identifying and Strengthening *Detachment*
   a. Are we so emotionally attached to someone or something that we cannot let go? If so, when? How can *flexibility*, *spirituality*, or other qualities support *detachment*?
   b. Do we react without thinking? If so, when? How can *discernment*, *self-discipline*, or other qualities assist us?
   c. When can *acceptance*, *forgiveness*, *generosity*, *humility*, *patience*, or other qualities assist us with strengthening *detachment*?
2. Identifying and Balancing Misuses of *Detachment*
   a. Are we insensitive and fail to consider the feelings of one another or others? If so, when? How can *caring*, *tactfulness*, or other qualities assist us in using *detachment* effectively?
   b. Do we say words or take actions that deliberately hurt one another or others to get even or to get our own way? If so, when? How can *mercy*, *responsibility*, or other qualities assist us?
   c. Do we isolate ourselves, plot secretly, reject one another coldly, or act unlovingly? If so, when? How can *compassion*, *love*, or other qualities assist us?
   d. When can using *helpfulness*, *integrity*, *service*, *spirituality*, *thankfulness*, or other qualities reduce our misuse of *detachment*?
3. When is the lack of or misuse of *detachment* a source of conflict for us? If necessary, how can we restore harmony?
4. What is the effect on our relationship when one of us is acting in a *detached* way? How do we understand the difference between loving *detachment* and a lack of concern for the other?
5. How can *detachment* enhance all types of intimacy between us?

STRENGTHEN OUR RELATIONSHIP

♥ Discuss how we reacted and responded to an upsetting situation, and what will we do differently another time
♥ Memorize a prayer or quotation that when said would support a *detached* response when we are tempted to react poorly instead
♥ Examine what expectations we have of one another
♥ Get rid of items in our life that *create* conflict or clutter
♥ How else are we *committed* to practicing *detachment*?

❧ Discernment ☙

EXPAND OUR INSIGHTS

...make your ear attentive to wisdom and your mind open to discernment.... You will then understand what is right, just, and equitable—every good course.

~ Judaism: *Tanakh*, Proverbs 2:2,9

♥

Discernment is clearly seeing the facts of a situation or seeing right from wrong. It assists us to set aside any prejudices or biases we might have. We can then observe and listen intently and with sensitivity to determine what is real and true about someone or a situation. As needed, we seek other perspectives and information. We do not take what we learn and use it inappropriately. We consult about issues that are troubling or unclear to discern their true nature, potential solutions, and actions to take. Discernment assists us to recognize when an issue from our past is affecting us negatively in the present. This gives us the opportunity to put it back in the past. Discernment also gives us keen perception of the blessings in our life and world. Even when others see only the negative, we can discern what is wonderful or find a hidden wisdom in it. We see things for what they are and understand them in their wider and deeper context. We can look at what is mysterious, discover its heart, and gain new knowledge from it.

♥

Conscience is the authentic voice of God to you.
~ Rutherford B. Hayes, *Diary and Letters of Rutherford Birchard Hayes*, Vol. V, p. 134

How are we practicing Discernment?
What new choices will we make?

CONSULT AND TAKE ACTION

1. Identifying and Strengthening *Discernment*
   a. Do we avoid, ignore, or fail to listen *carefully* to *wise* advice? If so, when? How can *courtesy, humility,* or other qualities support *discernment?*
   b. Are we careless in our choices without considering ethics, morals, values, or other standards? If so, when? How can *honesty, justice,* or other qualities assist us?
   c. When can *compassion, equality, flexibility, generosity, spirituality, wisdom,* or other qualities assist us with strengthening *discernment?*

2. Identifying and Balancing Misuses of *Discernment*
   a. Are we nosy about someone's business, even when it does not affect us? If so, when? How can *detachment, tactfulness,* or other qualities assist us in using *discernment* effectively?
   b. Do we look for flaws in circumstances and people and are critical and judgmental about them? If so, when? How can *acceptance, mercy,* or other qualities assist us?
   c. When can using *contentment, forgiveness, humility, mercy, moderation, respect, unity,* or other qualities reduce our misuse of discernment?

3. When is the lack of or misuse of *discernment* a source of conflict for us? If necessary, how can we restore harmony?

4. What areas of our lives feel confused and unclear? Are there issues from the past affecting us? Who or where could we turn to for advice or *wisdom?*

5. How can *discernment* enhance all types of intimacy between us?

STRENGTHEN OUR RELATIONSHIP

- ❤ Identify areas in our home and lives we have been neglecting
- ❤ Consult with family members to *discern* their unmet needs
- ❤ Consult about an issue in our community and identify a potential solution; act to implement it; assess if the solution worked
- ❤ Consult about issues we are avoiding assessing and handling
- ❤ How else are we *committed* to practicing *discernment?*

✒ *Encouragement* ✑

EXPAND OUR INSIGHTS

...love each other, constantly encourage each other, work together, be as one soul in one body, and in so doing become a true, organic, healthy body animated and illumined by the spirit.

~ Bahá'í Faith: *Wellspring of Guidance*, p. 39

Encouragement is sincere, positive affirmation of one another's character qualities, effective actions, or good intentions. We know what is important to one another and what our plans are. We provide positive words and actions that inspire one another into courageous action. We show confidence in one another's ability to succeed. Encouragement lifts our hearts and prompts us to try harder. Mutual encouragement brings us closer together, and we appreciate one another more. If we criticize one another's characters rather than encourage them, we know we are being highly destructive to our marriage. We do not compare one another unfavorably to others. Encouragement releases positive thoughts, emotions, and creative energy in our lives. It is one of the greatest ways we support one another and sustain our marriage.

♥

People form much more positive emotional connections when they encourage one another's dreams and aspirations.

~ John M. Gottman, Ph.D. and Joan DeClaire, *The Relationship Cure*, p. 209

How are we practicing Encouragement?
What new choices will we make?

CONSULT AND TAKE ACTION

1. Identifying and Strengthening *Encouragement*
   a. Do we behave or speak negatively about what is important to one another? If so, when? How can *enthusiasm, sincerity,* or other qualities support *encouragement?*
   b. Do we devalue one another's abilities or criticize one another's actions or character? If so, when? How can *equality, loyalty,* or other qualities assist us?
   c. Do we fail to point out one another's *strengths* and our belief in one another's ability to overcome difficulties? If so, when? How can *confidence, cooperation,* or other qualities assist us?
   d. When can *caring, generosity, helpfulness, love, respect, unity,* or other qualities assist us with strengthening *encouragement?*
2. Identifying and Balancing Misuses of *Encouragement*
   a. Do we use *encouragement* so much and so often that it seems insincere? If so, when? How can *truthfulness, wisdom,* or other qualities assist us in using *encouragement* effectively?
   b. Do we push or manipulate the other to do something harmful, unwise, or unwanted? If so, when? How can *gentleness, honesty,* or other qualities assist us?
   c. When can using *commitment, detachment, helpfulness, integrity, sincerity,* or other qualities reduce our misuse of *encouragement?*
3. When is the lack of or misuse of *encouragement* a source of conflict for us? If necessary, how can we restore harmony?
4. What words, actions, and results *encourage* each of us? When do we need them the most? Are our expectations realistic?
5. How can *encouragement* enhance all types of intimacy between us?

STRENGTHEN OUR RELATIONSHIP

❤ Acknowledge something great each of us did
❤ Give a gift to one another for a special event or occasion
❤ Tell one another five great qualities we especially appreciate in the other
❤ Leave notes of *encouragement* in unexpected places
❤ How else are we *committed* to practicing *encouragement?*

✄ *Enthusiasm* ✄

EXPAND OUR INSIGHTS

If anything is to be done...attack it vigorously!
~Buddhism: *The Gospel of Buddha*, XLVIII:11

♥

Enthusiasm occurs when authentic, genuine, and passionate emotions fill our spirits about something wonderful or extraordinary. We are excited and positive about something that is happening, or is about to happen. We clearly see the best in something or someone, and share sincerely and excitedly from the heart about it. We act wholeheartedly, with eagerness, giving full effort to our marriage and to whatever we do. We enthusiastically share our bodies, minds, hearts, and souls with one another. We create new adventures, possibilities, and experiences together. We do not get so carried away with enthusiasm that we neglect one another or our responsibilities. We embrace life without letting doubts and concerns interfere, and we enjoy what we do with smiles and laughter. We show enthusiasm when we greet one another with a smile and affection, and when we spend time together, with our family, and with our friends. When we are enthusiastic, we are inspired, happy, enjoying ourselves, and living life to its fullest.

Nothing great was ever achieved without enthusiasm.
~ Ralph Waldo Emerson, "Circles"

How are we practicing Enthusiasm?
What new choices will we make?

CONSULT AND TAKE ACTION

1. Identifying and Strengthening *Enthusiasm*
   a. Do we see everything as the same and nothing as great, extraordinary, or inspiring? If so, when? How can *beauty*, *joyfulness*, or other qualities support *enthusiasm*?
   b. Do we express negative, discouraging, resigned, bored, or cynical comments about what is happening? If so, when? How can *encouragement*, *idealism*, or other qualities assist us?
   c. When can *confidence*, *courage*, *creativity*, *friendliness*, *purposefulness*, *service*, *sincerity*, *spirituality*, *thankfulness*, or other qualities assist us with strengthening *enthusiasm*?
2. Identifying and Balancing Misuses of *Enthusiasm*
   a. Do we talk excessively about what we know and see? If so, when? How can *detachment*, *moderation*, or other qualities assist us in using *enthusiasm* effectively?
   b. Do we jump into a belief, project, or idea and negatively affect one another because it lacks substance or value? If so, when? How can *discernment*, *wisdom*, or other qualities assist us?
   c. When can using *honesty*, *humility*, *self-discipline*, *sincerity*, *tactfulness*, *truthfulness*, or other qualities reduce our misuse of *enthusiasm*?
3. When is the lack of or misuse of *enthusiasm* a source of conflict for us? If necessary, how can we restore harmony?
4. What aspects of our marriage and our activities most inspire us to be *enthusiastic*? When are we *enthusiastic* about different things?
5. What is our response when one of us is unenthusiastic about something? When the other is too *enthusiastic*?
6. How can *enthusiasm* enhance all types of intimacy between us?

STRENGTHEN OUR RELATIONSHIP

♥ *Create* a list of five things we are both *enthusiastic* about
♥ Tell one another what we look forward to each day
♥ Find at least one positive aspect of a tedious, boring, or difficult task and find something in it to be *enthusiastic* about
♥ *Create* an inspiring new adventure, such as a trip or project
♥ How else are we *committed* to practicing *enthusiasm*?

✣ *Equality* ✣

EXPAND OUR INSIGHTS

The world of humanity has two wings—one is women and the other men. Not until both wings are equally developed can the bird fly. ... Not until the world of women becomes equal to the world of men in the acquisition of virtues and perfections, can success and prosperity be attained as they ought to be.

~ Bahá'í Faith: *Selections from the Writings of 'Abdu'l-Bahá*, p. 30

Equality is a form of balance in our marriage where we respect one another as partners. We support and encourage one another, which assists us to develop ourselves to our fullest capacity. Both of us have the opportunity to seek education and employment. We are equally responsible for contributing to our family and community, and we respect one another's efforts. Equality does not mean we make the same choices or that our roles are identical. We stay aware of gender traditions and stereotypes, and we avoid making choices based on them without careful thought. Together we work out our responsibilities, and we do not treat the other as superior or inferior. We do not give one another unwelcome assistance or advice. We consult together and reach mutual decisions about our lives, marriage, family, and work. We carefully listen to one another's point of view. Each of us has a body, mind, heart, and soul worthy of equal respect.

The full measure of intimacy in marriage requires husbands and wives to be equals.

~ Blaine J. Fowers, Ph.D., *Beyond the Myth of Marital Happiness*, p. 18.

How are we practicing Equality?
What new choices will we make?

CONSULT AND TAKE ACTION

1. Identifying and Strengthening *Equality*
   a. Do we give orders or attempt to dominate or control the other? If so, when? How can *cooperation, respect,* or other qualities support *equality*?
   b. Do we treat one of us as more important than the other? If so, when? How can *humility, unity,* or other qualities assist us?
   c. Do we refuse to do our fair share of the work? If so, when? How can *commitment, justice,* or other qualities assist us?
   d. When can *assertiveness, caring, courage, honesty, idealism, helpfulness, integrity, love, responsibility, self-discipline, spirituality,* or other qualities assist us with strengthening *equality*?
2. Identifying and Balancing Misuses of *Equality*
   a. Do we rigidly insist that our roles and *responsibilities* be identical? If so, when? How can *discernment, flexibility,* or other qualities assist us in using *equality* effectively?
   b. Do we ignore or devalue our differences? If so, when? How can *acceptance, kindness,* or other qualities assist us?
   c. When can using *contentment, detachment, gentleness, loyalty, moderation, patience, peacefulness, thoughtfulness, wisdom,* or other qualities reduce our misuse of *equality*?
3. When is the lack of or misuse of *equality* a source of conflict for us? If necessary, how can we restore harmony?
4. How have we divided up household tasks? Does this structure reflect *equality*? Have we fallen into traditional gender roles inappropriately? What should we adjust or learn to do?
5. How can *equality* enhance all types of intimacy between us?

STRENGTHEN OUR RELATIONSHIP

♥ Teach one another a new skill
♥ Switch duties we each have in our home for a day (or accompany one another throughout a task or day) to increase understanding
♥ Take turns initiating intimate touch; initiating consultation
♥ Work together to prepare our home for guests
♥ How else are we *committed* to practicing *equality*?

❧ Excellence ❧

EXPAND OUR INSIGHTS

...in this world, aspirants may find enlightenment by two different paths. For the contemplative is the path of knowledge: for the active is the path of selfless action.

~ Hinduism: *The Song of God: Bhagavad-Gita*, III

Excellence is a high standard of achievement and quality. We commit to giving our best effort in our friendship and marriage. We consult together about what we want to achieve. We practice tasks, skills, and positive behaviors until we can do them consistently well. We focus on learning what most benefits our family and professions. Our efforts are done with care and guided by purposes and principles, including being of service to others. Our excellence is a humble example and inspiration to others. Aiming for balance, we do not strive so hard for excellence that we slip into perfectionism. We simply do our very best and focus on continual improvement. Part of the excellence in our marriage and family is visible in our growth, happiness, stability, and unity.

The excellent becomes the permanent.

~ Jane Addams

How are we practicing Excellence?
What new choices will we make?

CONSULT AND TAKE ACTION

1. Identifying and Strengthening *Excellence*
   a. Are we careless in our *responsibilities*? If so, when? How can *integrity*, *self-discipline*, or other qualities support *excellence*?
   b. Do we neglect our marriage or other relationships? If so, when? How can *faithfulness*, *loyalty*, or other qualities assist us?
   c. Do we deny or avoid striving for *excellence* and accept mediocrity? If so, when? How can *commitment*, *perseverance*, or other qualities assist us?
   d. When can *caring*, *creativity*, *discernment*, *idealism*, *purity*, *responsibility*, *spirituality*, *trustworthiness*, *thoughtfulness*, *unity*, or other qualities assist us with strengthening *excellence*?
2. Identifying and Balancing Misuses of *Excellence*
   a. Are we rigid, inflexible, and impatient with our achievements and ourselves, and take it out on those close to us? If so, when? How can *acceptance*, *humility*, or other qualities assist us?
   b. Do we impose our standards on other people? If so, when? How can *cooperation*, *flexibility*, or other qualities assist us?
   c. When can using *compassion*, *contentment*, *forgiveness*, *gentleness*, *mercy*, *patience*, *respect*, *spirituality*, *tactfulness*, or other qualities reduce our misuse of *excellence*?
3. When is the lack of or misuse of *excellence* a source of conflict for us? If necessary, how can we restore harmony?
4. Where are we trying too hard to "get it right?" When are we making the other "wrong" so we can be "right?"
5. Do we try to meet one another's expectations of *excellence*? How do we handle not meeting one another's expectations?
6. How can *excellence* enhance all types of intimacy between us?

STRENGTHEN OUR RELATIONSHIP

- ♥ Discuss and honor one another's *excellent* achievements
- ♥ *Create* a marriage enrichment goal to achieve together
- ♥ Complete a volunteer project in the community with *excellence*
- ♥ Teach one another a new skill and practice it to achieve *excellence*
- ♥ How else are we *committed* to practicing *excellence*?

❧ *Faithfulness* ❧

EXPAND OUR INSIGHTS

...faithfully observe their trusts and their covenants....
~ Islam: *The Qur'án*, 23:8

Faithfulness is maintaining a devoted commitment to a belief or a relationship. It supports the constancy of our marriage and friendship. We are loyal in thought, speech, and action—true to one another and worthy of trust. We do not look for nor establish close relationships with others that would lead to unfaithfulness. We consistently honor the integrity of our sacred, unified marriage commitment, supporting one another when we feel afraid or insecure. We know that we can rely on one another's faithfulness in maintaining our family bond. We are also steadfast in our love for God and search for truth, which allows us to travel a faith-filled path, even when it becomes difficult. When difficulties test our faithfulness, our trust, or our loyalty to God or one another, we can use the challenge as an opportunity to become stronger.

Having faith in someone commits a part of our energy to that person; having faith in an idea commits a part of our energy to that idea; having faith in a fear commits a part of our energy to that fear. ... Our faith and our power of choice are, in fact, the power of creation itself. We are the vessels through which energy becomes matter in this life. Therefore, the spiritual test inherent in all our lives is the challenge to discover what motivates us to make the choices we do, and whether we have faith in our fears or the Divine.
~ Caroline Myss, Ph.D., *Anatomy of the Spirit*, p. 224

How are we practicing Faithfulness?
What new choices will we make?

CONSULT AND TAKE ACTION

1. Identifying and Strengthening *Faithfulness*
   a. Do our actions differ from our beliefs? If so, when? How can *honesty, integrity*, or other qualities support *faithfulness*?
   b. Do we improperly share our bodies or hearts with others and negatively affect our marriage? If so, when? How can *chastity, respect*, or other qualities assist us?
   c. When can *commitment, excellence, love, loyalty, perseverance, purity, responsibility, self-discipline, strength, trustworthiness, truthfulness, unity*, or other qualities assist us with strengthening *faithfulness*?
2. Identifying and Balancing Misuses of *Faithfulness*
   a. Are we more *faithful* to friends or others than to family or God? If so, when? How can *discernment, wisdom*, or other qualities assist us in using *faithfulness* effectively?
   b. Do we unquestioningly follow religious beliefs without scrutiny or investigation of truth? If so, when? How can *courage, integrity*, or other qualities assist us?
   c. When can using *assertiveness, equality, honesty, justice, tactfulness*, or other qualities reduce our misuse of *faithfulness*?
3. When is the lack of or misuse of *faithfulness* a source of conflict for us? If necessary, how can we restore harmony?
4. What supports us in being *faithful* to one another and our marriage vows? To our beliefs?
5. What benefits do we see in being *faithful*? What is challenging about it? What assistance or support do we need?
6. How can *faithfulness* enhance all types of intimacy between us?

STRENGTHEN OUR RELATIONSHIP

♥ Share what we appreciate about one another's *faithfulness*
♥ Study our wedding vows and discuss how they relate to *faithfulness*
♥ *Forgive* for when we were not *faithful* in word, thought, or deed
♥ *Create* a spiritual practice together that *strengthens faithfulness* and try it out for a period of time to see if it works for us
♥ How else are we *committed* to practicing *faithfulness*?

ᴄ⁊ *Flexibility* ⱷ

EXPAND OUR INSIGHTS

If it be Thy pleasure, make me to grow as a tender herb in the
meadows of Thy grace, that the gentle winds of Thy will may stir me
up and bend me into conformity with Thy pleasure, in such wise that
my movement and my stillness may be wholly directed by Thee.

~ Bahá'í Faith: *Prayers and Meditations by Bahá'u'lláh*, p. 240

Flexibility is being able to adjust to life as it happens and enjoy
spontaneity. It supports us in changing direction as needed, while
remaining true to our values and beliefs. We welcome and celebrate
the unexpected. We do not get upset with the good intentions
of others, even when we are taken by surprise. We bend gently
and choose to flow without resistance, fear, or anger with what
happens in our lives. We are open to change and to one another's
opinions, ideas, choices, and feelings. We are able to see different
creative options, approaches, and perspectives. We consider spiritual
teachings, which can give us standards and guidance for being
flexible about choices or firm about principles. Flexibility helps us
to learn from challenges, adapt to new circumstances, change our
minds, eliminate bad habits, and try new behaviors that support our
marriage. It helps us to grow, change, and develop together.

Once you make a decision, you are committed to it. Yet, be flexible.
Monitor progress, make adjustments along the way when necessary
to achieve your goal.

~ Khalil A. Khavari, Ph.D., *Spiritual Intelligence*, p. 237

How are we practicing Flexibility?
What new choices will we make?

CONSULT AND TAKE ACTION

1. Identifying and Strengthening *Flexibility*
   a. Do we insist that nothing should change or become upset when it does? If so, when? How can *acceptance*, *detachment*, or other qualities support *flexibility*?
   b. Do we refuse to change anything about ourselves? If so, when? How can *humility*, *honesty*, or other qualities assist us?
   c. Do we have difficulty handling changes in plans? If so, when? How can *cooperation*, *unity*, or other qualities assist us?
   d. When can *courage*, *creativity*, *gentleness*, *patience*, *peacefulness*, or other qualities assist us with strengthening *flexibility*?
2. Identifying and Balancing Misuses of *Flexibility*
   a. Do we resist having a schedule, plan, structure, or goals? If so, when? How can *purposefulness*, *self-discipline*, or other qualities assist us in using *flexibility* effectively?
   b. Do we abandon or ignore our principles to adjust to or submit to one another or circumstances? If so, when? How can *courage*, *integrity*, or other qualities assist us?
   c. When can using *assertiveness*, *commitment*, *discernment*, *faithfulness*, *trustworthiness*, *wisdom*, or other qualities reduce our misuse of *flexibility*?
3. When is the lack of or misuse of *flexibility* a source of conflict for us? If necessary, how can we restore harmony?
4. How do we respond to small and large changes in our lives? What would help us be more *flexible* in handling change?
5. What assists us to change our points of view about issues?
6. How can *flexibility* enhance all types of intimacy between us?

STRENGTHEN OUR RELATIONSHIP

❤ Go *enthusiastically* on a spontaneous date where the destination and activity are unknown when we leave home and are new for us
❤ *Create* a new routine or end an old habit over the next 30 days
❤ Visit the worship services of another faith
❤ Sacrifice something to make the other happy
❤ How else are we *committed* to practicing *flexibility*?

❧ *Forgiveness* ❧

EXPAND OUR INSIGHTS

Bear with each other and forgive whatever grievances you may have against one another. Forgive as the Lord forgave you.
> ~ Christianity: *The Bible* (New International Version), Colossians, 3:13

Forgiveness is pardoning someone for doing or saying something hurtful. We give up any desire to get even with or hold it against them. We explore what happened, ask for or give forgiveness, then put the incident in the past. This helps us detach from any feelings of anger, resentment, or hurt, and releases us from feeling like a "victim." Even when it is very difficult, forgiveness helps us to accept what happened, reconcile, and give another chance. This includes forgiving ourselves so we can put pain in the past. Everyone makes mistakes, and we are each willing to be responsible for what we do, changing our behavior and ourselves, or making amends as needed. With forgiveness, we can move ahead in our marriage, ready to do things differently. It helps us restore love, respect, and unity in our marriage.

❤

When you forgive, you need to do more than say the words and mean them. You also have to extend a forgiving, helping hand. To truly forgive, you need to be gracious to your partner. Being kind and generous as well as granting pardon will put you back on the same footing and keep your love strong.
> ~ Howard J. Markman, Scott M. Stanley, Susan L. Blumberg, Natalie H. Jenkins, and Carol Whiteley, *12 Hours to a Great Marriage*, p. 207

How are we practicing Forgiveness?
What new choices will we make?

CONSULT AND TAKE ACTION

1. Identifying and Strengthening *Forgiveness*
   a. Do we refuse the other's apology for a mistake? If so, when? How can *acceptance, mercy,* or other qualities support *forgiveness?*
   b. Do we hold onto grudges and resentments about past errors and bring them back up? If so, when? How can *compassion, detachment,* or other qualities assist us?
   c. Do we withhold *forgiveness,* mistakenly thinking it means we are condoning the action? If so, when? How can *discernment, unity,* or other qualities assist us?
   d. When can *caring, flexibility, generosity, respect, spirituality,* or other qualities assist us with strengthening *forgiveness?*
2. Identifying and Balancing Misuses of *Forgiveness*
   a. Do we put up with repeated unjust or harmful actions with no resolution? If so, when? How can *assertiveness, justice,* or other qualities assist us in using *forgiveness* effectively?
   b. Do we act irresponsibly and assume it will be accepted? If so, when? How can *honesty, responsibility,* or other qualities assist us?
   c. Are we permissive with other's actions because we have made the same mistakes or choices? If so, when? How can *humility, integrity,* or other qualities assist us?
   d. When can using *confidence, discernment, strength, trustworthiness, truthfulness,* or other qualities reduce our misuse of *forgiveness?*
3. When is the lack of or misuse of *forgiveness* a source of conflict for us? If necessary, how can we restore harmony?
4. What helps us to *forgive* quickly? Do we wait a long time?
5. How can *forgiveness* enhance all types of intimacy between us?

STRENGTHEN OUR RELATIONSHIP

♥ Pray together and ask God for *forgiveness* for hurting one another
♥ Engage in frank and *loving* consultation about a hurtful issue
♥ *Create* a *forgiveness* ceremony with music, prayers, and more
♥ Make *sincere* amends by doing something *generous* and *loving*
♥ How else are we *committed* to practicing *forgiveness?*

❧ *Friendliness* ❧

EXPAND OUR INSIGHTS

Two are better off than one…. For should they fall, one can raise the
other….

~ Judaism: *Tanakh*, Ecclesiastes, 4:9-10

Friendliness is an outgoing and social attitude that connects us in
relationships with others. Together, we also reach out beyond our
marriage to bond socially with others. Friendliness is an outpouring
of the loving spirit of our marriage, which is founded on our strong
friendship. We talk with one another, laugh together, and work as
friends toward common goals. We greet one another with smiling and
friendly faces. Others see this happiness as we welcome them into our
home with warm and generous hospitality. We share our time, ideas,
feelings, touch, celebrations, struggles, and love together as friends
in our marriage. We support one another through difficult times,
listening compassionately, and offering comfort. Friendliness creates
a safe place in our marriage for us to share ourselves, influence one
another, and appreciate who we really are. We are confident that the
friendship of spirit we have will endure.

❤

Friendship is a single soul dwelling in two bodies.

~ Aristotle

How are we practicing Friendliness?
What new choices will we make?

CONSULT AND TAKE ACTION

1. Identifying and Strengthening *Friendliness*
   a. Do we behave in a cool way toward one another or others, waiting for someone else to be *friendly* first? If so, when? How can *caring, love*, or other qualities support *friendliness*?
   b. Do we avoid inviting people to our home? If so, when? How can *generosity, thoughtfulness*, or other qualities assist us?
   c. When can *compassion, cooperation, enthusiasm, respect, service*, or other qualities assist us with strengthening *friendliness*?
2. Identifying and Balancing Misuses of *Friendliness*
   a. Are we motivated by the desire to increase our status and importance? If so, when? How can *honesty, humility*, or other qualities assist us in using *friendliness* effectively?
   b. Do we spend so much time with *friends* that they excessively influence us, and we neglect *responsibilities* and family? If so, when? How can *detachment, self-discipline*, or other qualities assist us?
   c. When can using *chastity, responsibility, loyalty, moderation, wisdom*, or other qualities reduce our misuse of *friendliness*?
3. When is the lack of or misuse of *friendliness* a source of conflict for us? If necessary, how can we restore harmony?
4. When does *friendliness* to others make us happy? When does it cause us problems?
5. Do we value *friendly* and *loving* hospitality or avoid socializing? What ways do we *create* it? What new actions could we try?
6. How can *friendliness* enhance all types of intimacy between us?

STRENGTHEN OUR RELATIONSHIP

♥ Smile, greet, and treat one another as best *friends* each day
♥ Spend time, as a couple, talking with the neighbors
♥ *Commit* to regularly visiting family and *friends*
♥ Spend time together at the end of the day and share what went well, what was humorous, what was challenging, what we need to apologize for, and where we need support and assistance
♥ How else are we *committed* to practicing *friendliness*?

❧ *Generosity* ❧

EXPAND OUR INSIGHTS

Give of the good things which ye have (honorably) earned, and of the fruits of the earth which We have produced for you....

~ Islam: *The Qur'án*, 2:267

Generosity is open-hearted and open-handed sharing of what we have. At times, this requires us to willingly share or sacrifice what we have, trusting in a positive outcome. We freely and fully share our thoughts, feelings, touch, time, listening, and spirituality with one another. The other's happiness and pleasure are our own. We are generous outside our marriage with our families, friends, and community where it is truly helpful. We generously acknowledge other's service to us. We wish to bring one another and others happiness, and we generously offer needed support. We act without hesitation or reluctance. We ensure we handle our responsibilities, however, and do not neglect them by being overly generous. We do not expect praise, gratitude, or any reward in return for what we give. We stay confident in the generous abundance that is available to us.

Certain obligations are commonly understood to be part of being a spouse—being faithful, communicating clearly, helping one another, contributing to the household, and so forth. Being generous in a marriage means going beyond what is required and in some way offering more. There is an infinite variety of ways in which you can be generous with your spouse…acknowledging and appreciating your partner's best qualities, forgiving inevitable failings, and giving care and attention.

~ Blaine J. Fowers, Ph.D., *Beyond the Myth of Marital Happiness*, pp. 166-67

How are we practicing Generosity?
What new choices will we make?

CONSULT AND TAKE ACTION

1. Identifying and Strengthening *Generosity*
   a. Are we stingy with our affection, money, time, appreciation, *encouragement*, gifts, celebrations, positive feedback, resources, *wisdom*, and possessions? If so, when? How can *thoughtfulness*, *thankfulness*, or other qualities support *generosity*?
   b. Do we avoid sharing our beliefs, *friendliness*, or *forgiveness*? If so, when? How can *cooperation*, *enthusiasm*, or other qualities assist us?
   c. When can *caring*, *compassion*, *humility*, *idealism*, *joyfulness*, *love*, *service*, or other qualities assist us with strengthening *generosity*?
2. Identifying and Balancing Misuses of *Generosity*
   a. Do we give to the point where we are neglecting our well-being or *commitments* to our family? If so, when? How can *discernment*, *responsibility*, or other qualities assist us in using *generosity* effectively?
   b. Are we extravagant, wasteful, or gambling with our resources? If so, when? How can *detachment*, *wisdom*, or other qualities assist us?
   c. When can using *flexibility*, *integrity*, *loyalty*, *spirituality*, or other qualities reduce our misuse of *generosity*?
3. When is the lack of or misuse of *generosity* a source of conflict for us? If necessary, how can we restore harmony?
4. What are some of the gifts we share with one another or others?
5. What *responsibilities* do we need to handle and agreements do we need to make before being financially *generous*? How do we balance *generosity* with thriftiness, saving, investing, and spending?
6. How can *generosity* enhance all types of intimacy between us?

STRENGTHEN OUR RELATIONSHIP

- ♥ Donate a portion of our income to a worthy cause
- ♥ Celebrate our anniversary or other occasion in a special way
- ♥ *Create* or buy something together and give it away
- ♥ Participate together in a volunteer activity
- ♥ How else are we *committed* to practicing *generosity*?

✄ *Gentleness* ✄

EXPAND OUR INSIGHTS

Satisfy the necessities of life like the butterfly that sips the flower, without destroying its fragrance or its texture.

~ Buddhism: *The Gospel of Buddha*, XCIV:17

Gentleness is a caring expression of our hearts. It helps us move gracefully, touch softly, hold carefully, and speak quietly. We cherish our relationship, treating it as very special. We think gentle and loving thoughts instead of critical ones. We create soft and beautiful places in our home that invite us to be gentle. We enjoy listening to uplifting and flowing music that encourages gentleness. We use self-awareness, sensitivity, and self-discipline to be gentle. No matter how strong we are, we are careful to avoid ever physically hurting one another or others. We give one another affectionate smiles, tender caresses, and loving words. Gentleness helps bring safety, security, and peacefulness to our relationship and home.

Such is the power of love in gentle mind, that it can alter all the course of kind.

~ Edmund Spenser, Amoretti, XXX

How are we practicing Gentleness?
What new choices will we make?

CONSULT AND TAKE ACTION

1. Identifying and Strengthening *Gentleness*
   a. Do we handle one another or any possessions roughly? If so, when? How can *caring, self-discipline*, or other qualities support *gentleness*?
   b. Do we lose our tempers, yell, or speak harshly or forcefully? If so, when? How can *moderation, peacefulness*, or other qualities assist us?
   c. When can *beauty, compassion, courtesy, humility, love, mercy, patience, respect*, or other qualities assist us with strengthening *gentleness*?
2. Identifying and Balancing Misuses of *Gentleness*
   a. Do we avoid using appropriate firmness to handle someone, something, or an issue? If so, when? How can *confidence, strength*, or other qualities assist us in using *gentleness* effectively?
   b. Do we become docile and so easy-going that others can easily manipulate us? If so, when? How can *assertiveness, discernment*, or other qualities assist us?
   c. When can using *honesty, integrity, justice, truthfulness, wisdom*, or other qualities reduce our misuse of *gentleness*?
3. When is the lack of or misuse of *gentleness* a source of conflict for us? If necessary, how can we restore harmony?
4. When do we appreciate *gentleness* from one another? When do we prefer firmness? What is the difference between them? When is *gentleness* difficult?
5. How can *gentleness* enhance all types of intimacy between us?

STRENGTHEN OUR RELATIONSHIP

♥ Caress, stroke, or massage one another wherever it feels best
♥ Show *gentleness* toward a child, an elderly family member, or a pet
♥ Think and express positive and honoring thoughts about ourselves and one another
♥ Be *gently assertive* about something appropriate
♥ How else are we *committed* to practicing *gentleness*?

❧ *Helpfulness* ❧

EXPAND OUR INSIGHTS

...as we have opportunity, let us do good to all people....
~ Christianity: *The Bible* (New International Version), Galatians, 6:10

Helpfulness is seeing someone's need and taking action to meet it. We are considerate, thoughtful, and spontaneous in responding to one another. When we are short on time or cannot do something, we appreciate helpfulness from the other. Sometimes we take the initiative to do something helpful for the other, and it turns out to be annoying instead. We then consult about what works and what does not. Together we create solutions to meet one another's needs and make life easier for both of us. Offering and accepting help brings us both happiness and relaxation. We do our best to accept help lovingly when it is given to us. Sometimes the person who is helping does an action differently than we would do it. We refrain from criticizing one another or others for sincere efforts. We accept loving help gracefully from one another, from others as needed, and from spiritual sources.

Forget yourself by becoming interested in others. Do every day a good deed that will put a smile of joy on someone's face.
~ Dale Carnegie, *How to Stop Worrying and Start Living*, p. 147

How are we practicing Helpfulness?
What new choices will we make?

CONSULT AND TAKE ACTION

1. Identifying and Strengthening *Helpfulness*
   a. Do we focus only on our own needs and are unaware of other's needs? If so, when? How can *service, thoughtfulness*, or other qualities support *helpfulness*?
   b. Do we avoid taking action when it is requested or needed? If so, when? How can *excellence, unity*, or other qualities assist us?
   c. Do we *help*, but begrudgingly? If so, when? How can *cooperation, kindness*, or other qualities assist us?
   d. When can *caring, compassion, generosity, mercy, purity, spirituality*, or other qualities assist us with strengthening *helpfulness*?
2. Identifying and Balancing Misuses of *Helpfulness*
   a. Do we start *helping* without assessing a situation or asking if it is wanted? If so, when? How can *courtesy, discernment*, or other qualities assist us in using *helpfulness* effectively?
   b. Do we take actions that enable others to avoid their *responsibilities*? If so, when? How can *detachment, wisdom*, or other qualities assist us?
   c. Do we violate our moral values when we respond to requests for *help*? If so, when? How can *integrity, strength*, or other qualities assist us?
   d. When can using *contentment, courage, honesty, patience, respect, self-discipline*, or other qualities reduce our misuse of *helpfulness*?
3. When is the lack of or misuse of *helpfulness* a source of conflict for us? If necessary, how can we restore harmony?
4. What do we need *help* with? When and why do we decline or resist asking for *help*? What are the benefits or consequences?
5. How can *helpfulness* enhance all types of intimacy between us?

STRENGTHEN OUR RELATIONSHIP

♥ Handle a *responsibility* that the other does not have time to do
♥ Ask one another for *help* with something
♥ Cook dinner for the other after a stressful day
♥ Perform a *helpful* service for a neighbor, family member, or friend
♥ How else are we *committed* to practicing *helpfulness*?

❧ *Honesty* ❧

EXPAND OUR INSIGHTS

...you must love honesty and integrity.

~ Judaism: *Tanakh*, Zechariah, 8:19

♥

Honesty begins with knowing ourselves thoroughly and then sharing who we really are. We do and say what is moral and legal, even in the face of strong temptation. We can rely on one another to not cheat, steal, lie, or make false promises. We sincerely say what we mean, mean what we say, and our actions match our words. We create a safe environment in which to honestly share feelings and thoughts without judgment. We are willing to listen carefully to one another, being open to talk through any issue. We look deep within our hearts and communicate what is true for us with respect and tactfulness. We do not erect barriers between us or create distrust by withholding important information. We are clear and direct in our speech without burdening one another. We admit our mistakes and acknowledge that we are sorry. Our honesty helps people to believe in us.

♥

Relationships bring up your stuff, and feelings are the stuff we are made of. ... Very important love rule: You must learn to be as honest as possible about what you feel. A simple mental sentence should do the trick: "Right now I am feeling ___." Once you acknowledge what you feel, you have a choice whether or not to express it.

~ Iyanla Vanzant, *In the Meantime*, p. 211

How are we practicing Honesty?
What new choices will we make?

CONSULT AND TAKE ACTION

1. Identifying and Strengthening *Honesty*
   a. Do we withhold important information or conceal our behavior from one another? If so, when? How can *truthfulness, trustworthiness,* or other qualities assist us?
   b. Do we cheat at games, underpay taxes or fees, take credit for other's work, defraud people, or steal from one another or others? If so, when? How can *detachment, loyalty,* or other qualities support *honesty?*
   c. When can *chastity, confidence, excellence, humility, justice, purity, responsibility, sincerity, spirituality, unity,* or other qualities assist us with strengthening *honesty?*
2. Identifying and Balancing Misuses of *Honesty*
   a. Do we act or speak without discretion or timeliness, or engage in gossip or backbiting? If so, when? How can *forgiveness, wisdom,* or other qualities assist us in using *honesty* effectively?
   b. Do we use *honesty* to upset or hurt others? If so, when? How can *self-discipline, tactfulness,* or other qualities assist us?
   c. When can using *gentleness, respect, service, thoughtfulness, wisdom,* or other qualities reduce our misuse of *honesty?*
3. When is the lack of or misuse of *honesty* a source of conflict for us? If necessary, how can we restore harmony?
4. How do we know whether we are being *honest* or not?
5. When are we tempted to be less *honest* with one another? How can we support one another in being *honest?*
6. How can *honesty* enhance all types of intimacy between us?

STRENGTHEN OUR RELATIONSHIP

♥ Discuss if we are handling our financial matters *honestly*
♥ Share something we have not been *honest* about, make amends, and recommit to *honesty*; agree how to support the *commitment*
♥ Share our feelings openly about something important in our lives
♥ Share *honest* remorse when we have done something hurtful
♥ How else are we *committed* to practicing *honesty?*

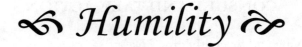

Humility

EXPAND OUR INSIGHTS

...enter the gate [of the town] with humility, in posture and in words, and We shall forgive you your faults and increase (the portion of) those who do good.

~ Islam: *The Qur'án*, 2:58

Humility is seeing our real selves and our real strengths in relation to God and to other people. It allows us to be equal partners in our marriage and not consider that one of us is more or less important. It helps us to acknowledge our imperfections and inability to have all the answers. We recognize our limitations, and we can ask for help. We respect ourselves, recognize our strengths, and are modest about our accomplishments. We do not speak of what we have done with excessive pride or boasting. We are happy to serve one another in a humble spirit of love. We know the other's needs are as valid and important as our own. We admit mistakes, learn from them, forgive, and let go of judgment. We are willing to seek and accept help from many sources, including spiritual ones. We acknowledge the best in others and ourselves. We are humbly thankful for the blessings in our life.

♥

...excessive pride is a familiar sin, but a man may just as easily frustrate the will of God through excessive humility.

~ Ken Follett, *The Pillars of the Earth*, p. 137

How are we practicing Humility?
What new choices will we make?

CONSULT AND TAKE ACTION

1. Identifying and Strengthening *Humility*
   a. Do we boast about our accomplishments? If so, when? How can *detachment, tactfulness,* or other qualities support *humility*?
   b. Do we believe we are better than one another and engage in overly *strong* and inappropriate competition? If so, when? How can *courtesy, self-discipline,* or other qualities assist us?
   c. Do we believe that we do not make mistakes, and we criticize others for their errors? If so, when? How can *equality, forgiveness,* or other qualities assist us?
   d. When can *compassion, honesty, patience, purity, service, thoughtfulness,* or other qualities assist us with strengthening *humility*?
2. Identifying and Balancing Misuses of *Humility*
   a. Do we lack self-*respect* and allow others to treat us poorly? If so, when? How can *assertiveness, justice,* or other qualities assist us in using *humility* effectively?
   b. Are we excessively self-centered about our imperfections? If so, when? How can *acceptance, thankfulness,* or other qualities assist us?
   c. When can using *confidence, contentment, kindness, moderation, respect,* or other qualities reduce our misuse of *humility*?
3. When is the lack of or misuse of *humility* a source of conflict for us? If necessary, how can we restore harmony?
4. Do we ever treat one another as more or less important?
5. How do we handle a big accomplishment? How do we handle it when one of us makes a mistake that affects the other?
6. How can *humility* enhance all types of intimacy between us?

STRENGTHEN OUR RELATIONSHIP

- Express appreciation of one another's *strengths*
- *Humbly* admit a mistake we have made, and make amends
- Share an accomplishment with one another without boasting
- *Create* a visual symbol of a *spiritual* power greater than we are
- How else are we *committed* to practicing *humility*?

ᨄ *Idealism* ᨃ

EXPAND OUR INSIGHTS

Let your acts be a guide unto all mankind.... It is through your deeds that ye can distinguish yourselves from others. Through them the brightness of your light can be shed upon the whole earth.

~ Bahá'í Faith: *Gleanings from the Writings of Bahá'u'lláh*, p. 305

Idealism is seeing what is possible to accomplish in the world, beyond what currently exists. We look together for ways to serve the needs of others. We are confident we can make a difference for them. We use creativity to imagine how to right injustices, and we set in motion actions that will address the issues. We know what our beliefs and values are, and what is important to accomplish in our lives and community. We have dreams and ideals for transforming our marriage and family. However, we do not lose track of the need for realistic plans and practical actions to carry them out. Idealism balances negative thinking and circumstances, and allows us to look for and create the best possible outcomes in all situations.

Man is born a predestined idealist, for he is born to act. To act is to affirm the worth of an end, and to persist in affirming the worth of an end is to make an ideal.

~ Oliver Wendell Holmes, Jr., *Speeches by Oliver Wendell Holmes*, pp. 96-97

How are we practicing Idealism?
What new choices will we make?

CONSULT AND TAKE ACTION

1. Identifying and Strengthening *Idealism*
   a. Do we only look after our day-to-day lives and not see what else around us could be improved? If so, when? How can *caring, excellence*, or other qualities support *idealism*?
   b. Are we pessimistic about our lives or the world? If so, when? How can *justice, purposefulness* or other qualities assist us?
   c. Do we look for the easiest pathway and settle for less than is *wise* or possible? If so, when? How can *courage, creativity* or other qualities assist us?
   d. When can *compassion, enthusiasm, generosity, spirituality*, or other qualities assist us with strengthening *idealism*?
2. Identifying and Balancing Misuses of *Idealism*
   a. Do we pay more attention to *idealistic* dreams than to reality? If so, when? How can *discernment, responsibility*, or other qualities assist us in using *idealism* effectively?
   b. Do we set our *ideals* so high and rigidly that we are intolerant of anything less than perfection? If so, when? How can *humility, moderation*, or other qualities assist us?
   c. When can using *acceptance, contentment, detachment, forgiveness, honesty, peacefulness, self-discipline, trustworthiness*, or other qualities reduce our misuse of *idealism*?
3. When is the lack of or misuse of *idealism* a source of conflict for us? If necessary, how can we restore harmony?
4. Do we have any conflicting *ideals*? How can we reconcile them? Do we have *respect* for one another's *ideals*?
5. What dreams do we want to fulfill? How can we fulfill them?
6. How can *idealism* enhance all types of intimacy between us?

STRENGTHEN OUR RELATIONSHIP

- ♥ *Create* a vision of what we want to have in our marriage
- ♥ Share our dreams for what we want to accomplish in our lives
- ♥ Volunteer time together at a community improvement project
- ♥ Identify and plan for an area in our life we want to improve
- ♥ How else are we *committed* to practicing *idealism*?

✺ *Integrity* ✺

EXPAND OUR INSIGHTS

May integrity and uprightness watch over me, for I look to You.

~ Judaism: *Tanakh*, Psalms, 25:21

Integrity is being in a state of balance and wholeness in our lives and marriage. Our ideals, intentions, words, and actions are honest, just, defensible, and in harmony. We choose the best words and behavior for each circumstance. Our clear moral and ethical code guides our lives and work. We do not allow others to influence us to lower our standards. Our integrity contributes to the harmony and trust in our marriage. We do not inappropriately keep secrets. We are responsible for making and keeping commitments and promises to one another, as well as to families, employers, and community leaders. We use reflection, prayer, consultation, and spiritual guidance to strengthen our integrity. Practicing integrity enables us to act in ways that are consistent with our deepest beliefs and highest values.

A person's word can have value and power or it can be cheap and meaningless. Persons of integrity have a reputation for keeping their word. What creates a strong reputation for integrity is behavior that is congruent, or consistent, with what we say. People listen to those who keep their word, and people organize their own behavior around promises made. ... When spouses keep their word to each other, predictability results, which creates security and trust. They can rely on each other.

~ Sandra Gray Bender, Ph.D., *Recreating Marriage with the Same Old Spouse*, pp. 150-51

How are we practicing Integrity?
What new choices will we make?

CONSULT AND TAKE ACTION

1. Identifying and Strengthening *Integrity*
   a. Do we break our agreements or promises? If so, when? How can *commitment, faithfulness,* or other qualities support *integrity*?
   b. Do we have a low standard of behavior? If so, when? How can *honesty, excellence,* or other qualities assist us?
   c. Do we act immorally or unethically? If so, when? How can *purity, self-discipline,* or other qualities assist us?
   d. When can *confidence, justice, purposefulness, respect, responsibility, strength, trustworthiness,* or other qualities assist us with strengthening *integrity*?
2. Identifying and Balancing Misuses of *Integrity*
   a. Do we have poor motives for our actions and avoid the consequences of poor choices? If so, when? How can *discernment, humility,* or other qualities assist us in using *integrity* effectively?
   b. Do we not see our own flaws and assume we cannot be led astray? If so, when? How can *truthfulness, wisdom,* or other qualities assist us?
   c. When can using *compassion, courage, detachment, sincerity, spirituality,* or other qualities reduce our misuse of *integrity*?
3. When is the lack of or misuse of *integrity* a source of conflict for us? If necessary, how can we restore harmony?
4. How do we keep track of our *commitments* and follow through? What excuses do we make? How can we restore any areas where we lack *integrity*?
5. How can *integrity* enhance all types of intimacy between us?

STRENGTHEN OUR RELATIONSHIP

- ❤ Identify any incomplete promises and follow through with them
- ❤ Pay all the bills on time
- ❤ Share with one another an ethical or moral dilemma we are struggling with, and consult together about how to address it
- ❤ Match a belief with our actions that reflect that belief
- ❤ How else are we *committed* to practicing *integrity*?

❧ *Joyfulness* ❧

EXPAND OUR INSIGHTS

...we also rejoice in our sufferings, because we know that suffering produces perseverance; perseverance, character; and character, hope.
~ Christianity: *The Bible* (New International Version), Romans, 5:4-5

Joyfulness is a feeling of high-spirited delight and happiness. It lifts us up from sadness, gives us energy, and overflows around us. It helps us to be optimistic, anticipating the best in life and from our marriage. Joy arises in our lives when we feel spiritually connected, spend loving time together as a couple, laugh, have fun, and share humor. Joyfulness comes when we are with people we love and care about deeply. We feel joyful when we excitedly share new knowledge and insights and give and receive gifts of all kinds. Joyfulness fills our hearts with vitality and gratitude for love and life. It assists us to be happy ourselves and to be a source of happiness for others.

❤

It is perfectly natural to feel a sense of joy when one feels love.
~ Betty Frost, *A Key to Loving*, p. 46

How are we practicing Joyfulness?
What new choices will we make?

CONSULT AND TAKE ACTION

1. Identifying and Strengthening *Joyfulness*
   a. Do we grumble and complain about our lives or fail to rejoice in the good fortune of others? If so, when? How can *enthusiasm*, *thankfulness*, or other qualities support *joyfulness*?
   b. Do we avoid happy and fun people, places, and experiences, and look for the bad instead of the good? If so, when? How can *beauty*, *friendliness*, or other qualities assist us?
   c. When can *chastity*, *creativity*, *equality*, *generosity*, *helpfulness*, *idealism*, *respect*, *spirituality*, *unity* or other qualities assist us with strengthening *joyfulness*?
2. Identifying and Balancing Misuses of *Joyfulness*
   a. Are we overly noticeable for our *joyfulness* at times when we should be quiet, sensitive, or *respectful* to other's feelings? If so, when? How can *self-discipline*, *tactfulness*, or other qualities assist us in using *joyfulness* effectively?
   b. Do we rejoice excessively over relatively minor events? If so, when? How can *detachment*, *sincerity*, or other qualities assist us?
   c. Do we disapprove of, discourage, or invalidate feelings of sadness or sorrow in others? If so, when? How can *encouragement*, *love*, or other qualities assist us?
   d. When can using *discernment*, *compassion*, *wisdom*, or other qualities reduce our misuse of *joyfulness*?
3. When is the lack of or misuse of *joyfulness* a source of conflict for us? If necessary, how can we restore harmony?
4. What brings *joyfulness* into our marriage and relationship? How do we practice it when we are feeling sad?
5. How can *joyfulness* enhance all types of intimacy between us?

STRENGTHEN OUR RELATIONSHIP

- ♥ Share funny stories from our day
- ♥ Use prayer or meditation together to experience *spiritual joy*
- ♥ Plan a fun activity or trip that will include laughter and *joy*
- ♥ Give gifts to one another that bring *joy*
- ♥ How else are we *committed* to practicing *joyfulness*?

ᕦ Justice ᕤ

EXPAND OUR INSIGHTS

Speak the truth to one another, render true and perfect justice….
~ Judaism: *Tanakh*, Zechariah, 8:16

Justice is assessing all the facts and feelings in a situation and doing what is in alignment with moral and ethical principles. It requires each of us to set aside biases and prejudices and to discern a situation's truth for ourselves. This releases us from relying on what others say. Justice helps us to be fair in our judgments and actions, to respect one another, and to search for equitable solutions. We are responsible for our own actions and their consequences. We do not choose to use our strength, words, or actions to hurt one another. We look for areas where there is injustice or harm occurring, and we work to restore integrity to the situations. There is fairness and equality in our marriage, resulting in stability, unity, and balance between us.

♥

Intimacy between husbands and wives is limited when there is a clear difference in power between them, because maintaining control requires the more powerful partner to stand apart from his or her spouse. You cannot share your vulnerabilities and secrets with your spouse if you want to have more power than your partner does. Intimacy between spouses requires a certain degree of fairness in marriage. Frequent experiences of injustice will make it difficult if not impossible for spouses to maintain the kind of trust necessary to clear communication and emotional closeness.
~ Blaine J. Fowers, Ph.D., *Beyond the Myth of Marital Happiness*, p. 185

How are we practicing Justice?
What new choices will we make?

CONSULT AND TAKE ACTION

1. Identifying and Strengthening *Justice*
   a. Do we treat others with disrespect and unfairness or allow others to do so to us? If so, when? How can *cooperation, trustworthiness,* or other qualities support *justice?*
   b. Do we act based on our prejudices or momentary feelings rather than on *truth?* If so, when? How can *equality, integrity,* or other qualities assist us?
   c. When can *confidence, courage, helpfulness, idealism, respect, self-discipline,* or other qualities assist us with strengthening *justice?*
2. Identifying and Balancing Misuses of Justice
   a. Do we try to be so fair that we become indecisive? If so, when? How can *acceptance, discernment,* or other qualities assist us in using *justice* effectively?
   b. Do we defend others inappropriately? If so, when? How can *flexibility, wisdom,* or other qualities assist us?
   c. Are we inappropriately focused on being *merciful?* If so, when? How can *assertiveness, strength,* or other qualities assist us?
   d. When can using *compassion, forgiveness, mercy, thoughtfulness,* or other qualities reduce our misuse of *justice?*
3. When is the lack of or misuse of *justice* a source of conflict for us? If necessary, how can we restore harmony?
4. How do we respond when one of us believes we are "right" and makes the other "wrong"?
5. What are the rights, *responsibilities,* and freedoms we each have in our marriage?
6. How can *justice* enhance all types of intimacy between us?

STRENGTHEN OUR RELATIONSHIP

- ♥ Identify a problem, and search for the facts that apply to solving it
- ♥ Admit a prejudice or bias and begin to eliminate it
- ♥ Identify an unjust social issue and consult about solutions
- ♥ Address something unfair that is happening in our marriage
- ♥ How else are we committed to practicing *justice?*

&ed; *Kindness* &ec;

EXPAND OUR INSIGHTS

...greater than all is lovingkindness. As the light of the moon is sixteen times stronger than the light of all the stars, so lovingkindness is sixteen times more efficacious in liberating the heart than all other religious accomplishments taken together.

~ Buddhism: *The Gospel of Buddha*, XX:22

Kindness is an attitude of thoughtful and warm-hearted consideration translated into actions that benefit and enrich each of us. With sympathetic kindness, our hearts are sincerely open to one another. We share words or gestures that show gentle love and caring to one another. We are kind to ourselves when we are going through a difficult time. We understand that both of us fail at times and need understanding and acceptance. Kindness from one another calms us when our emotions are in turmoil. A kind act influences us to smile when we are sad and feel hopeful and encouraged to go forward when life is difficult. Kindness to one another helps us to show kindness to those whose lives we touch.

Kindness is the life's blood, the elixir of marriage. Kindness makes the difference between passion and caring. Kindness is tenderness. Kindness is love....

~ Randolph Ray, *My Little Church Around the Corner*

How are we practicing Kindness?
What new choices will we make?

CONSULT AND TAKE ACTION

1. Identifying and Strengthening *Kindness*
   a. Do we act as if people deserve severe consequences for their mistakes? If so, when? How can *love*, *mercy*, or other qualities support *kindness*?
   b. Do we ignore the needs of those around us? If so, when? How can *compassion*, *helpfulness*, or other qualities assist us?
   c. Are we regularly mean or critical? If so, when? How can *gentleness*, *thoughtfulness*, or other qualities assist us?
   d. When can *caring*, *courtesy*, *encouragement*, *friendliness*, *respect*, or other qualities assist us with strengthening *kindness*?
2. Identifying and Balancing Misuses of *Kindness*
   a. Are we so *kind* to others we lose our moral perspective of their actions or we neglect our *responsibilities* and family? If so, when? How can *detachment*, *loyalty*, or other qualities assist us in using *kindness* effectively?
   b. Are we selectively *kind* only to those who *serve* our interests? If so, when? How can *honesty*, *sincerity*, or other qualities assist us?
   c. When can using *assertiveness*, *discernment*, *justice*, *self-discipline*, *purposefulness*, *truthfulness*, *wisdom* or other qualities reduce our misuse of *kindness*?
3. When is the lack of or misuse of *kindness* a source of conflict for us? If necessary, how can we restore harmony?
4. When do we most appreciate *kindness* from one another?
5. How can *kindness* enhance all types of intimacy between us?

STRENGTHEN OUR RELATIONSHIP

- Use positive, uplifting words when speaking with one another
- Share a gift with a friend that shares a *spiritual* or *helpful* perspective
- Surprise one another with an act of *kindness*
- Deliver and receive all messages and communications that come into our home from others in a *kind* and effective manner
- How else are we *committed* to practicing *kindness*?

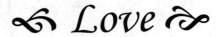

Love

EXPAND OUR INSIGHTS

It is He Who created you from a single person, and made his mate of like nature, in order that he might dwell with her in love.

~ Islam: *The Qur'án*, 7:189

♥

Love is the powerful magnetic and caring force that draws us to one another, to a loving God, and to others. It is a bond of intense feeling that holds us together even during very difficult times. Love in our hearts assists us to understand gentleness, kindness, patience, and all our character qualities, as well as see and encourage these qualities in others. Our love brings out the best in one another. We acknowledge and respect that we both have bodies, minds, hearts, and souls worthy of love. We do not take it for granted that we love one another. We ensure we let one another know what expressions of love we most appreciate receiving. We then consciously communicate love through our words, actions, and gestures. We do not withhold touch and affection to manipulate or punish one another. Love frees us from negative emotions and thoughts, and brings life, hope, and happiness to our marriage. We make the conscious choice to love one another every day.

♥

If you feel the flow of love in your life, you have a springboard to miracles under your feet with every step.

~ Gay Hendricks, Ph.D. and Kathlyn Hendricks, Ph.D., Lasting Love, xiii

How are we practicing Love?
What new choices will we make?

CONSULT AND TAKE ACTION

1. Identifying and Strengthening *Love*
   a. Are we bitter, critical, or contemptuous of one another? If so, when? How can *acceptance, respect,* or other qualities assist us?
   b. Do we act unloving toward one another? If so, when? How can *generosity, thoughtfulness,* or other qualities assist us?
   c. When can *caring, courtesy, enthusiasm, equality, faithfulness, kindness, patience, purity, service, sincerity, spirituality, unity,* or other qualities assist us with strengthening *love?*
2. Identifying and Balancing Misuses of *Love*
   a. Do we smother one another with so much time and attention that there is not space to be ourselves or live our own lives? If so, when? How can *detachment, moderation,* or other qualities assist us in using *love* effectively?
   b. Do we only express affection sexually? If so, when? How can *equality, gentleness,* or other qualities assist us?
   c. Do we enable each others weaknesses because of *love?* If so, when? How can *discernment, respect,* or other qualities assist us?
   d. When can using *chastity, contentment, service, sincerity, self-discipline, wisdom,* or other qualities reduce our misuse of *love?*
3. When is the lack of or misuse of *love* a source of conflict for us? If necessary, how can we restore harmony?
4. How do we express *love?* What makes us feel *loved?* How do we let one another know that we feel *loved?*
5. What circumstances might challenge us with maintaining *loving* feelings? How can we avoid this?
6. How can *love* enhance all types of intimacy between us?

STRENGTHEN OUR RELATIONSHIP

- ♥ Discover two new ways of expressing our *love* for one another
- ♥ Leave *love* notes in unexpected and obvious places
- ♥ Treat one another to a special evening out
- ♥ *Create* a sensuous/sexual time together that builds oneness
- ♥ How else are we *committed* to practicing *love?*

✧ Loyalty ✧

EXPAND OUR INSIGHTS

...we...should on no account slacken our efforts to be loyal, sincere and men of good will....we must be constant in our faithfulness and trustworthiness, and occupy ourselves in offering prayers for the good of all.

~ Bahá'í Faith: *Selections from the Writings of 'Abdu'l-Bahá*, p. 294

Loyalty is an expression of belonging, such as to a marriage partner, family, community, or country. We act in ways that contribute to the well-being of those we are loyal to. Loyalty devotedly binds our hearts to one another and supports us in keeping our marriage special and important. It includes firmly resisting temptation or opportunities to betray one another. Loyalty is vital for maintaining our friendship. We speak well of one another, respecting the integrity of our marriage bond. We defend the other from attack. Beyond our loyalty to one another, we are loyal to our family, friends, employers, ideals, country, and the global community. We consult together when there appears to be conflicting loyalties pulling us in different directions. This helps us focus on what is best for everyone over time.

Complaining about your spouse to your parents, friends, or others is deadly to marriage. If you have a grievance, the one who should know about it is your spouse—the one who has an investment in you and the relationship.

~ Khalil A. Khavari, Ph.D. and Sue Williston Khavari, M.A., *Together Forever*, p. 224

How are we practicing Loyalty?
What new choices will we make?

CONSULT AND TAKE ACTION

1. Identifying and Strengthening *Loyalty*
   a. Do we speak negatively about people behind their backs or undermine someone's authority? If so, when? How can *faithfulness*, *respect*, or other qualities support *loyalty*?
   b. Do we fail to defend one another? If so, when? How can *commitment*, *courtesy*, or other qualities assist us?
   c. Do we drop relationships and friendships easily? If so, when? How can *perseverance*, *trustworthiness*, or other qualities assist us?
   d. When can *acceptance*, *cooperation*, *friendliness*, *love*, *self-discipline*, or other qualities assist us with strengthening *loyalty*?
2. Identifying and Balancing Misuses of *Loyalty*
   a. Do we make *loyalty* so important that we ignore or excuse unjust, false, weak, or negative behavior toward one another or others? If so, when? How can *discernment*, *justice*, or other qualities assist us in using *loyalty* effectively?
   b. Are we so *loyal* to people that we act immorally or illegally to assist them? If so, when? How can *detachment*, *responsibility*, or other qualities assist us?
   c. Are we overly possessive of one another, or we cannot let go of an unwise friendship? If so, when? How can *detachment*, *flexibility*, or other qualities assist us?
   d. When can using *honesty*, *integrity*, *kindness*, *moderation*, *strength*, or other qualities reduce our misuse of *loyalty*?
3. When is the lack of or misuse of *loyalty* a source of conflict for us? If necessary, how can we restore harmony?
4. What and who are we *loyal* to in our lives?
5. How can *loyalty* enhance all types of intimacy between us?

STRENGTHEN OUR RELATIONSHIP

♥ Honor friends for their *loyalty* to us with a special occasion
♥ Discuss how our home does or does not reflect our *loyalties*
♥ Identify a misplaced *loyalty* and take steps to *detach* from it
♥ Affirm our *loyalty* to one another
♥ How else are we *committed* to practicing *loyalty*?

❧ *Mercy* ❧

EXPAND OUR INSIGHTS

Be ye therefore merciful, as your Father also is merciful.
~ Christianity: *The Bible* (King James Version), Luke, 6:36

♥

Mercy is a gentle and forgiving way of accepting that someone has made a mistake. It is giving pardon, even when undeserved. We tenderly and compassionately accept one another's apologies and amends. We avoid bringing up mistakes from the past. We care about the circumstances and challenges that the other faces, and we have faith that our partner can handle whatever is going on and grow from it. We can then be merciful in offering assistance or forgiveness when things do not go well. We mercifully avoid annoying one another with repeated comments, complaints, or requests. God is very merciful to us by giving us many chances to keep learning from our mistakes. We do our best to be merciful to one another in the same way.

♥

The quality of mercy is not strain'd. It droppeth even as the gentle rain from heaven upon the place beneath: it is twice bless'd; it blesseth him that gives and him that takes.
~ William Shakespeare, *The Merchant of Venice*, Act iv, Sc. 1

How are we practicing Mercy?
What new choices will we make?

CONSULT AND TAKE ACTION

1. Identifying and Strengthening *Mercy*
   a. Do we look down on, lecture, or patronize the other's imperfections and mistakes? If so, when? How can *compassion, love*, or other qualities support *mercy*?
   b. Do we reject pleas for *mercy* and second chances from one another or someone else who has hurt us? If so, when? How can *kindness, humility*, or other qualities assist us?
   c. Do we hold grudges and resentments? If so, when? How can *forgiveness, unity*, or other qualities assist us?
   d. When can *caring, flexibility, gentleness, patience, purity, spirituality*, or other qualities assist us with strengthening *mercy*?
2. Identifying and Balancing Misuses of *Mercy*
   a. Do we repeatedly tolerate and permit unkind, damaging, or unjust behavior? If so, when? How can *assertiveness, justice*, or other qualities assist us in using *mercy* effectively?
   b. Do we unreasonably expect or insist on *mercy* and no consequences for our poor actions? If so, when? How can *honesty, strength*, or other qualities assist us?
   c. When can using *discernment, excellence, respect, wisdom*, or other qualities reduce our misuse of *mercy*?
3. When is the lack of or misuse of *mercy* a source of conflict for us? If necessary, how can we restore harmony?
4. When we feel tempted to be judgmental with one another, what supports us to be *merciful* instead?
5. How can *mercy* enhance all types of intimacy between us?

STRENGTHEN OUR RELATIONSHIP

♥ *Forgive* one another for a time our feelings were hurt, let go of lingering resentment, and stop raising the issue
♥ Share how we feel about something difficult that is going on
♥ Give *mercy* to one another and stop reminding, complaining, or nagging the other about something
♥ Make a list of what we appreciate about one another
♥ How else are we *committed* to practicing *mercy*?

❧ *Moderation* ❧

EXPAND OUR INSIGHTS

Let a man be moderate in his eating and his recreation, moderately
active, moderate in sleep and in wakefulness.

~ Hinduism: *The Song of God: Bhagavad-Gita*, VI

Moderation is recognizing the extremes in all things and seeking
the balance in various aspects of our lives. Choices in our lives are
abundant—how we use our time, attention, and resources to name
just a few. We regularly take a step back to assess our situation,
consult about our priorities, and wisely choose steps toward
maintaining a balanced life. We include family, work, service, and
leisure in our life, but with appropriate boundaries and priorities.
Moderation helps us to have the time to share our thoughts and
feelings, lowers our stress level, and allows us to be more rested. We
handle our responsibilities with a higher level of integrity, and there
is more energy for fun, intimacy, and affection. We are able to keep
nurturing our marriage as one of our most important priorities.
When we practice moderation, we use self-discipline, control our
strong desires, and respond calmly when life gives us challenges. We
spend wisely, eat healthily, speak respectfully, and move through life
with purpose, grace, and ease.

Moderation is the silken string running through the pearl chain of all
virtues.

~ Joseph Hall, *Christian Moderation*, introduction

How are we practicing Moderation?
What new choices will we make?

CONSULT AND TAKE ACTION

1. Identifying and Strengthening *Moderation*
   a. Do we allow our actions and emotions to fluctuate from one extreme to another? If so, when? How can *detachment, self-discipline*, or other qualities support *moderation*?
   b. Do we become exhausted from attempting to handle too much? If so, when? How can *gentleness, wisdom*, or other qualities assist us?
   c. Do we over-indulge in activities or harmful or addictive behavior? If so, when? How can *purity, strength*, or other qualities assist us?
   d. When can *chastity, helpfulness, kindness, patience, spirituality*, or other qualities assist us with strengthening *moderation*?
2. Identifying and Balancing Misuses of *Moderation*
   a. Do we stop ourselves from fully enjoying life? If so, when? How can *acceptance, flexibility*, or other qualities assist us in using *moderation* effectively?
   b. Do we become over-cautious, timid, or reserved in our relationship to one another or to others? If so, when? How can *confidence, enthusiasm*, or other qualities assist us?
   c. When can using *assertiveness, equality, justice, responsibility*, or other qualities reduce our misuse of *moderation*?
3. When is the lack of or misuse of *moderation* a source of conflict for us? If necessary, how can we restore harmony?
4. How can we adjust areas of our life that are out of balance?
5. How can *moderation* enhance all types of intimacy between us?

STRENGTHEN OUR RELATIONSHIP

♥ Examine our schedules and *commitments* and re-prioritize our lives to make more time to be together
♥ Assess our financial situation and modify our spending as needed
♥ Identify an issue where our reactions and opinions are extreme, discuss how to *moderate* them, and practice new wording
♥ Examine our diets and learn how to make them more healthy
♥ How else are we *committed* to practicing *moderation*?

❧ Patience ❧

EXPAND OUR INSIGHTS

The end of a matter is better than the beginning of it. Better a patient spirit than a haughty spirit.

~ Judaism: *Tanakh*, Ecclesiastes, 7:8

♥

Patience is taking the time needed to handle a situation in a slow, levelheaded, and calm way. We wait appropriately for things to happen or someone to do something, accepting what we cannot change with humor and grace. We endure delays or troublesome situations calmly and tolerantly without complaints, criticisms, agitation, or anxiety. We give the attention, time, and practice needed to build our marriage and develop our characters. We give one another the freedom to go at our own best pace. We listen patiently and attentively as we each express ourselves. Patience helps us give the time needed to bring one another pleasure. We practice patience and self-discipline when things happen in our lives that we do not expect, or when someone's behavior is challenging. Patience is quiet hope and expectation based on trust that, in the end, everything will work out.

I have the patience to endure my tests. I see the gifts in suffering. I am patient with others. I am hopeful and expectant. I wait patiently for the gifts of life to unfold. I have trust and confidence in my Creator.

~ Linda Kavelin Popov, *Sacred Moments*, October 14

How are we practicing Patience?
What new choices will we make?

CONSULT AND TAKE ACTION

1. Identifying and Strengthening *Patience*
   a. Do we rush ahead or into a situation without assessing it, or speak before thinking it through? If so, when? How can *humility, self-discipline*, or other qualities support *patience*?
   b. Do we push for things to happen faster than is *wise*? If so, when? How can *detachment, wisdom*, or other qualities assist us?
   c. Are we unreasonable or short-tempered? If so, when? How can *contentment, unity*, or other qualities assist us?
   d. When can *acceptance, discernment, flexibility, moderation, spirituality*, or other qualities assist us with strengthening *patience*?
2. Identifying and Balancing Misuses of *Patience*
   a. Do we permit delays, passively ignore issues, or act too slowly without concern for the consequences? If so, when? How can *courage, purposefulness*, or other qualities assist us in using *patience* effectively?
   b. Do we make a demand and then withhold affection and attention for extended lengths of time to wait out the other and get our own way? If so, when? How can *honesty, mercy*, or other qualities assist us?
   c. When can using *assertiveness, commitment, confidence, justice, respect, responsibility*, or other qualities reduce our misuse of *patience*?
3. When is the lack of or misuse of *patience* a source of conflict for us? If necessary, how can we restore harmony?
4. How do we feel when the other is impatient? *Patient*?
5. What issues or projects in our life will benefit from more *patience*?
6. How can *patience* enhance all types of intimacy between us?

STRENGTHEN OUR RELATIONSHIP

- ♥ Wait with grace and ease when the other is busy
- ♥ Practice *self-discipline* in a difficult situation and be *patient*
- ♥ Assemble something that has many steps and pieces; if either of us become impatient, stop until it is possible to resume *patiently*
- ♥ Develop activities to do while waiting for something
- ♥ How else are we *committed* to practicing *patience*?

∽ℰ *Peacefulness* ℰ∾

EXPAND OUR INSIGHTS

Truth gives peace to the yearning mind; it conquers error; it quenches the flames of desires....

~ Buddhism: *The Gospel of Buddha*, III:12

Peacefulness is being calm and centered, working to reduce conflict, and building unity between others and ourselves. We seek points of agreement and harmony, which enhances our intimacy. We communicate in respectful and loving ways. We do not dominate one another or cause arguments. Peacefulness creates an inner sense of calm, tranquility, and happiness. Inner peace develops through regular moments of gratitude, meditation, and prayer. When we are peaceful inside, it is easier for us to create peace in our environments. We seek peaceful circumstances, such as spending time in nature or listening to uplifting music. When we struggle with situations that are triggering angry or upset feelings, peacefulness assists us to calm our emotions. Through peaceful hearts and language, we transform negative thoughts, emotions, and actions into love and reconciliation.

...nothing can be achieved through conflict and quarrel. Conflict begets further conflict...

~ Erik Blumenthal, *To Understand and Be Understood,* p. 37

How are we practicing Peacefulness?
What new choices will we make?

CONSULT AND TAKE ACTION

1. Identifying and Strengthening *Peacefulness*
   a. Do we fight with one another or provoke disagreements or conflicts? If so, when? How can *friendliness, unity,* or other qualities support *peacefulness?*
   b. Are we often anxious and worried about potential negative outcomes? If so, when? How can *detachment, joyfulness,* or other qualities assist us?
   c. When can *acceptance, cooperation, flexibility, forgiveness, honesty, love, moderation, patience, self-discipline, spirituality, thankfulness,* or other qualities assist us with strengthening *peacefulness?*
2. Identifying and Balancing Misuses of *Peacefulness*
   a. Do we calm our emotions so much that we cannot express positive feelings like *joyfulness* or excitement? If so, when? How can *confidence, enthusiasm,* or other qualities assist us in using *peacefulness* effectively?
   b. Do we suppress righteous anger about injustice? If so, when? How can *courage, responsibility,* or other qualities assist us?
   c. Do we avoid taking *strong* and decisive action? If so, when? How can *justice, purposefulness,* or other qualities assist us?
   d. When can using *assertiveness, creativity, helpfulness, sincerity,* or other qualities reduce our misuse of *peacefulness?*
3. When is the lack of or misuse of *peacefulness* a source of conflict for us? If necessary, how can we restore harmony?
4. How can we *create* a marriage that uses consultation instead of fighting and destructive disagreements?
5. What assists us with *creating peacefulness* in our extended family?
6. How can *peacefulness* enhance all types of intimacy between us?

STRENGTHEN OUR RELATIONSHIP

- ♥ Set up a *peaceful,* harmonious place for quiet time together
- ♥ Discuss *peaceful* actions to prevent or recover from arguments
- ♥ Plan and carry out a restful and relaxing activity together
- ♥ Make a list of our favorite *peaceful* music to play
- ♥ How else are we *committed* to practicing *peacefulness?*

✥ *Perseverance* ✥

EXPAND OUR INSIGHTS

Those who patiently persevere will truly receive a reward without measure!

~ Islam: *The Qur'án*, 39:10

Perseverance is using our strength and resources to persist in reaching our goals. One of our goals is having a happy and lasting marriage. We take a long-term view of our relationship, understanding that we have the ability to move steadily forward toward this goal. It takes time to learn the rhythm of one another's bodies, minds, hearts, and souls, so we persevere on this path of discovery over time. With our character growth, goals, and projects, we stay committed, no matter how long it takes, or what obstacles we encounter. We use discernment, however, to reflect on and evaluate whether we need to appropriately change our goals or direction. When challenges arise as we persevere, we are steadfast and work together to overcome them, trusting in positive outcomes. We focus on our tasks, encouraging and helping one another as needed to keep going. We finish the projects we begin, instead of leaving them partially done. We avoid distractions that lead us away from a task or off course. Perseverance supports our success.

♥

But I have discovered the secret that after climbing a great hill, one only finds that there are many more hills to climb.

~ Nelson Mandela, *Long Walk to Freedom*, p. 625

How are we practicing Perseverance?
What new choices will we make?

CONSULT AND TAKE ACTION

1. Identifying and Strengthening *Perseverance*
   a. Do we avoid the process it takes to accomplish something, or give up at the first sign of distress? If so, when? How can *patience*, *purposefulness*, or other qualities support *perseverance*?
   b. Do we skip from one task to another without completing them? If so, when? How can *integrity*, *self-discipline*, or other qualities assist us?
   c. When can *confidence*, *courage*, *encouragement*, *enthusiasm*, *loyalty*, *responsibility*, *strength*, or other qualities assist us with strengthening *perseverance*?
2. Identifying and Balancing Misuses of *Perseverance*
   a. Do we ignore repeated challenges as a possible signal to reconsider a goal, change course, or seek advice? If so, when? How can *discernment*, *flexibility*, or other qualities assist us in using *perseverance* effectively?
   b. Do we resist giving up or giving in when there are many indications it would be reasonable, *unifying*, or *wise*? If so, when? How can *detachment*, *mercy*, or other qualities assist us?
   c. When can using *acceptance*, *contentment*, *gentleness*, *love*, *peacefulness*, *wisdom*, or other qualities reduce our misuse of *perseverance*?
3. When is the lack of or misuse of *perseverance* a source of conflict for us? If necessary, how can we restore harmony?
4. What extraordinary, *persevering* efforts are we willing to do to maintain our marriage or overcome a hurdle in our relationship?
5. What do we find discouraging? What distracts us from our goals?
6. How can *perseverance* enhance all types of intimacy between us?

STRENGTHEN OUR RELATIONSHIP

- ♥ Discuss where we see our relationship in 1, 5, 10, 25, and 50 years
- ♥ *Create* a plan for overcoming an obstacle we are currently facing
- ♥ Identify and carry out a project we can complete together
- ♥ Add *encouragement* to a project we have started and are finding it challenging to finish; complete the project and celebrate
- ♥ How else are we *committed* to practicing *perseverance*?

 Purity

EXPAND OUR INSIGHTS

A man who is born with tendencies toward the Divine, is fearless and pure in heart.

~ Hinduism: *The Song of God: Bhagavad-Gita*, XVI

Purity is a combination of such aspects as physical cleanliness, positive and chaste thoughts, and a loving heart. The cleanliness of our bodies and clothes benefits the intimacy of our relationship. Our home is clean and orderly, which frees and uplifts our spirits. We replace negative, destructive, or inappropriate sexual thoughts with positive or spiritual ones. We fill our hearts with pure love instead of resentful or negative emotions. The words we use are positive, not destructive. We practice detachment from our possessions and concerns so we can stay focused on our spirituality. We work to overcome our negative habits. We maintain the purity of our motives for speaking and acting, so we do not manipulate others. Developing our character qualities increases our sense and feeling of purity. We live a pure and positive life, free of negative influences, according to our true values.

I go through my mental rooms and examine the thoughts and beliefs in them. Some I love, so I polish and shine them and make them even more useful. Some I notice need replacement or repair, and I get around to them as I can. Some are like yesterday's newspapers and old magazines or clothing that's no longer suitable. These I either give away or toss into the trash, and I let them be gone forever.

~ Louise L. Hay, *You Can Heal Your Life*, p. 61

How are we practicing Purity?
What new choices will we make?

CONSULT AND TAKE ACTION

1. Identifying and Strengthening *Purity*
   a. Do we neglect our bodies, clothes, vehicles, possessions, and home, and allow dirt and clutter regularly? If so, when? How can *beauty*, *excellence*, or other qualities support *purity*?
   b. Do we accept violence or pornography as our entertainment? If so, when? How can *chastity*, *self-discipline*, or other qualities assist us?
   c. Do we hold anger, hate, or jealousy in our hearts? If so, when? How can *love*, *forgiveness*, or other qualities assist us?
   d. When can *detachment*, *honesty*, *respect*, *spirituality*, *trustworthiness*, or other qualities assist us with strengthening *purity*?
2. Identifying and Balancing Misuses of *Purity*
   a. Are we so clean and neat that if people make a mess or are untidy with a project, they are afraid it will upset us? If so, when? How can *creativity*, *moderation*, or other qualities assist us in using *purity* effectively?
   b. Do we so elevate ourselves and our standards that we think we are better than other people? If so, when? How can *flexibility*, *humility*, or other qualities assist us?
   c. When can using *acceptance*, *contentment*, *discernment*, *enthusiasm*, *mercy*, *wisdom*, or other qualities reduce our misuse of *purity*?
3. When is the lack of or misuse of *purity* a source of conflict for us? If necessary, how can we restore harmony?
4. What will assist us with *purifying* our bodies? Minds? Hearts? Souls? Home? Environment?
5. How can *purity* enhance all types of intimacy between us?

STRENGTHEN OUR RELATIONSHIP

- Organize and clean a part of our home together
- Do a fun activity involving water (Examples: having a bubble bath, swimming, floating down a river, creating a fountain...)
- Write and share a prayer or meditation to assist us with *purity*
- Invent a funny replacement word for swearwords
- How else are we *committed* to practicing *purity*?

✌ *Purposefulness* ✌

EXPAND OUR INSIGHTS

To every thing there is a season, and a time to every purpose under the heaven: a time to weep, and a time to laugh; a time to mourn, and a time to dance; …a time to embrace, and a time to refrain from embracing; a time to get, and a time to lose; a time to keep, and a time to cast away; …a time to keep silence, and a time to speak; a time to love…and a time of peace.

~ Christianity: *The Bible* (King James Version), Ecclesiastes, 3:1, 3:4-8

Purposefulness is having a clear focus on a final goal and being determined to accomplish what we set out to do. Together, we choose the purposes and directions for our lives and marriage. We act with determination, efficiency, and effectiveness to fulfill our goals and dreams and to develop our character qualities. We understand there is a higher spiritual purpose in our lives that calls us to greater matters than our individual concerns. We do not sit around waiting for life to happen or other people instead of us to do things. We determine our priorities and act with purpose to fulfill our commitments and vision for our lives. We are purposeful in searching for what is true, for greater knowledge, and for ways to be of service to others.

We need not control our genetics, only our actions, because God helps those who help themselves, who behave well, who live on purpose.

~ Dan Millman, *Living on Purpose*, p. 148

How are we practicing Purposefulness?
What new choices will we make?

CONSULT AND TAKE ACTION

1. Identifying and Strengthening *Purposefulness*
   a. Do we avoid *creating* plans or goals? If so, when? How can *idealism, responsibility*, or other qualities support *purposefulness*?
   b. Do we simply work to live and live to work without having any real meaning to our lives? If so, when? How can *service, spirituality*, or other qualities assist us?
   c. When can *confidence, commitment, encouragement, enthusiasm, excellence, faithfulness, joyfulness, loyalty, perseverance, self-discipline, strength*, or other qualities assist us with strengthening *purposefulness*?
2. Identifying and Balancing Misuses of *Purposefulness*
   a. Do we focus so much on our goals that we neglect our relationships or *responsibilities*? If so, when? How can *detachment, moderation*, or other qualities assist us in using *purposefulness* effectively?
   b. Do we find it difficult to bend or change plans as needed when new information or circumstances arise? If so, when? How can *cooperation, flexibility*, or other qualities assist us?
   c. When can using *courtesy, discernment, humility, trustworthiness*, or other qualities reduce our misuse of *purposefulness*?
3. When is the lack of or misuse of *purposefulness* a source of conflict for us? If necessary, how can we restore harmony?
4. What goals as a couple are we *purposeful* in accomplishing?
5. What is distracting us from being *purposeful*? How do we want to handle this?
6. How can *purposefulness* enhance all types of intimacy between us?

STRENGTHEN OUR RELATIONSHIP

- ♥ *Create* at least three goals to accomplish in our relationship within the next year, and ways and times to measure progress
- ♥ Participate in an activity outside our marriage and home
- ♥ *Create* a structure to finish any partly-done projects
- ♥ Choose a character quality to *purposefully* practice for a week
- ♥ How else are we *committed* to practicing *purposefulness*?

❧ *Respect* ❧

EXPAND OUR INSIGHTS

...[the marriage of husband and wife should be a] relationship of mutual respect and equality...a relationship governed by the principles of consultation and devoid of the use of force to compel obedience to one's will.

~ Bahá'í Faith: *Compilation of Compilations, Vol. II*, p. 458

Respect is treating people and what is important to them as worthy of our esteem. We listen to and value one another's thoughts, feelings, needs, boundaries, and rights. This respect contributes to the harmonious functioning of our marriage and home on a foundation of equality. It increases our attraction to one another and our intimacy. We speak, act, and touch in ways that reflect love, courtesy, consideration, responsibility, and other character qualities. We treat one another's possessions respectfully, honoring their value to the other. We show respect for one another's spiritual beliefs and practices. Our families know we respect them because we stay in contact and seek their companionship. We take respectful care of our home and our neighborhood, and we receive respect from our neighbors in return. Respect makes life more peaceful and orderly for us.

In a good marriage, respect permeates the relationship. This doesn't mean that the two are cautious or formal in their interaction. It simply reflects—in things that they do and say—that they genuinely respect each other. Where there is respect, love can thrive.

~ Khalil A. Khavari, Ph.D. and Sue Williston Khavari, M.A., *Together Forever*, pp. 43-44

How are we practicing Respect?
What new choices will we make?

CONSULT AND TAKE ACTION

1. Identifying and Strengthening *Respect*
   a. Do we speak critically or rudely toward one another or others? If so, when? How can *courtesy*, *sincerity*, or other qualities support *respect*?
   b. Are we careless with possessions, irreverent with spiritual things, or do we borrow and not return? If so, when? How can *responsibility*, *thoughtfulness*, or other qualities assist us?
   c. Do we ignore the rights and boundaries of others and society and behave in an intrusive, immoral, or unethical way? If so, when? How can *integrity*, *spirituality*, or other qualities assist us?
   d. When can *chastity*, *cooperation*, *equality*, *honesty*, *justice*, *tactfulness*, or other qualities assist us with strengthening *respect*?
2. Identifying and Balancing Misuses of *Respect*
   a. Do we so value some people we *accept* or defend whatever they do and not stop cruel, unjust, or unwise behavior? If so, when? How can *assertiveness*, *strength*, or other qualities assist us in using *respect* effectively?
   b. Do I/we get weak and helpless in the presence of certain people, try to please them in every way they ask, say, or do anything to make them happy? If so, when? How can *courage*, *equality*, or other qualities assist us?
   c. When can using *detachment*, *flexibility*, *integrity*, *love*, *truthfulness*, *wisdom*, or other qualities reduce our misuse of *respect*?
3. When is the lack of or misuse of *respect* a source of conflict for us? If necessary, how can we restore harmony?
4. What shows that we have *respect* for one another? For marriage?
5. How can *respect* enhance all types of intimacy between us?

STRENGTHEN OUR RELATIONSHIP

- ♥ Listen to the other without formulating a response or speaking
- ♥ *Create* areas that *respect* our need for personal space and privacy
- ♥ Share with a friend what we honor and *respect* about our spouse
- ♥ Remember and commemorate special and important occasions
- ♥ How else are we *committed* to practicing *respect*?

❧ *Responsibility* ❧

EXPAND OUR INSIGHTS

A capable wife is a crown for her husband.... He who tills his land shall have food in plenty.... ...One is repaid in kind for one's deeds.

~ Judaism: *Tanakh*, Proverbs 12:4,11,14

Responsibility is taking ownership of our happiness and choices, as well as the agreements we make with others. We practice initiative, leadership, empowerment, and responsibility in our marriage, home, and community. We keep our promises and ensure that what is important to us receives our attention and best efforts. We do not need to remind one another to handle responsibilities. This helps us to avoid taking on one another's tasks inappropriately. We humbly accept credit when things go right. When things do not go well, we are willing to be accountable, clear up misunderstandings, make amends, and address the need for improvement. We trust one another to respect the truth, use good judgment, make smart choices, and obey laws. We have confidence in one another's ability to respond maturely when issues arise. We are responsible for the quality of our lives.

♥

Living successfully with a partner means making the mental switch from being someone who operates alone to someone who operates with a teammate. You and your partner must be committed to the view that the only good deal is the deal that's good for both of you, and that each of you are responsible for making sure that you *both* get a good deal. If either gets a good deal at the other's expense, you both lose.

~ Virginia Scott, George Doub, Peggy Runnels, *Raising a Loving Family*, p. 29

How are we practicing Responsibility?
What new choices will we make?

CONSULT AND TAKE ACTION

1. Identifying and Strengthening *Responsibility*
   a. Do we break promises, ignore rules, and not apologize or make amends? If so, when? How can *caring, respect,* or other qualities support *responsibility*?
   b. Do we leave important tasks undone, or avoid looking for ways to *help* or make a difference? If so, when? How can *helpfulness, self-discipline,* or other qualities assist us?
   c. Do we defend or deny when we make a mistake or negatively affect one another? If so, when? How can *truthfulness, unity,* or other qualities assist us?
   d. When can *honesty, integrity, purposefulness, service, trustworthiness,* or other qualities assist us with strengthening *responsibility*?
2. Identifying and Balancing Misuses of *Responsibility*
   a. Do we treat everything as deeply significant, take charge, and rarely relax, have fun, or laugh? If so, when? How can *joyfulness, moderation,* or other qualities assist us in using *responsibility* effectively?
   b. Do we handle tasks that others can and should do, sometimes to make ourselves look or feel good? If so, when? How can *respect, wisdom,* or other qualities assist us?
   c. When can using *detachment, flexibility, humility, love, mercy,* or other qualities reduce our misuse of *responsibility*?
3. When is the lack of or misuse of *responsibility* a source of conflict for us? If necessary, how can we restore harmony?
4. Where do we allow *responsibility* to become a joyless burden?
5. How can *responsibility* enhance all types of intimacy between us?

STRENGTHEN OUR RELATIONSHIP

❤ Consult and divide household and outdoor chores in ways that consider our abilities, desire to learn new skills, and fairness
❤ Invite coaching and correction about errors we made
❤ Follow through with an incomplete *commitment* we have made
❤ Identify our highest priorities and how we will handle them
❤ How else are we *committed* to practicing *responsibility*?

ᔕ Self-Discipline ᔐ

EXPAND OUR INSIGHTS

...show patience, firmness and self-control....

~ Islam: *Qur'án*, 3:17

Self-discipline is the inner control, outer guidelines, and structures we create that support us in fulfilling our personal goals and life purposes. We each monitor and control our thoughts and behaviors so they do not harm one another or ourselves. We do what is important in an orderly and timely way without needing one another to watch over us or remind us. At times, this means doing what we need to do, rather than what we would prefer to do, and being timely in doing it. Sometimes we set up a system of rewards and consequences to support appropriate action. We make wise choices about our nutrition, exercise, and sleep. We choose our actions and words wisely, calmly, and appropriately. We do not lose control of ourselves when we feel hurt or angry. Self-discipline assists us with creating routines, orderliness, and harmony in our home and marriage.

Choosing to lead our lives with self-control and self-directedness is at the heart of feeling good. Self-control is something we learn from others. If the models we have are spiritual and cheerful, then we may be motivated to follow their example.

~ Khalil A. Khavari, Ph.D., *Spiritual Intelligence*, p. 8?

How are we practicing Self-Discipline?
What new choices will we make?

CONSULT AND TAKE ACTION

1. Identifying and Strengthening *Self-Discipline*
   a. Do we discard rules, principles, and *commitments*, and live the way we want to with few good habits or routines? If so, when? How can *detachment, purposefulness*, or other qualities support self-discipline?
   b. Do we give up on worthwhile goals for other easier activities? If so, when? How can *commitment, trustworthiness*, or other qualities assist us?
   c. When can *chastity, cooperation, integrity, perseverance, responsibility*, or other qualities assist us with strengthening *self-discipline*?

2. Identifying and Balancing Misuses of *Self-Discipline*
   a. Do we enforce strict rules with a harsh attitude with one another, reducing intimacy and sharing? If so, when? How can *friendliness, unity*, or other qualities assist us in using *self-discipline* effectively?
   b. Do we find it difficult to set aside our rigid work schedule for our relationship and family? If so, when? How can *flexibility, love*, or other qualities assist us?
   c. When can using *acceptance, caring, creativity, enthusiasm, gentleness, kindness, mercy, respect, spirituality, wisdom*, or other qualities reduce our misuse of *self-discipline*?

3. When is the lack of or misuse of *self-discipline* a source of conflict for us? If necessary, how can we restore harmony?

4. When can using *self-discipline* effectively avoid a problem between us? What supports us in being *self-disciplined*?

5. How can *self-discipline* enhance all types of intimacy between us?

STRENGTHEN OUR RELATIONSHIP

❤ Spend time each week tidying and cleaning our home
❤ Review our priorities and determine how to address them
❤ Develop a budget, follow it, and evaluate how it worked
❤ Follow a law, such as the speed limit, and assess the outcome
❤ How else are we *committed* to practicing *self-discipline*?

❧ *Service* ❧

EXPAND OUR INSIGHTS

You, my brothers, were called to be free. But do not use your freedom to indulge the sinful nature; rather, serve one another in love. ... Love your neighbor as yourself.
~ Christianity: *The Bible* (New International Version), Galatians, 15:13-14

Service is a humble attitude and a pattern of sacrificial action that makes an appreciable difference in the quality of people's lives. In our marriage, we put the other's needs and comforts before our own. We handle tasks quietly, without any expectation of notice, reward, or appreciation. The more we do acts of service for one another in our marriage and our home, the deeper the bond between us grows. We look for opportunities to do the everyday actions that make life easier for the other, no matter how small. Our attitude of service is inspired by and strengthened through our spiritual faith, which encourages us to put others before ourselves. This attitude of service assists us to address the social issues in our community. We reach out to make a difference for others who may be less fortunate in some ways than we are. Through generously spending time doing service for others, we increase love and happiness in their lives and ours. Service that is sincere, joyful, and compassionate, with our hearts full of love, makes our marriage happier, healthier, and stronger.

Be consistently aware of the need to serve God and to serve others in any and all of your actions. That is the way of the miracle worker.
~ Dr. Wayne W. Dyer, *Everyday Wisdom*, p. 129

How are we practicing Service?
What new choices will we make?

CONSULT AND TAKE ACTION

1. Identifying and Strengthening *Service*
   a. Do we sit and expect one another or others to wait on us? If so, when? How can *caring, thoughtfulness,* or other qualities support *service?*
   b. Do we assume others will handle what needs to be done? If so, when? How can *commitment, helpfulness,* or other qualities assist us?
   c. Do we act as though it is enough to take *care* of our own troubles without being concerned for others? If so, when? How can *compassion, humility,* or other qualities assist us?
   d. When can *encouragement, generosity, love, purity, sincerity, spirituality,* or other qualities assist us with strengthening *service?*
2. Identifying and Balancing Misuses of *Service*
   a. Do we enable others to be overly dependent on us? If so, when? How can *detachment, wisdom,* or other qualities assist us in using *service* effectively?
   b. Do we agree to do so much that we neglect our relationships, *commitments,* and *responsibilities?* If so, when? How can *moderation, self-discipline,* or other qualities assist us?
   c. Do we *serve* others expecting a favor in return? If so, when? How can *integrity, thoughtfulness,* or other qualities assist us?
   d. When can using *assertiveness, equality, honesty, respect, responsibility, tactfulness,* or other qualities reduce our misuse of *service?*
3. When is the lack of or misuse of *service* a source of conflict for us? If necessary, how can we restore harmony?
4. What *service* brings the most happiness to us?
5. How can *service* enhance all types of intimacy between us?

STRENGTHEN OUR RELATIONSHIP

❤ Do regular acts of *service* for one another
❤ Volunteer together for an organization or a *spiritual* community
❤ Do a household task that the other would usually do
❤ Request others participate in a *service* activity
❤ How else are we *committed* to practicing *service?*

❧ *Sincerity* ❧

EXPAND OUR INSIGHTS

Right speech will be his dwelling-place on the road…. Right efforts will be his steps: right thoughts his breath; and right contemplation will give him the peace that follows in his footsteps.

~ Buddhism: *The Gospel of Buddha*, XVI:21

Sincerity is being genuine and honest with our words and actions, so we build trust between others and us. It is the authentic expression of deep and heartfelt feelings in our marriage. It allows us to listen attentively to one another, knowing that we can trust the other's words. Sincere words penetrate deep within us. Sincerity ensures our interactions are full of integrity. We reveal our true selves without pretending to be something we are not. We do not fake our responses to one another. We truly care about others and live consistently according to our values. We look for the best in one another and others so we can sincerely celebrate character qualities in all of us.

Sincerity is impossible, unless it pervade the whole being, and the pretence of it saps the very foundation of character.

~ James Russell Lowell, *Lectures on English Poets*, "Essay on Pope"

How are we practicing Sincerity?
What new choices will we make?

CONSULT AND TAKE ACTION

1. Identifying and Strengthening *Sincerity*
   a. Do we use our words or actions to manipulate one another to change? If so, when? How can *detachment, purity,* or other qualities support *sincerity*?
   b. Do we pretend that something is okay when it really is not? If so, when? How can *honesty, integrity,* or other qualities assist us?
   c. Do we present a view of ourselves to others that is different from who we really are in secret? If so, when? How can *confidence, truthfulness,* or other qualities assist us?
   d. When can *caring, courage, equality, justice, purposefulness, spirituality,* or other qualities assist us with strengthening *sincerity*?
2. Identifying and Balancing Misuses of *Sincerity*
   a. Do we give too much serious attention to each aspect of our lives so that it affects the way we live, work, and play? If so, when? How can *joyfulness, wisdom,* or other qualities assist us in using *sincerity* effectively?
   b. Do we allow ourselves to be easily fooled by others' intentions? If so, when? How can *discernment, self-discipline,* or other qualities assist us?
   c. When can using *assertiveness, helpfulness, patience, service, thoughtfulness,* or other qualities reduce our misuse of *sincerity*?
3. When is the lack of or misuse of *sincerity* a source of conflict for us? If necessary, how can we restore harmony?
4. How do we feel when words said to us do not seem *sincere*?
5. What is the effect on us when words and actions are *sincere*?
6. How can *sincerity* enhance all types of intimacy between us?

STRENGTHEN OUR RELATIONSHIP

- ♥ Offer a *sincere* compliment to one another
- ♥ Say or read aloud a prayer in a *sincere* manner; discuss or meditate on how this *sincerity* moves or inspires each of us
- ♥ Acknowledge something about one another that we truly appreciate
- ♥ Make a *sincere* request for assistance from one another or others
- ♥ How else are we *committed* to practicing *sincerity*?

✌ *Spirituality* ✍

EXPAND OUR INSIGHTS

The need is very great, everywhere in the world...for a true spiritual awareness to pervade and motivate people's lives. No amount of administrative procedure or adherence to rules can take the place of this soul-characteristic, this spirituality which is the essence of Man.

~ Bahá'í Faith: *Compilation of Compilations, Vol. II*, p. 14

Spirituality is an interactive closeness to the Creator and a connection to Divine guidance in our lives. We strengthen our marriage by nurturing one another's spiritual lives and by carrying out spiritual practices both separately and together. We pray and meditate regularly for guidance and for our marriage. We turn to God in conversation, as we would turn to a friend for companionship and advice. Reverence in our attitudes and behavior helps to connect us to the Creator and the precious gift of life. We treat spiritual books as special, turning to them for understanding and strength. We feel awe and wonder in beautiful and sacred places. We base our words, actions, work, and service on spiritual values. These, in turn, support our words, actions, work, and service. We authentically share our spiritual lives and beliefs with others. As we develop our spirituality, we become both more tranquil inside as well as more active in our lives. The strength of our faith becomes the foundation for all our actions.

Prayer is the fair and radiant daughter of all the human virtues, the arch connecting heaven and earth, the sweet companion that is alike the lion and the dove; and prayer will give you the key of heaven.

~ Honoré De Balzac, *Seraphita*, Ch. VI

How are we practicing Spirituality?
What new choices will we make?

CONSULT AND TAKE ACTION

1. Identifying and Strengthening *Spirituality*
   a. Do we focus on our everyday practical life and exclude *spiritual* practices? If so, when? How can *faithfulness, service,* or other qualities support *spirituality?*
   b. Do we deny *spirituality* as an important part of life? If so, when? How can *joyfulness, love,* or other qualities assist us?
   c. Are we showing *respect* for our best qualities, or do we engage in character attacks? If so, when? How can *honesty, sincerity,* or other qualities assist us?
   d. When can *beauty, chastity, peacefulness, purity, thankfulness, unity,* or other qualities assist us with strengthening *spirituality?*
2. Identifying and Balancing Misuses of *Spirituality*
   a. Do we shut ourselves away from others for long periods to focus solely on our *spiritual* life? If so, when? How can *friendliness, moderation, wisdom,* or other qualities assist us in using *spirituality* effectively?
   b. Do we separate ourselves from those we consider less *spiritual* than us? If so, when? How can *equality, humility,* or other qualities assist us?
   c. When can using *detachment, flexibility, generosity, honesty,* or other qualities reduce our misuse of *spirituality?*
3. When is the lack of or misuse of *spirituality* a source of conflict for us? If necessary, how can we restore harmony?
4. How does *spirituality* build *unity* between us? How do we want to develop it further?
5. How can *spirituality* enhance all types of intimacy between us?

STRENGTHEN OUR RELATIONSHIP

- Plan an evening at our home with prayer, *spiritual* readings, and music for the two of us, or invite our family and friends to join us
- Attend a religious or *spiritual* service or occasion
- Set up a reverent place for *spiritual* books or daily meditation
- Memorize a quotation or prayer and share it with a friend
- How else are we *committed* to practicing *spirituality?*

❧ *Strength* ❧

EXPAND OUR INSIGHTS

Persevere in patience and constancy; vie in such perseverance;
strengthen each other; and fear God; that ye may prosper.

~ Islam: *Qur'án*, 3:200

Strength is a binding and intense force that is durable in the face of
challenges. We handle problems and responsibilities in an effective
way that strengthens our characters. We practice our qualities until
they are strong and consistent. It is this strength of character that
helps us to choose to do the right thing, even when it is difficult.
When others come to us because of our strength, we carefully assess
whether to help them or encourage them to take responsibility for
themselves. We do not give in to destructive fears and weaknesses.
Sometimes we have strong emotional reactions to one another
or incidents in our lives. We moderate them as needed, so we do
not react in hurtful ways. We stand firm on our convictions and
beliefs when others confront us. We draw on all available resources
to reinforce us. Our physical strength grows with regular fitness
and health routines. However, we do not use our strength to harm
one another. We rely on the united strength of our marriage and
friendship to support us in all circumstances.

♥

In union there is strength.

~ Aesop, *Aesop's Fables*, "The Bundle of Sticks"

How are we practicing Strength?
What new choices will we make?

CONSULT AND TAKE ACTION

1. Identifying and Strengthening *Strength*
   a. Do we fall into self-pity, resist and complain about difficulties, or deny and run away from our problems? If so, when? How can *confidence, perseverance*, or other qualities support *strength*?
   b. Do we abandon or threaten one another or others during times of need? If so, when? How can *courage, responsibility*, or other qualities assist us?
   c. Do we let go of our convictions and beliefs? If so, when? How can *faithfulness, integrity*, or other qualities assist us?
   d. When can *acceptance, assertiveness, enthusiasm, loyalty, purposefulness, self-discipline*, or other qualities assist us with strengthening *strength*?

2. Identifying and Balancing Misuses of *Strength*
   a. Are we stubborn and unable to be *flexible* in our approach? If so, when? How can *flexibility, tactfulness*, or other qualities assist us in using *strength* effectively?
   b. Are we strong-willed and find it difficult to see when it is time to do something different or listen to other's advice? If so, when? How can *humility, wisdom*, or other qualities assist us?
   c. When can using *detachment, friendliness, respect*, or other qualities reduce our misuse of *strength*?

3. When is the lack of or misuse of *strength* a source of conflict for us? If necessary, how can we restore harmony?

4. When has our *strength* benefited our relationship? When has it interfered with us changing in a new and appropriate direction?

5. How can we use our *strength* to contribute to others?

6. How can *strength* enhance all types of intimacy between us?

STRENGTHEN OUR RELATIONSHIP

- ♥ Set up a regular exercise routine
- ♥ Choose the actions we will take when faced with a crisis
- ♥ Work on a character quality that will help us during problems
- ♥ Assess and practice our consultation skills
- ♥ How else are we *committed* to practicing *strength*?

✌ *Tactfulness* ✍

EXPAND OUR INSIGHTS

Let your conversation be always full of grace, seasoned with salt, so that you may know how to answer everyone.

~ Christianity: *The Bible* (New International Version), Colossians, 4:6

Tactfulness is speaking words in a gentle and kind way so someone's feelings are not hurt. We carefully assess what we are about to say, and we determine whether our words are timely, constructive, and wise. We stay aware of the effect of our words, body language, and tone of voice on one another. Sometimes we wait for our emotions to be calm before speaking. Other times, we choose to delay or not speak at all out of sensitivity for the other. We create gentle and appropriate communications. We are wise and careful so that we do not hurt one another's heart nor cause embarrassment. We do not use tactfulness as an excuse to avoid saying what is true and important, however. We use it when we speak the truth, and we do it with kindness, courtesy, and love.

If we wish truly to communicate with our partner about a problem, we must share our own point of view with him. To do this, we must accept that our partner, too, will have a point of view about the subject and this may well be different from ours.

~ Mehri Sefidvash, *Coral and Pearls,* p. 100

How are we practicing Tactfulness?
What new choices will we make?

CONSULT AND TAKE ACTION

1. Identifying and Strengthening *Tactfulness*
   a. Do we blurt out *truthful* words without pausing to consider the effect on one another? If so, when? How can *discernment*, *thoughtfulness*, or other qualities support *tactfulness*?
   b. Are we insensitive about relationships or circumstances? If so, when? How can *love*, *wisdom*, or other qualities assist us?
   c. When can *compassion*, *courtesy*, *gentleness*, *purity*, *respect*, *sincerity*, or other qualities assist us with strengthening *tactfulness*?
2. Identifying and Balancing Misuses of *Tactfulness*
   a. Does our excessive concern for the reactions of others cause us to withhold what we would like to say? If so, when? How can *responsibility*, *truthfulness* or other qualities assist us in using *tactfulness* effectively?
   b. Are we over-sensitive or easily offended in response to others when we think they have not been *tactful* to us? If so, when? How can *peacefulness*, *unity*, or other qualities assist us?
   c. When can using *assertiveness*, *confidence*, *forgiveness*, *friendliness*, *honesty*, *trustworthiness*, or other qualities reduce our misuse of *tactfulness*?
3. When is the lack of or misuse of *tactfulness* a source of conflict for us? If necessary, how can we restore harmony?
4. When do we see *tactfulness* preventing disunity?
5. What is the difference between lying and *tactfulness*? How can we communicate without hurting one another and still tell the *truth*?
6. How can *tactfulness* enhance all types of intimacy between us?

STRENGTHEN OUR RELATIONSHIP

- ♥ Let one another *lovingly* know that we prefer a different color or type of clothing or outfit than he or she has chosen
- ♥ Give one another *tactful* feedback about an upsetting behavior
- ♥ Identify a facial expression or gesture we each have that communicates the *truth* with *love*
- ♥ Request something from one another in a *tactful* way
- ♥ How else are we *committed* to practicing *tactfulness*?

৬ *Thankfulness* ৫

EXPAND OUR INSIGHTS

It is good to praise the Lord, to sing hymns to Your name, O Most
High....

~ Judaism: *Tanakh,* Psalms, 92:2

Thankfulness is gratitude for blessings of all kinds in our lives
and marriage. We appreciate the gifts God has given us of life,
understanding, spirit, intellect, and one another. We appreciate our
marriage, special friendship, and partnership that bring a feeling of
contentment to our lives. We let one another know how thankful
we are for what each of us does for the other. Though difficulties
challenge us at times, we are thankful that the outcome is growth and
strength in our relationship and ourselves. We focus on the positive.
Thankfulness helps us willingly receive and acknowledge what others
offer. We demonstrate our gratitude in our happiness and in our
actions as we show kindness and love to others.

At home the only currency exchange is how you and your mate
express your feelings about each other, and gratitude is an often-
overlooked commodity. It's easier to say "Thanks" when you're
feeling good about your marriage. It's harder when you're dissatisfied.
But gratitude, and its expression, is not just a *reflection* of a happy
marriage; it is one of the causes.

~ Dr. Paul Coleman, *The 30 Secrets of Happily Married Couples*, p. 161

How are we practicing Thankfulness?
What new choices will we make?

CONSULT AND TAKE ACTION

1. Identifying and Strengthening *Thankfulness*
   a. Do we take one another's actions for granted and not acknowledge them? If so, when? How can *courtesy*, *generosity*, or other qualities support *thankfulness*?
   b. Do we pity ourselves, and see nothing positive in our lives or circumstances, including lessons to be learned? If so, when? How can *contentment*, *service*, or other qualities assist us?
   c. Do we ignore nature, art, music, or the nice things of life that we could gratefully enjoy? If so, when? How can *beauty*, *joyfulness*, or other qualities assist us?
   d. When can *acceptance*, *creativity*, *enthusiasm*, *love*, *patience*, *purity*, *self-discipline*, *spirituality*, or other qualities assist us with strengthening *thankfulness*?
2. Identifying and Balancing Misuses of Thankfulness
   a. Do we use such excessive compliments, flattery, or *thanks* that others feel uncomfortable or manipulated? If so, when? How can *responsibility*, *truthfulness*, or other qualities assist us?
   b. Do we give *generously* to others so their gratitude will prompt them to do us favors? If so, when? How can *honesty*, *humility*, or other qualities assist us?
   c. When can using *compassion*, *courage*, *purposefulness*, *wisdom*, or other qualities reduce our misuse of *thankfulness*?
3. When is the lack of or misuse of *thankfulness* a source of conflict for us? If necessary, how can we restore harmony?
4. What assists us to be *thankful* for our gifts and blessings?
5. What assists us to be *thankful* during tests and difficulties?
6. How can *thankfulness* enhance all types of intimacy between us?

STRENGTHEN OUR RELATIONSHIP

❤ List what we are *thankful* for, using each letter of the alphabet
❤ Create three *thank*-you/appreciation cards to give to others
❤ Identify something we are *thankful* for and give it away
❤ Post an ongoing list of the things we are *thankful* for
❤ How else are we *committed* to practicing *thankfulness*?

❧ Thoughtfulness ❧

EXPAND OUR INSIGHTS

Good thoughts will produce good actions....

~Buddhism: *The Gospel of Buddha*, XLVIII:12

Thoughtfulness is concern for others' well-being or happiness and anticipating their needs and wants. We think of ways to be supportive of one another, and then we act in a thoughtful way. Often this means doing small considerate actions, such as bringing a cup of tea or coffee, putting the laundry away, or giving a hug. We are thoughtful of one another's needs, wants, and circumstances, and support one another with loving actions. We think ahead about how to have our experiences together be positive and pleasurable. Thoughtfulness also assists us to take great care in major decisions. We consider and consult together about the effects of our choices before making them. It helps us to move beyond being self-centered to being committed to what is best for our marriage, our family, and both of us. It is a gift of love to one another.

All too often we underestimate the importance of a smile, an embrace, a kind word, a sincere compliment, or the giving of one's attention. It is precisely the small things that can change difficult moments into special ones.

~ Mehri Sefidvash, *Coral and Pearls*, pp. 11-12

How are we practicing Thoughtfulness?
What new choices will we make?

CONSULT AND TAKE ACTION

1. Identifying and Strengthening *Thoughtfulness*
   a. Do we act impulsively and cause harm? If so, when? How can *courtesy*, *respect*, or other qualities support *thoughtfulness*?
   b. Are we unresponsive to one another in the ways and at the times it is most needed? If so, when? How can *compassion*, *helpfulness*, or other qualities assist us?
   c. Are we selfish, insensitive, and focused only on our own needs and not on one another's? If so, when? How can *caring*, *equality*, or other qualities assist us?
   d. When can *friendliness*, *generosity*, *love*, *patience*, *purposefulness*, *service*, or other qualities assist us with strengthening *thoughtfulness*?
2. Identifying and Balancing Misuses of *Thoughtfulness*
   a. Do we try so hard to be *thoughtful* that we end up being intrusive? If so, when? How can *discernment*, *flexibility*, or other qualities assist us in using *thoughtfulness* effectively?
   b. Are we so analytical about details and the right approach to take, we become fussy and self-absorbed over it? If so, when? How can *detachment*, *self-discipline*, or other qualities assist us?
   c. When can using *mercy*, *tactfulness*, *wisdom*, or other qualities reduce our misuse of *thoughtfulness*?
3. When is the lack of or misuse of *thoughtfulness* a source of conflict for us? If necessary, how can we restore harmony?
4. What *thoughtful* actions do we most appreciate?
5. When is it important to talk to one another before doing something we think is *thoughtful*?
6. How can *thoughtfulness* enhance all types of intimacy between us?

STRENGTHEN OUR RELATIONSHIP

💙 Buy something *thoughtful* for one another spontaneously
💙 Develop a regular habit that is *thoughtful*, or eliminate one that is challenging for the other
💙 Consider our schedules and *responsibilities* before making plans
💙 Express appreciation for specific *thoughtful* actions
💙 How else are we *committed* to practicing *thoughtfulness*?

❧ *Trustworthiness* ❧

EXPAND OUR INSIGHTS

...truly the best of men for thee to employ is the (man) who is strong and trusty...

~ Islam: *Qur'án*, 28:26

Trustworthiness is the ability to handle all our responsibilities with integrity and honesty. This allows us to have consistent confidence in one another's words and actions. We are truthful and faithful to one another. We trust that we will treat one another with respect and fairness. We keep our commitments, appropriate confidences, do not gossip or backbite, handle money with integrity, and give honorable service to others. We rely on one another, and others rely on the promises we make together. We can be trusted to do what aligns with our values. We make choices that are for the greater good of our marriage, our family, and society. We do not act in ways that would result in suspicion or distrust. Trustworthiness is vital in our marriage, because it provides stability and consistency to us and our family members.

When all is said and done, friendship is the only trustworthy fabric of the affections.

~ Miles Franklin, *My Career Goes Bung*, Ch. 19

How are we practicing Trustworthiness?
What new choices will we make?

CONSULT AND TAKE ACTION

1. Identifying and Strengthening *Trustworthiness*
    a. Do we say we will do something and then not follow through? If so, when? How can *commitment, truthfulness,* or other qualities support *trustworthiness?*
    b. Do we accept *responsibilities* but handle them carelessly? If so, when? How can *excellence, integrity,* or other qualities assist us?
    c. Do we avoid positions of leadership, ignore *responsibilities,* avoid *service* to others, and live just for ourselves? If so, when? How can *cooperation, responsibility,* or other qualities assist us?
    d. When can *chastity, equality, faithfulness, helpfulness, patience,* or other qualities assist us with strengthening *trustworthiness?*
2. Identifying and Balancing Misuses of *Trustworthiness*
    a. Do we so want others to see us as *trustworthy* that we try to over-please people or over-extend ourselves until our relationships suffer? If so, when? How can *detachment, honesty,* or other qualities assist us in using *trustworthiness* effectively?
    b. Do we unreasonably keep a *commitment* or promise even when it will cause more harm than good? If so, when? How can *discernment, humility,* or other qualities assist us?
    c. When can using *flexibility, justice, mercy, peacefulness, purity, unity, wisdom,* or other qualities reduce our misuse of *trustworthiness?*
3. When is the lack of or misuse of *trustworthiness* a source of conflict for us? If necessary, how can we restore harmony?
4. How do we handle broken *trust* between us? Between others?
5. Do we share important information with one another? Allow intimate touch? What increases our sharing and *trust?*
6. How can *trustworthiness* enhance all types of intimacy between us?

STRENGTHEN OUR RELATIONSHIP

- Agree on our boundaries for keeping our marriage issues private
- Identify and complete an outstanding promise or *commitment*
- Blindfold one of us and let the other lead over/around obstacles
- Handle an outstanding financial matter
- How else are we *committed* to practicing *trustworthiness?*

❧ *Truthfulness* ❧

EXPAND OUR INSIGHTS

Truthfulness is the foundation of all human virtues…. When this holy attribute is established in man, all the divine qualities will also be acquired.

~ Bahá'í Faith: *Compilation of Compilations, Vol. II*, p. 338

Truthfulness is speaking accurate words and searching for what is factual about all circumstances. We actively seek to find the truth inside ourselves and share it. When we are clear what is true about ourselves and about our marriage, we can be open and sharing with others. We admit when we make a mistake, and we do not lie about it, even to defend ourselves. We look at the facts, without creating imaginary stories or assumptions about what is occurring. Truthfulness protects us from the damage and destruction that exaggeration, deceit, and lies cause. It is the foundation of our trust in one another. Sometimes we need to draw on courage to speak the truth in a timely and wise way. Truthfulness brings peacefulness to us and builds trust and love. Truthfulness supports the development of all the other character qualities we practice.

❤

Let there be truth between us two forevermore.

~ Ralph Waldo Emerson, *The Conduct of Life*, "Behavior"

How are we practicing Truthfulness?
What new choices will we make?

CONSULT AND TAKE ACTION

1. Identifying and Strengthening *Truthfulness*
   a. Do we lie to one another or give false information to get what we want? If so, when? How can *purity*, *trustworthiness*, or other qualities support *truthfulness*?
   b. Do we misuse our imagination to *create* information that is inaccurate or misleading? If so, when? How can *creativity*, *self-discipline*, or other qualities assist us?
   c. Do we consult using distorted information? If so, when? How can *excellence*, *integrity*, or other qualities assist us?
   d. When can *chastity*, *courage*, *faithfulness*, *honesty*, *justice*, *sincerity*, or other qualities assist us with strengthening *truthfulness*?
2. Identifying and Balancing Misuses of *Truthfulness*
   a. Do we communicate the truth rudely, bluntly, and hurtfully? If so, when? How can *kindness*, *tactfulness*, or other qualities assist us in using *truthfulness* effectively?
   b. Do we backbite and gossip, and then defend what we are doing as telling the *truth*? If so, when? How can *responsibility*, *unity* or other qualities assist us?
   c. When can using *caring*, *compassion*, *discernment*, *love*, *respect*, *wisdom*, or other qualities reduce our misuse of *truthfulness*?
3. When is the lack of or misuse of *truthfulness* a source of conflict for us? If necessary, how can we restore harmony?
4. What signals do we display when we are telling the *truth*? When we are lying? How do we handle hearing the *truth*? Hearing lies?
5. How can *truthfulness* enhance all types of intimacy between us?

STRENGTHEN OUR RELATIONSHIP

💙 Tell one another an accurate story with no backbiting or gossip
💙 Communicate our *true* intentions about something we are doing
💙 Each *create* a collage of photos and words from magazines that expresses the *truth* about ourselves, and then together *create* a third one that expresses the *truth* about our marriage
💙 Tell the *truth* about our thoughts and feelings on an issue
💙 How else are we *committed* to practicing *truthfulness*?

☙ *Unity* ❧

EXPAND OUR INSIGHTS

Behold, how good and how pleasant it is...to dwell together in unity!
~ Christianity: *The Bible* (King James Version), Psalms 133:1

Unity is consciously looking for points of harmony and commonality between people. We bring people together in love, commitment, and cooperation. We focus on finding points of agreement between us. We regard disunity as destructive to our relationship. We build unity through using the character qualities effectively with one another. We draw on one another's strengths and abilities. We use consultation as an important tool to understand our differences and reach a unified decision. We recognize that the success of our marriage is more important than the attainment of one person's goals at the expense of the other. The unity of our marriage is a vital and stable foundation for our children and other family members. It is a force that connects us to people everywhere. It is the bond that keeps our marriage intact, strong, and thriving.

A good marriage thrives on unity—not on who is right and who is wrong.
~ Khalil A. Khavari, Ph.D. and Sue Williston Khavari, M.A., *Together Forever*, p. 193

How are we practicing Unity?
What new choices will we make?

CONSULT AND TAKE ACTION

1. Identifying and Strengthening *Unity*
   a. Do we separate ourselves from people who are different than us, because we think we are better than them? If so, when? How can *courtesy, peacefulness*, or other qualities support *unity*?
   b. Do we boss one another instead of consulting? If so, when? How can *equality, respect*, or other qualities assist us?
   c. Do we decide we do not like people and leave them out or gossip and backbite about them? If so, when? How can *acceptance, friendliness*, or other qualities assist us?
   d. When can *beauty, cooperation, flexibility, generosity, love, sincerity, spirituality*, or other qualities assist us with strengthening *unity*?
2. Identifying and Balancing Misuses of *Unity*
   a. Do we insist that everyone do the same thing, and not allow room for leadership and individual initiative? If so, when? How can *flexibility, responsibility*, or other qualities assist us in using unity effectively?
   b. Do we ignore actual differences and unequal values between people and circumstances and try to promote *unity* without *responsibility*, reconciliation, or amends? If so, when? How can *truthfulness, trustworthiness*, or other qualities assist us?
   c. When can using *creativity, encouragement, gentleness, wisdom*, or other qualities reduce our misuse of *unity*?
3. When is the lack of or misuse of *unity* a source of conflict for us? If necessary, how can we restore harmony?
4. What signals to us we are out of harmony with one another? How do we restore it?
5. How can *unity* enhance all types of intimacy between us?

STRENGTHEN OUR RELATIONSHIP

♥ Agree on a practice that will call us back to *unity* as needed
♥ Experiment with using music as a means of pulling us together
♥ Consult about how to increase *unity* in our families or community
♥ Agree on boundaries and needs for together and alone time
♥ How else are we *committed* to practicing *unity*?

✒ *Wisdom* ✒

EXPAND OUR INSIGHTS

Be humble, be harmless, have no pretension, be upright, forbearing...
calmly encounter the painful, the pleasant...seek this knowledge and
comprehend clearly why you should seek it...such, it is said, are the
roots of true wisdom....

~ Hinduism: *The Song of God: Bhagavad-Gita*, XIII

Wisdom is drawing on experience and knowledge to see the best
actions and words for any circumstance. It increases in our marriage
as we learn from one another and mature together. We also learn
wisdom from our mistakes and challenges. We use reflection,
discernment, good judgment, and common sense to assess whether
our words and actions will be timely and appropriate. We specifically
seek for wisdom to guide us. It helps us know when to request
assistance, provide guidance, take action, or be still and silent. We
build wisdom as we seek to see and tell the truth and understand
the potential consequences of our words or actions. We can learn
knowledge and wisdom from both spiritual and scientific sources. We
are truly wise when we are humble enough to admit that no matter
how much we strive to understand, there will always be much we do
not know.

It is the province of knowledge to speak and it is the privilege of
wisdom to listen.

~ Oliver Wendell Holmes, *The Poet at the Breakfast Table*

How are we practicing Wisdom?
What new choices will we make?

CONSULT AND TAKE ACTION

1. Identifying and Strengthening *Wisdom*
   a. Do we act without planning or reflection? If so, when? How can *patience, responsibility*, or other qualities support *wisdom*?
   b. Do we resist experiences instead of learning and improving from them? If so, when? How can *discernment, excellence*, or other qualities assist us?
   c. Do we ignore all the various sources of *wisdom* and guidance available to us? If so, when? How can *self-discipline, spirituality*, or other qualities assist us?
   d. When can *purposefulness, respect, trustworthiness, truthfulness*, or other qualities assist us with strengthening *wisdom*?
2. Identifying and Balancing Misuses of *Wisdom*
   a. Do we think we know everything, and everyone should listen to our advice and knowledge? If so, when? How can *humility, mercy*, or other qualities assist us in using *wisdom* effectively?
   b. Do we share what we know without assessing its timeliness and effect, or criticize others for not listening? If so, when? How can *flexibility, tactfulness* or other qualities assist us?
   c. When can using *courtesy, detachment, gentleness, love*, or other qualities reduce our misuse of *wisdom*?
3. When is the lack of or misuse of *wisdom* a source of conflict for us? If necessary, how can we restore harmony?
4. What valuable lessons have we learned in our marriage?
5. What unwise decisions or actions have we taken? Why?
6. How can *wisdom* enhance all types of intimacy between us?

STRENGTHEN OUR RELATIONSHIP

♥ Read quotes from people who are considered *wise* and *spiritual*, and discuss what we agree with and what we do not
♥ Write down *wise* advice that we want to pass to our children
♥ Apologize to someone who was upset when we gave them unasked-for advice
♥ Assess the timeliness and *wisdom* of an action we are considering
♥ How else are we *committed* to practicing *wisdom*?

Appendices

Appendix A:
COMMUNICATION SKILL: CONSULTATION IN MARRIAGE

DIRECTIONS: Often the way you speak, listen to, and respond to one another during your consultations will affect the quality of your interactions, the harmony in your relationship, and your ability to reach a decision.

1. Individually, look at each consultation item, consider how often you *currently* do these behaviors, and rate each item from 1- 5. You may wish to mark your responses on separate pieces of paper and only complete the chart below when consulting together.

2. Individually, go back through the list and put a checkmark (✓) on the line to the right of your rating, for items where you need more *practice* and *skill development* and intend to adjust your behavior.

3. Consult together and identify growth areas for you as a couple.

Note: Marriage Therapist Keyvan Geula contributed to this worksheet.

Rarely	1	2	3	4	5	Usually
	<-->					

When you consult with your spouse, how often do you:	His	✓	Hers	✓
1. Ensure the problem to be solved is clear at the beginning and whether we are simply exploring a subject or intent on a prompt decision?				
2. Gather and clarify all input early in the process, including facts, feelings, and points of view?				
3. Identify the guiding principles and character qualities that apply?				
4. Pray before or during consultation, for wisdom, clarity, unity, and strength to follow principles?				
5. Stay focused on one subject at a time?				
6. Dominate the consultation (voices are not equal)?				
7. Focus on the present and avoid bringing up potentially "hot" issues from the past?				
8. Carefully consider views already expressed before speaking, and avoid unnecessary repetition?				

When you consult with your spouse, how often do you:	His	✓	Hers	✓
9. Graciously accept your spouse's view if you believe he/she is right?				
10. Share your views frankly but with courtesy, kindness, love, and goodwill?				
11. Express opinions as contributions, not "truth"?				
12. Consciously adjust your tone or body language to show you are a caring friend?				
13. Suspend judgment to see if your spouse's views makes sense to you?				
14. Willingly offer your opinion to be challenged in the interest of truth?				
15. Pause and ask for a break or prayer if you feel strong anger or frustration?				
16. Limit how long you talk, so that you do not lose your spouse's attention?				
17. Praise your spouse for his/her sound views and fairness?				
18. Patiently listen to your spouse?				
19. Speak very slowly, too softly, or too little to control, shame, or belittle him/her?				
20. Speak faster or louder than your spouse, or constantly interrupt to dominate him/her?				
21. Interrupt your spouse or inappropriately finish his/her sentences?				
22. Take offense if your spouse disagrees with you?				
23. Summarize what has been said before responding, to ensure you understand?				
24. Use remarks or gestures that ridicule your spouse or others?				
25. Humbly ask the other to summarize what you have said, to ensure accuracy and understanding?				
26. Search for differing views and ideas to expand understanding and awareness?				
27. Honestly say what you think, instead of saying one thing, but thinking and feeling differently?				
28. Remember that being united and searching for truth is far more important than being right?				
29. Steer away from telling your spouse what he/she should and should not think, feel, want, or do?				

When you consult with your spouse, how often do you:	His	✓	Hers	✓
30. Briefly reflect, pause, and take a deep breath before you respond?				
31. Respect your spouse's personal space (closeness/distance), and back up or move as needed?				
32. Sincerely pause and ask if you are making sense?				
33. Rethink and reframe your initial thoughts out of tactful consideration for your spouse's feelings?				
34. Use appropriate humor to de-escalate a tense conversation?				
35. Use a kindly manner and voice to express concerns?				
36. Try to understand and respect your spouse's point of view?				
37. Complain to and criticize your spouse for disagreeing with you?				
38. Let go of your own thoughts and feelings in the interest of emerging ones, if they are better?				
39. Avoid voicing your opinion as right and defending it with great passion?				
40. Avoid belittling your spouse's thoughts or opinions?				
41. Apologize when you are in the wrong?				
42. Acknowledge your spouse's character qualities and strengths?				
43. Put yourself in your spouse's situation and seek to understand his/her feelings?				
44. Share your feelings and be responsible for them?				
45. Trust the consultation process as a channel for guidance and creative ideas?				
46. Allow yourself to be distracted by the phone, computer, television, video games....?				
47. Peacefully and appropriately defer to your spouse?				
48. Avoid rushing through consultation to make a quick decision?				
49. Evaluate if there is a unifed decision?				
50. Fully support the mutual decision in deeds and words?				

Appendix B:
COMMUNICATION SKILL: AGREED CONSULTATION PRACTICES

DIRECTIONS:
1. Pray or do some other spiritual or unifying practice together.
2. On a separate piece of paper, brainstorm the possible things that you might want to have as spiritual, mental, emotional, and physical practices in your consultations. Include what you would do both separately and as a couple. (Examples: Pray before beginning; eat before discussing anything serious)
3. Think through what would prevent miscommunications, arguments, conflicts, and so on.
4. Ask yourselves, "What would best support us in achieving unified agreements?"
5. Consider, "If we cannot agree, how do we want to handle one of us deferring to the other?"
6. When you have created the list, then review it together, consult, and choose the practices that are most meaningful for you as a couple. As you agree on each one, enter it in the space below.

We are committed to establishing the following behaviors and practices in our consultations:
1.
2.
3.
4.
5.
6.
7.

Note: You may wish to add more than 7 to your list, and consider posting the final agreed list somewhere in your home.

Appendix C:
CONSULTATION PRACTICE: SERVICE AND TIME COMMITMENTS

Note: It is best to reflect on how you each currently use your time and manage your entire schedule before completing this worksheet.

DIRECTIONS: This worksheet will help you to look at your major commitments and decide on the best uses of your time. Many people participate in and are of service to several different organizations or activities. It is very easy to get "too busy" to really pay attention to your spouse, focus on your family, or take time to relax and enjoy life. Are your choices moderate and in balance? Consider the following:

✓ Amount of time devoted to this activity each week
✓ Level of importance (Example: Is this a priority based on personal preference, spiritual guidance, or continuing education requirements to fulfill for your profession?)

As a couple, complete the chart below, ranking each item with a number in the priority column. Answer the questions that follow it.

ASSESSMENT OF TIME USE

Husband's Major Activities and Commitments	Activity Done on Behalf of? (self, family, organization, religious institution...)	Time Per Week	Priority
Ex: Meeting	Non-profit Board of Directors	1 hr.	3

Wife's Major Activities and Commitments	Activity Done on Behalf of? (self, family, organization, religious institution...)	Time Per Week	Priority
Ex: Yard work	Family	2 hrs.	4

Shared Major Activities and Commitments	Activity Done on Behalf of? (self, family, organization, religious institution...)	Time Per Week	Priority
Ex: Study session	Religious group	2 hrs.	2

Service and Time Commitments Discussion:

1. How important is it to you to participate in the same activities? In different activities? _____

2. What are your motivations for participating in these activities? Are you doing some to be of service to others? _____
_____

3. Which activities make you happy?_____
_____

4. Which activities simply take up your time and do not really bring joy or fulfillment? _____
_____

5. Which activities use a large amount of time, but have a low priority? _____
_____

6. Which activities can be done by others instead? _____
_____

7. Which activities use your special/best skills and talents?
_____

8. Which activities represent the highest and best use of your time, skills, and abilities? _____
_____

9. Which activities most contribute to your character growth?
_____

10 How do your activities affect your relationship and family?
_____

11. What would happen if you stopped doing each activity?
_____

12. Which activities are you committed to continue? Why?_____
_____

Appendix D:
CONSULTATION PRACTICE: YOUR HISTORY WITH MONEY

DIRECTIONS: Often when you talk about money, the discussion is influenced by emotions and issues from the past. Everything that people, parents, and experience have taught you as individuals affect how you handle money within your marriage. Individually, reflect on your financial history using the questions below and the Notes section that follows. Add your own history as well. After this is complete, go through the Discussion section together.

Reflection Questions:
- Were you taught to save, spend but be thrifty, or spend lavishly?
- Were you trained in how to make wise investments?
- Did you give to religious or charitable organizations?
- Did you ever steal money as a child? How was it handled?
- Did your parents trust or distrust banks?
- Did your grandmother (or other older relative) hide her money under the bed or in the freezer?
- Did a bully extort your lunch money? How was this handled?
- Were you taught to live and spend in the moment and not plan for the future?
- Were you taught to save everything for the future and not enjoy spending any money as you earn it?
- Were you taught that children should work for the family out of love and not be paid for it?
- Did you get an allowance? If so, how much? Did your friends get more or less? How did you feel about that?
- Do you think parents should pay all college expenses and not require their children to work during college?
- Do you think people over 18 should pay their expenses for everything and not count on parents for financial help?
- Did either of you have relatives who gave you large sums of money that affected your attitudes and spending habits?
- Were you required to work or did you choose to work once you were old enough? At what age? How did you manage your earnings?

Notes: How is your history affecting you today? How do you manage money? What do you think about or react to when your spouse manages, spends, or saves money?

_____

_____

_____

_____

_____

_____

_____

_____

Discussion: How can understanding the histories you both have with money assist you in preventing conflict in your relationship? Consult about any new financial management choices you want to make.

How would you handle these scenarios?

1. Person #1 shops all the time with the credit card, while his/her spouse, Person #2, prefers to only charge or spend money on items if he/she is sure the bill can be paid off immediately. What are the issues? What are some potential guiding principles? Consult through the challenges and reach agreement on how the couple could manage their money.

2. The wife's brother has asked her to lend him $150 so he can fix his car, which he uses to get to work. The money would come out of the joint checking account, and you, as the husband and wife, need to agree about lending the money. The brother did not pay back a $300 loan made five months before. Lending him the money might mean delaying paying off a credit card bill. What are the issues? What are some potential guiding principles? What do you decide?

Appendix E:
COMMUNICATION SKILL: TONE OF VOICE

DIRECTIONS: Say a few of the following phrases to one another in a variety of different tones of voice and with varied expressions on your faces. Ensure that you say each one with both a positive and a negative tone. Watch the listener's reactions to these different tones. Take turns so each of you has the opportunity to both speak and listen.

a.	Sorry	k.	Fine
b.	Excuse me	l.	Thanks
c.	Stop it	m.	Come with me
d.	Don't touch me	n.	What do you want
e.	Will you call me	o.	Why did you do that
f.	Whatever you want	p.	Yes, dear
g.	All right, I'll do it	q.	Can you hear me
h.	Sit down	r.	Leave it alone
i.	I don't want to talk now	s.	Can you help me
j.	How are you	t.	Good morning

Discussion:

1. Which tones of voice did you like?

2. Which ones would you prefer *not* to have as part of your communications – either giving or receiving?

3. Were any phrases difficult to say in a positive tone?

4. Were there any phrases that you added "please" to automatically to make it sound more positive?

5. Did any cultural accents affect the meaning of the statements?

6. How did you feel when you spoke in different tones of voice?

7. What did you learn about the use of different tones of voice and your mutual communication?

Appendix F:
COMMUNICATION SKILL: MAKING REQUESTS

It is an important communication technique to be lovingly direct with one another, either about a concern or with a request for assistance, without using criticism.

Making requests develops partnership between you and creates action. The ability to make them is a reflection of the equality between you. When you are in a relationship, internal signals can indicate when you need to raise an issue or make a request. These might include feelings of resentment, tension, annoyance, frustration, or sadness. If you notice that you are complaining or feeling tense, for example, you may wish to initiate direct communication.

It is important to reflect first on your emotions and understand the best means of conveying the root issue you are addressing and your feelings about it in a manner that your spouse will be able to receive. Without this reflection, often problems can become worse by your unwitting negative tone of voice or any defensiveness or anger that your spouse may already feel.

As you learn to be clear in your communications, you will minimize conflicts and misunderstandings and better maintain family unity. Try to use "I" statements, speaking for yourself, rather than "You" statements, which might sound accusatory.

Review these examples of direct requests:

"Honey, can I talk to you about something? I'm unhappy because _____ did not get done and I am feeling _____. Would it be possible for you to handle it by _____ (date and time)?" or

"Sweetheart, it is not working well for me that _____ is not being handled. Could we please talk about what would work for both of us?"

If you are feeling emotionally low, you can consider asking your spouse to bring you flowers. Or, if you are both struggling with something, you can make mutual requests for support.

When you want to make a request of your spouse, you can say, "It would help me in doing _____ if you would do _____."

You can also make direct offers of assistance to him/her by saying, "How can I help you?" Offering support and giving your spouse an opportunity to clarify what he/she needs can be a very loving act in a relationship. Support might include asking your spouse how he/she is feeling, sharing honest emotions, and reflecting back to the other what he/she said in a way that indicates empathetic understanding.

DIRECTIONS: Take turns phrasing a direct request to one another related to one of the issues below, or some other issue that is particularly meaningful to you. Consult briefly to resolve the issue. Remember that the person receiving the request has the opportunity to respond in many different ways. He or she could say "yes," "no," "maybe," or come up with an alternate solution to the issue.

Issues:

a. One leaves dirty clothes on the floor, and the other requests that they be picked up.

b. One arrives home in a dirty and sweaty condition from work or an outdoor activity, and the other requests that he or she shower or bathe before sitting down on the furniture.

c. One has difficulty paying bills on time, and the other requests that they work together to devise a solution, so late payments stop happening.

d. One requests that the other spend time with their children for an evening.

Appendix G:
COMMUNICATION SKILL:
STOP MISUSING CREATIVE IMAGINATION

Often challenges arise in relationships when people respond to one another and communicate without fully understanding a situation. Often this is complicated by reactions that are based on what one of them is *imagining*, rather than on what is actually happening. This includes jumping to conclusions; for example, seeing a receipt or bill for a purchase you do not recognize, and assuming your partner is spending money inappropriately.

You might react in your head to something that happens and imagine negative scenarios for how you will respond. For example, imagining your spouse becoming ill or dying when he or she schedules a medical test.

Or, you might dwell on something small and build up a high level of anxiety. For example, a wife might expect a husband home by a certain time. When he is a half hour late, she might start to imagine that he has been in an accident and is badly hurt. By the time he arrives home, she is highly anxious or perhaps angry. What happened, objectively, is that he was late. Her reaction is due to what she imagined might be happening. In another situation, a husband might see a tool missing from the garage and start imagining someone stole it or a family member was careless with it. He becomes angry based on his imagination, and only later remembers where he left it.

DIRECTIONS: In this activity, the object is to begin to distinguish between what is actually happening, the interpretation that the other imagines, the behavior that results, and the effect on the communication between the couple.

1. Role-play and analyze at least one of the scenarios below. The person reacting negatively to what happened should say what they are imagining in their minds aloud for the other person to hear. Then talk through how to respond more effectively.

a. The husband promises to call the wife at 5:15 p.m. after he is through working, and the call does not happen. What goes through her head, and how does she interact with him the next time they communicate? How could she handle the communication instead?

b. The man asks the woman about having a couple over for dinner. She has an unhappy look on her face, does not really respond, and changes the subject. What goes through both of their heads, and how does this affect their communication? How could they handle the communication instead?

c. One person asks the other to stop at the grocery and buy a can of icing for their child's birthday cake. The person arrives home without it. What goes through both of their heads, and how does this affect their communication? How could they handle the communication instead?

d. One person accidentally drops a receipt for a $200 item, the other person picks it up and reacts, knowing that the family is short of money. What goes through the head of the person who picked up the receipt, and how does that affect their communication? How could they communicate instead?

Discussion: When have you observed this pattern? What have been the consequences? Does it ever have a positive outcome? What can you do to shift the pattern and focus on what is happening instead of creating other scenarios in your minds?

2. Using an example from your own life, use the first row of circles on the next page to map out what occurred, what interpretation you gave to the circumstances, and how you behaved as a result. In the second row fill in how you could have interpreted the situation in a more positive and empowering way.

Discussion: What insights have you learned from this activity?

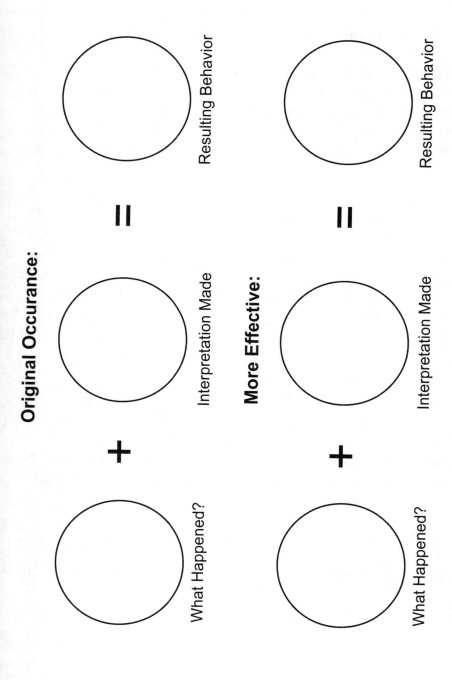

Appendix H:
COMMUNICATION SKILLS: HUMOR AND FUN

DIRECTIONS: Humor and having fun together have the power to strengthen your marriage and draw you closer together. Talk through whether you have balanced amounts of both in your marriage through discussing the questions below. Consider whether you are meeting your needs in these areas.

Humor

1. Is laughing together important to you?

2. What two things are almost guaranteed to make the other laugh?

3. What can you do to increase the amount of laughing you do (if this is needed)?

Fun

1. What is fun for you to do together?

2. What is your commitment to having fun/dating/engaging in social activities together in your marriage? How often? What types of activities?

3. What new activities do you want to try?

4. What adjustments do you need to make to have more or less fun?

Appendix I:
WHAT'S CHARACTER GOT TO DO WITH IT?
ENHANCING SEXUAL INTIMACY IN YOUR MARRIAGE

The majority of the following material was first published as a booklet. This was a comment made about it: **"This should be on every married couple's bedside table as great bedtime reading. It's a wise, unique, and instantly helpful perspective on sexual intimacy."**

~ Diane Sollee, Founder and Director of smartmarriages.com

Goal: Explore the intimacy of sex and understand how character qualities relate to it.

1. Read through the following qualities, and discuss how you currently use them or might include them in your lovemaking.
2. Choose three character qualities and use them during your next sexually intimate experience.
3. What is a request you each have of the other for the next time(s) you make love?

Below are brief descriptions of ways to integrate character qualities into your lovemaking. Explore how a *"high quality"* sexual experience can build conscious intimacy into your in marriage. It can be more thrilling and fulfilling than you ever imagined.

Acceptance ~ No one is perfect. Give one another the grace of accepting each other and your desires, bodies, and souls just the way they are.

Assertiveness ~ Ask one another for what you want and need. Share your preferences for being invited into a sexual interaction, preparation time, foreplay, touch, holding, and sexual intercourse. Also share how and when you prefer to communicate your desires with one another.

Beauty ~ Deeply appreciate and acknowledge the beauty of one another's mind, heart, body, and soul. Ensure the environment around you when you make love is also comfortable and beautiful. Recognize, together, that all beauty comes from the Creator.

Caring ~ Show that you passionately care about the wellbeing and sensual experience of one another by being considerate of one another's needs and wishes.

Chastity ~ This is a gift to one another of spiritual, mental, and physical faithfulness and focus, so your sexual thoughts and actions are moderate and pure and directed toward your spouse, not to others. Replace thoughts of attraction to others with strong positive thoughts of love for one another to bring you back to the sanctity of your marriage.

Commitment ~ When you speak the words and take the actions that show you are committed to your relationship, you can both relax, knowing you will stay together. Commitment allows you each the freedom to work through any relationship and sexual challenges together.

Compassion ~ Sometimes life is tough, and you can take the time to hold and comfort one another. Listen to what is on one another's mind and heart, and together you may choose to postpone lovemaking for another time.

Confidence ~ Be an active, not passive, participant in the sexual process, inviting touch and initiating action to achieve full mutual enjoyment and satisfaction.

Contentment ~ Every time you make love will be a new experience, as your bodies go through their natural rhythms over time, and your lives change. Contentment allows you to flow with these rhythms without unreasonable expectations of one another. It assists you to accept the valleys of experience along with the peaks.

Cooperation ~ Limbs get tangled and tongues get twisted, so help one another move and maneuver smoothly. Cooperation in building oneness is broader than your physical experience as well. It includes sharing with one another, supporting each of your goals and dreams, and listening to one another's minds and hearts.

Courage ~ Speak up about your needs and desires, reach out to create a full sensual experience, take risks, connect with one another, and remain focused on your partner. After an experience disrupts your lives, it may take courage to re-initiate physical intimacy and sexual activity.

Courtesy ~ Manners are as important in the bedroom as they are in the dining room. "Please," "Thank you," and gracious interactions support your experience together.

Creativity ~ Variety, something new, can spice up your experience, whether it's a new outfit, a new position or location, adding music, or any number of other choices. Use your imagination and have fun together creating what is special for you.

Detachment ~ Sometimes you can detach from your own immediate needs and offer focused touch and attention to your spouse. Detachment can also assist you to accept that while a particular sexual experience was positive, a climax wasn't possible or necessary. Sometimes it just is not the right time.

Discernment ~ The inviting or disinterested cues you give one another are often subtle, so discernment helps you pay close attention. Throughout lovemaking, it also supports you in being sensitive to one another's responses and in making appropriate adjustments.

Encouragement ~ Where and how to touch, frequency, and pacing can all be enhanced with encouraging words and positive feedback.

Enthusiasm ~ Ah, now that is encouraging! Have a great time!

Equality ~ One-sided and selfish sex just doesn't work. Mutual respect, balance, and pleasing one another is definitely more fun.

Excellence ~ Go for the best experience you can have—it's a worthy goal. This includes excellence in listening, in being compassionate, and in supporting and looking after one another.

Faithfulness ~ Yes, it means sticking together, but it also means inviting God to be present and making sex a sacred experience of oneness between you. You might experiment with praying before you begin lovemaking, or simply be conscious that your experience is bonding your hearts and souls, not just your bodies.

Flexibility ~ Sometimes you're hot, sometimes you're not; sometimes it works, sometimes it doesn't. Flexibility allows you to find other creative ways of connecting with your spouse, such as a sensual massage or a great conversation.

Forgiveness ~ It is difficult to be in harmony when something is unresolved between you. Forgiveness frees you from resentment and blame and allows you to move forward in your relationship and lovemaking.

Friendliness ~ Laughing together, enjoying each other's company, and supporting one another as friends are all a great foundation for lovemaking. In turn, a bonding experience of lovemaking can enhance your friendship.

Generosity ~ Give to one another in every way possible, so the other's pleasure and happiness become your own.

Gentleness ~ Passion should never hurt, and pain destroys true pleasure. Be gentle and considerate in your mutual approach and touch.

Helpfulness ~ Be aware of and ask what will help one another relax, be focused on the experience, and reach a climax. Each of your needs may vary, so don't assume that the same action will work every time.

Honesty ~ Honest sharing, listening, and learning will guide you to know what works well and what doesn't in your lovemaking. It is best to be clear and build understanding, without barriers between you.

Humility ~ Be who you are, honestly, without pretense. Ego won't build a strong relationship in your bedroom—lovemaking between married partners is not about being a performer on stage. Humility assists you to be authentic, loving, and available.

Idealism ~ It's a great idea to dream about what could happen between you … and then try to create it together.

Integrity ~ Clearly communicate about your pasts, your experiences, your promises, and your commitments when they affect one another. Honesty and openness will create a deeper bond between you, both in the bedroom and in your marriage.

Joyfulness ~ Lovemaking can be fun, exhilarating, and bring happiness and closeness to you both. Joy happens when your hearts are attuned to one another and you are grateful for the gifts in your lives.

Justice ~ Kick dominance or anything that is unfair, unwise, or hurtful out the door of the bedroom … and the house. Justice supports your equality and your respectful interactions with one another.

Kindness ~ Perform sweet acts in lovemaking for one another, such as lighting a candle, smoothing lotion on each other, offering a massage, or bringing a glass of water to the other. Kindness will bring your hearts together.

Love ~ Love is the magnetic force that draws you together over and over again and is expressed in a variety of ways throughout your relationship. One way is through your shared sexual experiences. Choosing each day to love one another, continually re-creates the bond between you.

Loyalty ~ Be sensitive about how you speak of one another when you are with friends and relatives. When you are loyal, you keep the details of your sexual experience private and intimate.

Mercy ~ Your moods and emotions affect your relationship, and you may need to give one another time and space to work through them. Sometimes one of you just can't last as long as the other, or has less desire or motivation, so give one another a break as needed.

Moderation ~ Anything done to excess loses its ability to be special. Work together to balance your mutual sensual and sexual rhythms. Practicing moderation in your entire lives will assist you to have the energy and focus needed for lovemaking.

Patience ~ Sometimes you need to wait until the best time for lovemaking, and this time of patience can increase your anticipation of being together. When you are engaged in lovemaking, being patient with one another and moving at a slower pace can prolong enjoyment.

Peacefulness ~ Agitation, aggravation, and conflict interfere with having a peaceful bedroom and intimate and joyful lovemaking. Inner peace and harmony between you bring calm centeredness to your sexual experience.

Perseverance ~ It takes time to learn the rhythm of one another's bodies, minds, hearts, and souls, so be understanding and keep working at it.

Purity ~ Your positive thoughts and motivations elevate your shared experiences. Manipulation has no place in true intimacy. Purity in the form of cleanliness is a great contributor to physical and spiritual intimacy. It is an indicator of self-respect and consideration for your spouse, as well as freeing you to touch one another without concerns.

Purposefulness ~ It's important to pay attention to what you are doing, the other person, and why you are touching one another. This is not the time to plan a business strategy, make a grocery list in your head, or emotionally remove yourself from the experience. Be focused on building your intimacy in positive ways.

Respect ~ Demonstrating respect is vital in maintaining your bond and having a mutual experience. Respect begins with valuing oneself and then valuing your spouse's wants, needs, and desires. Mutual respect allows you to be intimate with one another, yet have healthy boundaries and equality.

Responsibility ~ Seeking knowledge about the functioning of male and female sexual biology allows you to support one another's experiences effectively. Responsibility for your actions and their consequences is an important part of an honest marriage, including not exposing your spouse to diseases or unplanned conception of a child.

Self-Discipline ~ Your self-control is a way to show your respect for your spouse, and it allows you to practice patience and gentleness as needed.

Service ~ An attitude of service will help you look for ways to arrange your environment, reduce distractions, and relax your spouse. And, sometimes, it has you focus on his/her pleasure and postpone your own.

Sincerity ~ Enjoy sexual intimacy and don't fake your responses. Sincerity builds trust.

Spirituality ~ Let your souls join as your bodies do. Lovemaking is a powerful connection between you, and achieving oneness in this way can be the ultimate pleasure for both of you. Sex is a spiritual gift to a marriage.

Strength ~ It is powerful to show the strength of your passion for one another. Your physical abilities allow you to explore many sexual positions. Ensure your strength supports, not hurts, one another.

Tactfulness ~ Frank words about what you perceive as your partner's shortcomings can be hurtful and are unlikely to improve your sexual experience with one another. Gentle and kind words, while still truthful, will be more likely to guide the other in new directions and enhance the experience for both of you.

Thankfulness ~ It's a great idea to affirm your partner's sexual performance and express gratitude for him/her in your bed and in your life.

Thoughtfulness ~ Prepare ahead of time to make your sexual/sensual time together even more special, such as allowing time to unwind from the day, spending time together, or bathing/showering separately or together. Sometimes you may need to accommodate for your partner's fears or trauma from a past negative experience through using different positions, touch, or increased light in the room. Other times, you may need to minimize distractions or make arrangements for your children so you have private time together.

Trustworthiness ~ Trust helps dispel fears or concerns that might arise for one of you about sex or during lovemaking. Your ability to trust one another allows you to relax and know that your spouse has your best interests in mind. Trustworthiness builds from truthfulness and faithfulness.

Truthfulness ~ This is the foundation of the other qualities, and it builds your store of trust in one another. As you truthfully share what you are thinking and feeling, you gain deeper knowledge of one another and strengthen your friendship.

Unity ~ A key outcome of your lovemaking is achieving a high level of oneness. The more unified your lives are generally, the more unity you will be able to create in the bedroom.

Wisdom ~ Sex is an important part of your relationship; however, it is important to keep it in perspective. You are married to one another and engaged in a lifetime commitment with or without sex.

The content of Appendix I is also available in booklet form;
Order your copies at www.marriagetransformation.com!
Susanne M. Alexander, ISBN 0972689346; $3.95 (Quantity Discounts Available)

Appendix J:
PERMISSIONS AND COPYRIGHT NOTICES

This page constitutes an extension to the copyright page.

Note: Every effort has been made to give credit and obtain permission where required for the content contained in this book by other authors and from other sources. Any omissions are completely unintentional. Upon notification, the publisher will be happy to make corrections in future printings and editions of this work.

The following terms have been trademarked: Marriage Transformation, Solving Conflicts, The Virtues Project, The Art of Spiritual Companioning, and Spiritual Companioning.

Reprinted with permission of Hay House, Inc. (Carlsbad, CA) from *You Can Heal Your Life* by Louise L. Hay; Copyright © 1999 Louise L. Hay

Reprinted with permission of Images International, Publisher, and Linda Kavelin Popov from *Sacred Moments* by Linda Kavelin Popov; Copyright © 1996 Linda Kavelin Popov

Reprinted with permission of John Wiley & Sons, Inc. from *Beyond the Myth of Marital Happiness* by Blaine J. Fowers, Ph.D.; Copyright © 2000 Jossey-Bass Inc., Publishers

Reprinted with permission of John Wiley & Sons, Inc. from *12 Hours to a Great Marriage* by Howard J. Markman, Scott M. Stanley, Susan L. Blumberg, Natalie H. Jenkins, and Carol Whiteley; Copyright © 2004 John Wiley & Sons, Inc.

Reprinted with permission of John Wiley & Sons, Inc. from *Fighting for Your Marriage* by Howard J. Markman, Scott M. Stanley, Susan L. Blumberg; Copyright © 2001 John Wiley & Sons, Inc.

Original quotations by Linda Kavelin Popov and Dan Popov, Ph.D., printed with their permission

Reprinted with permission of Khalil A. Khavari from *Spiritual Intelligence* by Khalil A. Khavari, Ph.D.; published by White Mountain Publications; Copyright © 2000 Khalil A. Khavari, Ph.D.

Reprinted with permission of Khalil A. Khavari and Sue Williston Khavari from *Together Forever* by Khalil A. Khavari, Ph.D. and Sue Williston Khavari; published by Oneworld; Copyright © 1993 Khalil and Sue Khavari

Reprinted with permission of Moody Publishers from *The Five Love Languages* by Gary Chapman; Copyright © 2004 Gary D. Chapman

Permission to publish quotations from the writings of the Bahá'í Faith by the National Spiritual Assembly of the Bahá'ís of the United States

From *101 Things I Wish I Knew When I Got Married*. Copyright © 2004 by Charlie and Linda Bloom. Reprinted with permission of New World Library, Novato, CA.; www.newworldlibrary.com or 800/972-6657 ext. 52

From *Living on Purpose*; Copyright © 2000 by Dan Millman. Reprinted with permission of New World Library, Novato, CA.; www.newworldlibrary.com or 800/972-6657 ext. 52

Appendix K:
ABOUT THE AUTHORS

Susanne M. Alexander and *Craig A. Farnsworth* have been married since August 1999, a second marriage for both of them. Between them, they have more than 50 years of marriage experience and four adult children.

Susanne and Craig are marriage educators, certified by Life Innovations, Inc. in PREPARE/ENRICH, and Susanne has also been trained by PREP Inc. They facilitate marriage preparation and marriage enrichment workshops with people of all ages. Susanne and Craig are principals of Marriage Transformation LLC, which empowers people globally to create happy, lasting, spiritually-based marriages (www.marriagetransformation.com). Their first book, published in 2003, was *Marriage Can Be Forever—Preparation Counts!* The first edition of *Pure Gold* was published in 2004.

The couple's commitment is to spread marriage education globally. They are engaged in doing this through creating practical resources and powerful learning opportunities that support relationships and marriages. They are part of creating a culture where people will not dream of being in relationships without learning the knowledge and skills to be successful.

છ∽ભ

Susanne is a journalist and writer and has a B.A. in Communications from Baldwin-Wallace College in Ohio. Her articles have been published in *Strengthening Marriage, Newsweek Japan, The (Cleveland) Plain Dealer, Crain's Cleveland Business, Writer's Digest,* and *Massage Magazine* among others. Susanne is a member of the American Society of Journalists and Authors. She is part of an author team that has written a college textbook, *College & Career Success Simplified,* published in July 2003. Susanne is a frequent speaker at writer's conferences, and she co-hosted a talk radio show in 1998-1999.

Craig is a full-time market manager for Radix Wire Company and holds a B.A. in Physics and a B.A. in Elementary Education from Hiram College in Ohio. He has had technical articles published in a variety of industry publications. He is a member of the American Society of Gas Engineers and serves on the steering committee for the International Appliance Technical Conference. Craig is a musician, playing many types of flutes and the guitar. He sings bass in various choirs, and he has performed nationally in the United States with the Voices of Bahá choir, including in Carnegie Hall.

ဆဘဗ

John S. Miller is a Character Coach and holds a B.S. in Psychology from Union College, Lincoln, Nebraska. In 1994, John married his best friend, Cindy, a second marriage for both of them. While college honed his writing, research, and intellectual abilities, John considers the best classroom to be real-life experience combined with the quest for truth. He comes from five successive generations ravaged by divorce, so he is an expert at understanding how divorce destroys families.

Within the context of an inherent personal need to find better ways for relationships to function, John has spent 25 years studying character and conflict. He and his wife founded Solving Conflicts LLC (www.solvingconflicts.com) in 2005 to offer their unique system of character assessment. It comes from their own personal use of character to solve conflicts and John's research into the meaning of character strengths. John and Cindy attribute the success of their eleven-year marriage to this focus. It is John and Cindy's mission to make this cutting-edge system of character education and assessment available to all people.

Please contact us as follows:
It will be a gift to us and other readers of *Pure Gold* to hear back from
you about your experiences with this book, and for you to share
anything that would improve its usefulness in future editions.

Marriage Transformation LLC
P.O. Box 23085, Cleveland, OH 44123
E-mail: staff@marriagetransformation.com
Website: www.marriagetransformation.com
Telephone: 216-383-9943
(9:30 a.m. to 8:30 p.m. Eastern U.S. Time Zone)

Be sure to visit our website, www.marriagetransformation.com,
for announcements of exciting new books, products, services, and
recommended resources for relationship and marriage education.

You may find this booklet useful to keep on your bedside table:
What's Character Got To Do With It?
Enhancing Sexual Intimacy in Your Marriage
ISBN: 0972689346

Marriage Transformation™ Project-Related News
and Announcement Listserve:
MarriageTransformation-subscribe@yahoogroups.com

For Coaching to Be a Marriage Educator:
MarriageTransformationEducator-subscribe@yahoogroups.com

Subscribe, on our home page, to our free, monthly e-newsletter,
filled with great information about relationships and marriage.

Our books are also available through your favorite local
or on-line bookseller!